THE BRAHMASTRA UNLEASHED

THE BRAHMASTRA UNLEASHED

A first-person account of how the Mumbai underworld was annihilated

D. SIVANANDHAN, IPS (RETD.)

Former Police Commissioner of Mumbai and Former Director General of Police, Maharashtra

Indus Source Books

Indian Spirit, Universal Wisdom

Praise for the Book

"Finally, it was only the enactment of the MCOCA, a brain-child of the author, and its rigid enforcement under his command and directions, that put an end to the dominance of the ganglords on the streets of Mumbai city."

~ J.F. Ribeiro, Former Police Commissioner of Mumbai and Former Director General of Police, Punjab

"The book, *The Brahmastra Unleashed* is a timely reminder of what Mumbai (then called Bombay) endured during the final decades of the twentieth century – earning the opprobrium of the Crime Capital of India . . . This is a must-read book, and I commend D. Sivanandhan in particular, for what he did after he took over as the Jt. CP, Bombay.

~ M.K. Narayanan, Former National Security Adviser of India, Former Director of Intelligence Bureau, and Former Governor of West Bengal

"A comprehensive account of the Mumbai underworld as it was a few decades ago. Imaginatively chronicled, it is a valuable addition to police literature. Policemen in the field and elsewhere will benefit greatly from the pen of a versatile professional."

~ Dr. R.K. Raghavan, Former Director of the Central Bureau of Investigation

"Few books can inspire you, fascinate you, make you feel nostalgic, motivate you, give a historical perspective, be a case study, be well documented and also give us hope and positivity . . . *The Brahmastra Unleashed* is one such book. All aspects rolled into one. Read this book to understand what strategy, leadership, honesty, and integrity can do..."

~ Dr. Radhakrishnan Pillai, Author, Leadership and Strategy Adviser

Indus Source Books
42/43C, Balaji Bhavan,
Sakal Bhavan Road, Sector 11,
CBD Belapur, Navi Mumbai 400614
INDIA
Email: info@indussource.com
www.indussource.com

The Brahmastra Unleashed:
A first-person account of how the Mumbai underworld was annihilated

ISBN (HB): 978-93-85509-90-2
(PB): 978-93-85509-91-9

First printed by Indus Source Books in 2025

Cover design: Neena Gupta

Printed at Thomson Press

*"The most valuable asset you own isn't money.
It's your ability to think clearly in a world designed
to confuse you. Mental clarity is wealth."*
~ Scott D. Clary

Words I live by . . .

This book is dedicated to the brave policemen of Mumbai Police and my family: wife Lalita, daughters Archana and Jyotsna, and grandchildren Layla and Eliot.

CONTENTS

Foreword:	*J.F. Ribeiro, Former Police Commissioner of Mumbai and Former Director General of Police, Punjab*	xi
Foreword:	*M.K. Narayanan, Former National Security Adviser of India, Former Director of Intelligence Bureau, and Former Governor of West Bengal*	xiii
Preface		xv
Acknowledgements and Gratitude		xviii
Introduction		1
Chapter 1:	Organised Crime and Its Genesis	6
	• Why People Turn to Crime	14
Chapter 2:	Why Mumbai?	17
	• Real Estate and Construction Industry	23
	• Hotel Industry	25
	• Cable TV Industry	26
Chapter 3:	Vintage Gangsters of Mumbai	27
	• Karim Lala	28
	• Haji Mastan	29
	• Vardarajan Mudaliar	32
Chapter 4:	Bloody and Messy Underworld – The Dawood Era	34
	• Dawood and Bollywood	49
	• Dawood and Cricket	49
	• Dawood Ibrahim – Convergence of Crime and Terrorism	50
	• Shift to a Religiously Motivated Terror Network	51
	• Conclusion	54
Chapter 5:	Gangsters and Their Genealogy – Evolution of the Mumbai Mafia	56
	• Abu Salem	56
	• Rajendra Sadashiv Nikhalje, a.k.a. Chhota Rajan	62
	• Arun Gawli, a.k.a. Daddy	76
	• Chhota Shakeel	94
	• Suresh Manchekar	99
	• Subhash Singh Thakur	100
	• O.P. Shrivastava, a.k.a. Babloo Shrivastava	102
	• The Pujaris – Ravi and Hemant	105

- D.K. Rao 109
- Ejaz Lakdawala 110
- Rohit Verma – The Hammer Man 113
- Ashwin Naik 115

Chapter 6: The Underworld-Terrorism Nexus 117
- The 1993 Serial Bomb Blasts in Mumbai 117
- IC 814 Hijacking – The Mumbai Angle 119

Chapter 7: The Underworld-Bollywood Nexus 133
- Film Industry 133
- Mafia Connections in the Film Industry 135

Chapter 8: Underworld Murders That Shook Mumbai 148
- The Murder of Rajan Nair by Chandrashekhar Safalika on 21 September 1983 148
- The Sensational Killing of Ashok Joshi on 3 December 1983 154
- The Abdul Kunju Murder in 1987 159
- The Gut-wrenching Killing of Babu Reshim on 5 March 1987 161
- The Dramatic Shootout at Sir J.J. Hospital on 12 September 1992 164
- The Murder of Tanya Koli on 17 September 1993 171
- The Murder of Pradeep Jain on 7 March 1995 174
- The Murder of Dr. Datta Samant on 16 January 1997 182

Chapter 9: The Justice Aguiar Commission Report 185

Chapter 10: The Multi-Pronged Attack by the Mumbai Police 195

Chapter 11: The Brahmastra: Unleashed 215

Chapter 12: MCOCA's First Salvo Sends the Underworld Reeling 220
- The Milind Vaidya Firing Case 220

Chapter 13: The Future – The War Is Won, But Battles Continue… 232

Chapter 14: My Personal Roller Coaster Ride 236

Chapter 15: Colleagues Speak 240

Chapter 16: Bridging Hunger to Deposit Smiles – The Roti Bank Story 247

About the Author 251

FOREWORD

D. Sivanandhan is a police officer after my own heart. He is a leader in the true sense – leading from the front, leading by example and taking all his officers and men along.

His concern for other human beings is apparent in his initiative of starting three schools, one each in Chandrapur, Gadchiroli and Thane city, where children of police personnel get preference in admission. After retiring from active service he started Roti Bank where 15,000 children of the less privileged are fed every single day. This facility, his single largest contribution to helping those in need, is a testimony to his concern for social justice and the quality of his compassion.

Towards the end of the book are some testimonials penned by officers who had served under him, chiefly in Mumbai city when it was reeling under the depredations of the underworld gangs led by the notorious ganglords Dawood Ibrahim, Chhota Rajan and Arun Gawli. One officer has testified that in the 34 years he served in the police he came across none who matched Siva's calibre.

Another officer wrote that his guidance during the investigation of complex cases was unmatched – something you rarely see in senior police officers today.

Yet another officer cited Siva's *"great ability of spotting particular talents in his juniors."* A good leader makes optimum use of personnel detailed to assist him in his allotted tasks.

The testimonials of these junior officers are what makes this book compulsory reading for I.P.S. (Indian Police Service) probationers at the N.P.A. (National Police Academy) and also for other senior officers. The book recounts the stories of different sensational crimes committed by organised gangs in the city of Mumbai as also the history of different gang leaders and how they were finally neutralised. This part of the book caters to the reader's curiosity about crime and criminals.

But what excited an old professional like me was the knowledge that encounters and specialists who were involved in such encounters only helped to worsen the crime scenario. Finally, it was only the enactment of the MCOCA (Maharashtra Control of Organised Crime Act, 1999), a brain-child of the author; and its rigid enforcement under his command and directions, that put an end to the dominance of the ganglords on the streets of Mumbai city.

D. Sivanandhan comes out as a remarkable police officer who deserves the gratitude of the citizens of my city of Mumbai.

~ **Padma Bhushan J.F. Ribeiro,**
Former Police Commissioner of Mumbai,
and Former Director General of Police, Punjab

◆◆◆◆◆◆

FOREWORD

The book, *The Brahmastra Unleashed* is a timely reminder of what Mumbai (then called Bombay) had endured during the final decades of the twentieth Century – earning the opprobrium of being the Crime Capital of India. One had to live through the period to understand how dangerous it was, and the bravery of those who, against the odds, fought the criminal gangs and succeeded in vanquishing them. The author of this work, Mr. D. Sivanandhan, was one of the prime movers in this effort, and together with a band of courageous police officers embarked upon the task of taking on the city's mafia, that had deeply entrenched itself in almost every aspect of Bombay's life, not excluding Bollywood.

The book projects the unvarnished truth of the situation that existed at that time, and how a band of brave officers such as Mr. Sivanandhan and Mr. Mendonca, Former Mumbai Police Commissioner, put their lives at risk in the process. This is, hence, a book that anyone who seeks peace and security should read.

Far more gripping than the saga of Al Capone in the U.S., are the actions of Dawood Ibrahim (who is still at large in Pakistan) and Chhota Rajan and the band of lesser dons like Arun Gawli. What comes out loud and clear from a perusal of this narrative is that bravery and fearlessness are essential requirements for the police, and the author and others mentioned, exemplify this in ample measure. If

Mumbai is an oasis of peace today, it is because of brave men like the author and a lot of other unsung heroes, who need to be extolled.

This is a must-read book, and I commend D. Sivanandhan in particular, for what he did after he took over as the Deputy Commissioner of Police, Bombay, (1987) and till he left the force years later (2011) as DGP Maharashtra. The nation must also pay a tribute to those unsung heroes who do not find specific mention for what they did.

The author, whom I regard as one of the finest members of the Indian Police Service, having been his senior in service, well exemplifies the finest qualities of the Indian Police Service.

~ **M.K. Narayanan**
Former National Security Adviser of India,
Former Director of Intelligence Bureau,
and Former Governor of West Bengal

◆◆◆◆◆◆

PREFACE

A child born in 2000 will be 25 years old today. He or she will never know what it was to live in the Mumbai of the 1970s, 1980s, 1990s and early 2000s. The decades were marked by street fights, gang wars, lynchings, kidnappings and abductions, extortions and more, which were a far cry from the 'safe' Mumbai of today. Even stranger was the way that the underworld functioned and how it had a stranglehold over Mumbai.

The incidents of violence that would spur fear and anxiety in working-class families in those days, will just be stories a the child today.

Tales of the infamous Mumbai underworld are legion. The *bhais*, the *goondas*, their gangs and how they ran what was almost a parallel economy that was more powerful and richer than the state government and even the richest industrialists, is now part of our urban myth.

What the current generation knows is the glorification of the underworld and its gangsters, shown through the lenses of Bollywood that churns out movies centred around dons and fugitives as Robin Hood-esque hero figures. A fugitive, notoriously brutal criminal like Dawood Ibrahim who has evoked terror in the name of crime and religion, is portrayed as a glamorous don.

However, what the current generation and everyone else should know is how the mighty underworld was finally vanquished; how the financial capital, one of the most cosmopolitan, fastest growing cities in the world, fought hard to neutralise the blight of the underworld and reclaim the safety of its citizens, as well as revive their faith in the Mumbai Police.

This book is an attempt to document the rise and fall of the underworld in Mumbai through real-life stories – some never heard before – sourced directly from first-person accounts given by various arrested gangsters, case diaries, First Information Reports (FIRs) and charge sheets. The domination of the underworld over Mumbai has been described. These are spine-chilling, blood-curdling accounts of how gangs wreaked havoc in Mumbai.

The Mumbai Police, after having tried various strategies such as implementing the Bombay Prohibition Act, MISA – Maintenance of Internal Security Act (1971), COFEPOSA – Conservation of Foreign Exchange and Prevention of Smuggling Activities Act (1974), TADA – Terrorist and Disruptive Activities (Prevention) Act (1985) and POTA – Prevention of Terrorism Act (2002) – failed to find a solution.

The police even tried to engage the gangsters in direct conflict, which resulted in several of them being killed in operations. However, none of these strategies were successful in curbing the underworld for prolonged periods of time.

When this author was the Chief of the Mumbai Crime Branch, heralded to be an elite unit within the Mumbai Police, the then Chief Minister and Home Minister had exhorted the Mumbai Police Commissioner to end the underworld menace in a way that would ensure no resurgence. The responsibility was handed to the Crime Branch.

How the Mumbai Police unleashed its *Brahmastra* (one of the most powerful and destructive weapons described in Indian mythology) on the underworld, neutralising it irrevocably, forms the central chapter of this book.

The epithet is befitting, as the Mumbai Police's 'weapon' had so much power that just like the Brahmastra annihilated everything in its path, it uprooted the underworld that has since never been able to re-establish itself in Mumbai.

It has been more than two decades and running that the people of Mumbai live their lives fearlessly thanks to the efforts of the Mumbai Police and its *Brahmastra*. This fact is not widely known and needs to be highlighted and recorded for posterity. This book is an effort to etch this on public memory.

Even though the author of this book led the counter-attack by the Mumbai Police which eventually destroyed the underworld, the credit for the work should be given to the entire Mumbai Police force. This is a fact-based narrative of the work of the Mumbai Police and its brave and dedicated soldiers, who led the fight with the unflinching support of Mumbaikars.

The information in this book is based on police records. Some cases are pending in the courts.

ACKNOWLEDGEMENTS AND GRATITUDE

First and foremost, I wish to thank the Almighty for having always blessed me and helped achieve all my aims, goals and dreams. Writing this book was a dream that I had cherished for a long time, and it is finally seeing the light of day due to His blessings.

I thank my family – my wife and children – for having always stood by me and backing me to the fullest. A special thanks to my wife for having borne the brunt of my work-related stress and frustration which I would inevitably bring home. In spite of that, she has always supported me wholeheartedly.

I am grateful to each and every policeman who I worked with from the beginning. Even though I wish to thank each one of them personally, it will be difficult to mention each one by name. I am grateful to all my seniors who helped me, guided me, supported me and advised me. I thank all my colleagues, fellow policemen, junior officers and the entire constabulary who worked relentlessly as a team, withstood insurmountable pressure, overcame some of the most difficult challenges, and succeeded despite all odds. I also thank all my mentors who were senior IPS officers.

I wish to thank Assistant Commissioner of Police (Retd.) Vilas Tupe for pushing and encouraging me to write this book. It was due to his prodding that I finally decided to write.

I also wish to thank Nikhil Dixit for helping me write this book.

Without his help this book would not have seen the light of the day.

I also wish to thank Ms. Aiswarya Iyer, for having helped in editing and polishing the language of the book.

I also thank Ms Ramya Sarma for the final edit of this book. A huge thank you to the publisher Ms. Sonavi Desai of Indus Source Books for putting her faith and trust in me and agreeing to publish this book.

Thank you!

◆◆◆◆◆◆

INTRODUCTION

It was an unusually balmy October evening in 1998. Inside the Birla Krida Kendra Auditorium, situated near the Girgaon Chowpatty, temperatures were rising amongst the gathering of 800-odd traders. The evening was going to probably be the most important one, the legendary hall had held until then. Little did anyone know that this peculiar gathering and what was about to follow, would permanently alter the history of Mumbai city.

While the entire world was grappling with the fear of Y2K and what its effects were going to be, this crowd was preparing to dissent against the political heavyweights of Maharashtra's ruling government and the (in)famous 'high and mighty' Mumbai Police.

As the event prepared to commence, the air was palpably fraught with simmering anger. Sitting on the stage were the then Chief Minister (CM) of Maharashtra (late) Manohar Joshi, Deputy Chief Minister (Deputy CM) (late) Gopinath Munde, Mumbai Police Commissioner (CP) R.H.M. Mendonca, myself and other senior police officers. Never had such a scene been witnessed - that a CM, Deputy CM, CP and Joint CP (Crime) were facing direct public ire and were being held accountable in an open public gathering.

Several traders, businessmen and industrialists of Mumbai had convened the meeting to directly question the government and the police about their inability to tackle the underworld menace that had engulfed the city of Mumbai. Things had become so adverse in the past decade that the business community was in virtual lockdown mode.

Businessmen feared abduction, blackmail or murder, so much so that they were holding off organising their children's weddings in Mumbai, fearing that they would be targeted by the Mumbai underworld to extort money.

The situation had reached boiling point a few days earlier, spurred by the cold-blooded murder of Bharat Shah, owner of Roopam showroom, (not to be confused with his namesake – the film producer who was arrested in the *Chori Chori Chupke Chupke* case) who was shot dead by three assailants in broad daylight, outside his showroom, on 8 October 1998.

The showroom is just a stone's throw away from the Mumbai Police Headquarters and the office of the Mumbai Police chief at Crawford Market in South Mumbai. This incident sent shockwaves through the business community of Mumbai, because of the audacity of the murder and the fact that the underworld had sent a clear message to traders: "Pay up or be killed, and the police will not come to your rescue."

The city was barely limping back to normalcy when it was hit by the proverbial last nail in the coffin – a daylight shootout that resulted in the killing of the restaurateurs, the Kurup brothers, in Bhandup, a few days after Bharat Shah's murder.

The day was 13 October 1998, when two motorcycle-borne assailants stopped outside the Madras Café in Bhandup and shot dead Krishnadas and Haridas Kurup. One moment the brothers were standing behind the cash counter of their hotel and within seconds their lifeless, bullet-riddled bodies were slumped over the cash counter in a pool of blood. The killing was done so speedily that customers who were sitting inside the hotel, the hotel staff, bystanders and other eyewitnesses barely had time to react. They gawked in shock as the shooters climbed back on the motorcycle and sped away.

A few days later, on 18 October, three businessmen were shot dead in a single day. One shootout happened in the morning, another in the afternoon and the third that evening.

In a span of just 15 days, the underworld had killed 12 businessmen across the city, spreading fear and panic. The killing of the Kurup brothers had pushed the morale of the Mumbai Police to its lowest point. Though later, through investigation it was established that the hoteliers had been targeted by the underworld, initially no one, including the police, had any idea why they had been chosen. An exasperated police force was grappling for answers and a way to deal with this hydra-headed monster – the Mumbai underworld.

Such was the fear that people had stopped stepping out and families had stopped going out to eat at luxury hotels, lest they be targeted by the underworld. A majority of the business community had moved their trade and families to the neighbouring state of Gujarat. Business families stopped conducting lavish weddings, receptions and other parties, because they would invariably get a phone call or visit from an underworld member to shell out money.

Inside the auditorium the atmosphere was heating up with anger and resentment. It was as if the frustration, fear, helplessness and anger towards the underworld, which had been piling up for more than two decades, had finally spilled over. The angry traders were like wounded lions waiting to devour those whom they believed had failed to protect them from the wrath of the gangsters.

Traders had armed themselves with placards; they wore black bands around their arms and foreheads and had decided to observe a Black Diwali that year as a mark of protest against the government and the police. Diwali is the biggest festival of the year for a majority of Indians. It is celebrated with fervour and festivity. The trading or business community – the biggest in Mumbai – observing a Black Diwali was a major embarrassment to the government and police and was a major win for the underworld as it denoted the supremacy of fear and the failure of governance.

Chief Minister Manohar Joshi, Deputy Chief Minister Gopinath Munde, Police Commissioner Ronnie Mendonca and I were being pelted with questions. The angry reprimands felt as if we were being taken to the cleaners in a public court (old Mumbai street parlance – *sarvajanik dhulai* literally translated into English means public washing).

The fuming crowd wanted answers. They wanted to know what was being done to ensure their safety, and that of their families and businesses. Neither the CM nor the Deputy CM or CP had any answers to give.

The situation on the streets of Mumbai during the mid-to-late 1990s was almost like a live crime scene. Every other day there were shootouts, intergang rivalry killings and rioting, kidnappings, extortion, looting and muggings. Innocent businessmen, industrialists and traders were being targeted and those who refused to obey the underworld diktat were hunted and gunned down. Those who were born in this century or were toddlers during the last decade of the previous century can never imagine the reign of fear that the underworld had spread across the city.

In the auditorium, as the evening progressed, the crowd was getting livid. Platitudes and pleas from the CM, Deputy CM and CP fell on deaf ears. The businessmen were not willing to accept any more assurances and promises; the dignitaries looked at each other, clueless, even as they were publicly ridiculed.

With no answers coming their way, the traders gave a very stern warning: After Black Diwali they would have no choice but to leave the city and take their business elsewhere. Mumbai's status of being the financial capital of the country and a safe city was under threat if the government and the police did not act fast to tackle the underworld menace.

The nature of public grilling and verbal flogging being extended to government and police would have been a source of mirth and vindication for the members of the underworld who were holed up in Mumbai and in various countries across the world. But they would soon realise that it was the Mumbai Police that was going to have the last laugh.

As the angry traders left, shouting slogans against the government and the police, something had changed. That balmy October evening at Birla Krida Kendra Auditorium played a pivotal role in the Mumbai Police's fight against the underworld.

While leaving the auditorium, I could not help but remember the day in the first week of June 1998 when I met Chief Minister Manohar Joshi in Chandrapur. I was posted as DIG (Nagpur Range) then, and the CM had come to Chandrapur for a visit. The CM told me that the government planned to select me for a very special task and that I should be prepared for it. Within a few days, the government transferred me to Mumbai with a promotion as Special Inspector General of Police and posted me as Joint Commissioner of Police to head the Mumbai Crime Branch.

I took charge as the new chief of the Mumbai Crime Branch on 29 June 1998. Within minutes of my taking charge, two people were killed in a shootout in the western suburbs. Fugitive gangster Chota Rajan's gang-members had shot dead Mohammad Jindran, a real estate developer, along with one other person. The incident got a lot of attention from the media, some members of the press touting it as 'underworld welcomes the new chief of the Mumbai Crime Branch with a double shootout'.

I realised that the special task the government had chosen me for was to end the menace of the Mumbai underworld and free the city and its people from the clutches of crime and terror. When I visited the shootout spot on my first day as the chief of the Mumbai Crime Branch, I vowed to myself that I would leave no stone unturned to finish the underworld and the organised crime syndicate that had held the city hostage with an iron grip around its neck.

♦♦♦♦♦♦

Chapter 1

ORGANISED CRIME AND ITS GENESIS

A general understanding of organised crime could be: when two or more individuals come together to conduct any form of criminal activity for financial gain and/or power.

Crime has been in existence ever since the advent of mankind. The nature and type of crime has changed over time and will keep changing. However, 'organised crime' is a type that has been most dangerous and has caused maximum damage and destruction.

In the latter half of the 1800s, the world was fast turning towards industrialisation. As industries grew, so did the need for an organised work culture. The more organised an industrial unit, the more successful it was. Everyone started realising the importance of an organisation… of being organised.

The world was standing up and taking notice. Amongst the first to realise the importance of organisation was the American mafia, established in 1869, and known as the 'Mob' or the 'Family'. It was the Italian Americans who first started the mob culture in U.S., taking a leaf out of the book of the original Italian Mafia which was simply referred to as the 'Mafia', or the Sicilian Mafia.

High profile criminals across the world soon realised that being organised was more efficient. It gave them more power and control over their men, their territories and the establishment. Within a quarter of a century, the Mob, the Mafia, the Yakuzas of Japan, the Bratva (Brotherhood) from Russia and the Triad from China became internationally organised crime syndicates and they spread their reign of terror across the globe.

Purists define organised crime as an urban phenomenon that revolved around economic activity. So, any activity, when committed by a network of career criminals on a continuing basis for pecuniary gains by using muscle and/or arms power is an organised crime.

Before being organised, criminal gangs were primarily operated by individuals based on their own machismo and charisma. And, when those individuals went out of action because of arrest or murder or death, the gang would become redundant.

What being organised did was that it made the gang or the group bigger than the individual. It ensured that the team continued to operate even if the individual leader was no longer 'operational'. Gang leaders were quick to understand the importance of this and changed their functioning to accommodate this aspect of an organisation.

The one aspect that changed the face of organised crime and helped gangs establish their supremacy across the world was the understanding of the importance of having a structure. They adopted a corporate style of functioning, with a formal hierarchy. Instead of the ringleader doing everything and the whole gang collapsing when left headless, a hierarchy was formed, with specialists brought in for each job.

Another change they made was to establish white-collar and clean businesses – akin to shell companies – to be run by relatives who were (deliberately) not exposed to the crime world. This was done to ensure that family members were not exposed to the police or rival gang members. Gang members were asked to take an oath of 'Omerta' or code of silence and be loyal to it.

Soon they had lawyers who would not only be instrumental in getting imprisoned gang members out on bail, but who also made inroads into the judicial system and found ways to manipulate it. These legal brains told the mobs how to carry out a hit so that the gangs could hoodwink the law.

In the 1980s and 1990s the Mumbai underworld had its own set of lawyers who made a name for themselves in the organised crime world. Some of them became victims of underworld shootouts as well.

Interpol defines organised crime as "any enterprise or group of persons engaged in continuing illegal activity which has its primary activities that bring together a client-public relationship which demands a range of goods and services which are illegal".

Organised crime can involve any group of individuals that is structured, sophisticated and distributed across nations. It is a section of society that seeks to operate outside the control of the people and their government. It is a self-perpetuating, continuing criminal conspiracy for profit and power, using fear and corruption, and seeking protection from law.

The Maharashtra Control of Organised Crime Act (MCOCA) of 1999 defines organised crime as "any continuing unlawful activity by an individual, singly or jointly, either as member of an organised crime syndicate or on behalf of such syndicate by use of violence or threat of violence or intimidation or coercion, or other unlawful means with the objective of gaining primary benefits or gaining undue economic or other advantage for himself or any other person promoting insurgency."

The whole purpose of organised crime was to make money – the authorities knew that. Hence, to hit the underworld where it hurt most, the Government of India enacted laws such as:

- The Conservation of Foreign Exchange and Prevention of Smuggling Activities Act (COFEPOSA), 1974
- The Benami Transactions (Prohibition) Act, 1988
- The Narcotic Drugs and Psychotropic Substances (NDPS) Act, 1985

- The Prevention of Illicit Traffic in Narcotic Drugs and Psychotropic Substances Act, 1988

As law enforcement agencies started chasing the underworld's money, experts and professional financial advisors like chartered accountants (CAs) became part of the organised crime syndicate. While sharpshooters were busy targeting their victims, the CAs used their skills to ensure that dirty money was channelled and hidden in safe havens within and outside the country, so that authorities couldn't lay their hands on it.

Anyone operating in India, whether a corporate entity or an organised crime syndicate, needs one very important individual: a pandit, astrologer or Vaastu expert. There have been instances when gangsters have consulted astrologers before planning a hit. They would be very particular about the day and time of a hit in order to avoid hurdles for their shootouts.

Soon enough, an organised crime syndicate had a corporate-like structure, with the Don being the head (MD or Chairman). One step below would be a Chief Executive Officer (CEO), responsible for the day-to-day functioning of the gang. Whenever a major operation was to be carried out, the MD and the CEO would plan the whole process.

The CEO would then be in charge of implementing it, first identifying and hiring a General Manager or Project Manager, who would be responsible for planning and implementing the entire operation on the ground. The General Manager would always be an established gang-member and a close confidant of the CEO.

It was the General Manager's job to hire specialists for a hit. The trend was to hire horses-for-courses and, in most cases, the specialists would be those who had a track record and had made a name for themselves in the crime world. In the mid-1990s it became common practice to hire gangsters and shooters from Uttar Pradesh and Bihar. The reasoning behind it was that these individuals would have no criminal record in Mumbai and Maharashtra, so the police would find it extremely difficult to identify them after a shootout. It was also a financially sound strategy, as these hitmen came cheap.

Depending on the hit, the number of people involved in a project would be decided. It was the Project Manager's responsibility to arrange for a safe haven for the shooters before the hit was carried out and to ensure a safe passage for them to flee after the deed was done.

Training camps would be organised in old and abandoned mills or forests situated on the outskirts of the city.

In case someone was hit or injured during an operation, doctors would be arranged for their treatment, and thus medical staff were also inducted into the organised crime hierarchy.

There have been instances when policemen and judges were included in the crime syndicate to ensure passage of timely information and help in those cases.

All these made an organised crime syndicate a robust 'professional' structure, which became extremely successful in carrying out criminal activities and at the same time managing to hoodwink the police and the law.

As their structure and organisation grew, these criminal gangs became more and more strict about whom they recruited. Each potential member was thoroughly vetted to see if he was in any way associated with a rival gang or had links to the police. The criminal organisation also wanted to ensure that they recruited specialists for each position and not anyone who could become a liability.

The ultimate selling proposition of any gang is the fear it generates in the minds of the public and the ability to successfully commit crimes. In the 1980s and 1990s, underworld gangs took their operations very seriously. The success of any operation was a matter of ego and money. Unsuccessful operations would become the target of ridicule in the underworld and were frowned upon by the bosses.

Another rule followed by these gangs involved the use of violence against its own gang members and those of rival gangs. This was to ensure that members remained loyal to their own gangs and did not spill trade secrets to rivals or to law enforcement agencies, and to instil fear in them.

Violent acts against gang members always had an impact on others in the gang. It would ensure that the other gang members or any of their family members did not speak to anyone about gang-related activities. Another rule followed during the early days of operations of the underworld was that no family members of any operatives of rival gang members would be targeted.

Even though earning as much money as possible through legal and illegal means is the core principle of any organised crime syndicate, another aspect which is of equal if not more importance, is power. Crime syndicates and gangs thrive on it and want to be in the corridors of power. Being in or proximate to power is like opium for a criminal organisation. Not only is it considered to be good for business, but it is also a massive ego boost for the gang and its members. However, power, especially that earned at the behest of fear or money, is fickle and can dissipate as fast as the results.

After running his smuggling empire for more than two decades, yesteryear don Haji Mastan dabbled in movie making and politics. He formed his own party (The Dalit Muslim Suraksha Maha Sangh) and even contested elections, but without much success.

Gangster Arun Gawli, after running his own gang for more than a decade, formed his own political outfit (Akhil Bhartiya Sena) and was even elected as a Member of the Legislative Assembly (MLA) in Maharashtra. That did not last too long. Gawli is currently in jail serving life imprisonment after being convicted under the MCOCA in the murder case of Shiv Sena leader Kamlakar Jamsandekar.

There are several such instances in India as well as across the world, where a crime syndicate boss or gangster has entered politics, sometimes even at the cost of his gang. Mexican drug lord Pablo Escobar is one such example – he spent millions of dollars to enter politics and even got himself inducted into the country's parliament. However, he did so at the cost of his syndicate and by the time he realised his folly, it was too late.

Another tool used by gangsters as part of organised crime is intimidation. And it is wielded for forcing someone to do or not to do something. A person could be intimidated into selling or handing over a plot of land for a throwaway price or could be stopped from buying a property because it is beneficial for the gangsters.

The murder of builder Pradeep Jain in 1995 is one such case, when gangster Abu Salem committed the crime. Jain and his brothers owned a property in the Kol-Dongri area of Andheri (East) in Mumbai, and Salem wanted it. However, Jain refused to part with it. Salem first tried to intimidate Jain and, when he did not relent, he had him murdered.

Abu Salem, along with his paramour, actress Monica Bedi, was extradited to India from Portugal in 2005. In 2017, the Special Terrorist and Disruptive Activities Act (TADA) Court pronounced him guilty of involvement in the 1993 serial bomb blasts in Mumbai and sentenced him to life imprisonment. He also stood trial in the Pradeep Jain murder case and in 2015 a special court convicted Salem and sentenced him to life imprisonment in that case as well.

When Abu Salem and Monica Bedi were arrested in Lisbon in 2002, India did not have an extradition treaty with Portugal. India had to fight a prolonged legal battle in the Supreme Court of Portugal for the extradition. Salem appealed to the Portugal Supreme Court not to extradite him to India, as he feared being targeted on the pretext that he belonged to a minority community and could be sentenced to death by Indian law.

Portugal has abolished capital punishment, while India still upholds the death penalty in the rarest of rare cases. To ensure that Salem was extradited and faced the law for the crimes that he had committed in India, the Government of India had to give an undertaking to the Portugal Supreme Court that Salem would not be sentenced to more than 25 years' imprisonment if found guilty of his crimes.

As organised crime started becoming lucrative, the industry started attracting more talent into it – newer criminals were recruited, and with them came newer crimes and forms of crimes. Apart from indulging in conventional crimes, gangs also now started getting involved in non-conventional activities that raked in more moolah for them.

Their activities included creating public disorder – whenever there was a need for civil unrest or public disorder, gangs would be summoned to incite it (given the contract, as it was known). As their involvement in such cases wasn't reported earlier, it took a few instances before the police and government realised who was responsible for organising these flare ups.

They also indulged in booth capturing during elections for influential politicians and political parties. This was a dual opportunity for them as not only was this a lucrative venture, but it also helped them build alliances with politicians who eventually became powerful as ministers.

Criminals also found that monopolising a business with the help of muscle power brought in big bucks. They did so by grabbing major government contracts in coal mines, Indian Railways, labour contracts in Special Economic Zones (SEZ) and transport contracts.

A paucity of water and electricity supply gave rise to various groups like the water mafia and electricity mafia. The rise and reach of cable television in the early 1990s resulted in the cable TV mafia. In Mumbai, every gang had its own cable mafia across the city.

With an increasing population and scarcity of land, land and property prices in Mumbai skyrocketed; this resulted in gangsters indulging in land-grabbing, illegal encroachments, extortion, kidnappings and murder for land/property.

The more organised they got, the more confident they became. With the increasing number of people in a gang there was a need to ensure that they were protected each time they got into trouble. The age-old system of corruption often did the trick. Wherever possible, gang members bribed their way through the system. They already had corrupt police officers and lawyers on their roster – these people would identify officials who were susceptible to corruption.

All kinds and types of incentives were deployed, from paying out money to payment in 'kind'. Money was used to directly bribe officials, but where that was not possible, other methods were used. Getting government officials transferred to postings of their choice, funding children's education abroad, arranging international vacations, buying property, expensive jewellery, cars, alcohol and other valuables... the rewards were diverse and limitless. Gangs also had several actresses, escorts and sex workers on their payroll, who were offered as enticement and used as honeytraps.

All this was part of an organised racket; once a government official was entangled in this web, he would always remain there and would have to work for the syndicate. There are allegations that as part of the racket, gangs kept records of bribes paid to government officials. They would often stealthily record officials taking bribes or in compromising positions with sex workers and escorts. This damaging evidence would then be used to blackmail the officials, who would thereby be on the payroll forever.

- **Why People Turn to Crime**

    - Economic and social inequality
    - Outdated laws
    - Cumbersome procedures in court
    - Inadequate manpower in the police force
    - Lack of resources with the police force, e.g., archaic machinery
    - General apathy of the public
    - Crash in real estate prices
    - Fluctuation in the share market
    - Globalisation and liberalisation of the economy
    - Influx of population in Mumbai
    - Ever-growing floating population
    - Increasing numbers of unemployed youth
    - High degree of anonymity
    - Introduction of pre-paid SIM cards
    - Lack of extradition treaties with various countries
    - Undue delays in trials
    - Liberal grant of bail and anticipatory bail facility
    - Glamorisation of criminals in the print and electronic media

It was observed that as the numbers of gangs and their members grew, with an influx of money and patronage, the nature of their operations evolved too. For instance:

- Commission of sensational crimes, especially attacks on policemen, to grab the limelight
- Calculated efforts to gain media attention
- Claiming patronage of politicians and government officials
- Concentrating in a particular area of influence and making efforts to monopolise it
- Phone calls for terror and extortion

Mafia activities carried out globally are irrespective of borders and very similar, such as:

- Smuggling
- Drugs – production, sale and smuggling
- Bootlegging
- Gambling
- Cricket match fixing (could be any sport!)
- Horse racing
- Pornography
- Bank fraud
- Extortion
- Illegal travel documents
- Employment rackets
- Export of antiques
- *Hawala* transactions
- Land grabbing
- Settlement of property disputes
- Dealing in animal skins
- Gun running
- Prostitution
- Contract killing
- Insurance fraud
- Theft from mines
- Export of labour, girls and children
- Booth capturing and rigging
- Piracy
- Dacoities and robberies
- Computer crimes

Almost all countries are increasingly confronted by the challenge of transnational organised crime, the major patterns of which have been documented in recent years:

- Illicit drug trafficking
- Smuggling

- Money laundering
- Financial fraud
- Counterfeiting
- Illegal arms trafficking
- International car theft rings
- Prostitution
- Economic offences
- Cybercrimes and frauds

◆◆◆◆◆◆

Chapter 2

WHY MUMBAI?

Mumbai – Bombay or Bombaim, as the Portuguese called it – has always been the most coveted crown jewel of every regime since the 1300s. From the Muslim rulers of Gujarat who were governing the areas of modern-day Thane and Vasai, to the Portuguese and later the British, everyone has wanted Mumbai for its location as a strategic natural harbour, and the fact that it has been almost impossible to attack from the mainland.

The Portuguese built ports, forts and churches, converting the seven islands of Bombaim into an important centre for trade and business. Merchant ships from across the world were soon passing through the city and international trade started flourishing.

Even though they entered India from Calcutta (now Kolkata), the British had always understood Bombay's importance. They had kept an eye on it from the start and were in constant confrontation with the Portuguese to take over control of Bombay, to no avail.

After having failed several times, the British took a different route to gain the territory. In 1662, Charles II of England got married to

Catherine of Braganza, daughter of King John IV of Portugal. As part of Catherine's dowry, the whole of Bombay was given to the British.

The British further developed the city and converted Bombay into a major port for trade and transport. Soon, it became the nerve centre for employment and business. People started to flock to the city from all corners of the country to set up their businesses or look for employment.

By the time India achieved its independence, Bombay had become the financial capital of the new India. While Delhi became the political centre, Bombay was a magnet for people looking to earn money. There were opportunities galore for anyone who was willing to work hard. Several success stories became part of Bombay folklore, giving the city its reputation of the 'City of Dreams' or *'Maya Nagari'*.

The financial successes of those who had fared well for themselves here, and the *Maya Nagari* tag, also attracted unwanted attention from anti-social elements.

India achieved independence in 1947 and the state of Maharashtra was formed on 1 May 1960, with Bombay as its capital. By then it was already an international destination, a port city, a centre for trade and business. The Hindi film industry – Bollywood, as it is known today – was already established and becoming a huge attraction for people from all over the country.

As the license raj came into existence, its loopholes were leveraged by some who began exploiting it. Thus began the era of smuggling in Bombay with bootleggers, gambling lords, gold and silver smugglers, and drug cartels leading it.

Because it was an important port, most of the import and export transportation by sea happened through the docks in Bombay. This gave ample opportunity to those who wanted to make quick money.

The prohibition policy of the Maharashtra government provided a lucrative ground for bootlegging, or trade in illicit liquor. This business was associated with *matka*, the illegal gambling racket.

In the 1960s, Varadarajan Muniswamy Mudaliar, nicknamed Vardhabhai, who started his career in crime with petty theft in the

Mumbai docks, emerged as the sole controller of bootlegging from Gujarat to southern Mumbai. With the acquisition of considerable wealth, he subsequently attained 'Godfather' status among the poor by providing them protection and speedy justice.

To gain legitimacy Vardhabhai also played an important role in organising the annual Ganapati festival. He was the first criminal in the history of Mumbai crime who could subvert the law enforcement system effectively. He created a Robin Hood-like image of himself by indulging in charity work in service of the poor people he treated as the constituents of his area.

He achieved cult-status, especially in areas like Dharavi, touted as Asia's biggest slum. Such was his popularity that he was immortalised in movies like *Nayakan* (made in Tamil on the life of Varadarajan, the protagonist played by famous actor Kamal Hasan) and *Dayavan* (the Hindi remake, starring actor Vinod Khanna).

Haji Mastan and Yusuf Patel, who specialised in smuggling gold and silver, and later invested their money in construction and real estate businesses, were contemporaries of Varadarajan. Smuggling being their main focus, their hold was limited to South Mumbai and the dockyard area. Later, Haji Mastan became a self-styled politician, while Patel established himself in the construction business.

By the 1970s Mumbai had become a major hub for smuggling operations. Everything from gold and silver to electronic goods, clothes, hooch, etc. was being smuggled in and out of the city. The gangsters were making impressive amounts of black money, and they soon expanded to organised crime, with Karim Lala, Haji Mastan and Varadarajan Mudaliar forming their own gangs.

They also had exclusive areas of operation, with a clear understanding that they would not interfere in the others' area of operation. Another important unwritten pact was that there would be no bloodshed or gang rivalry. The gangs would stay away from targeting rival gangsters or their family members, as well as from the others' respective businesses.

The imposition of the national Emergency in 1975 broke the

supremacy of these gangs in Mumbai, but it also provided an opportunity for unemployed youth and small-time smugglers to make a living through illicit activities.

It was fugitive gangster Dawood Ibrahim, in the late 1970s and early 1980s who changed the game. As a youngster he joined the Haji Mastan gang and was part of the gold smuggling syndicate. Dawood soon realised that if he had to succeed and make money, he would need to break the rules. 'Creating chaos through disruption and gaining control' was the mantra that he used. It was Dawood who first violated the unwritten rule of non-interference and resorted to violence by attacking rival gang members and stealing their goods.

All this while, Bombay had witnessed only smuggling operations and stray incidents attributed to the crime world. Ordinary citizens were not affected by these; hence smuggling activities also went unreported as few knew about them, and those who knew did not want to interfere.

However, Dawood's entry and rise in the crime world changed this. To strengthen his hold over smuggling and criminal activities, Dawood started kidnapping and extortion rackets. He began abducting businessmen and industrialists and released them in exchange for huge sums of money. With this started the era of extortion and kidnapping as organised crime in Bombay.

Soon, Dawood and his gang members resorted to killing rival gangsters, and the once silent and peaceful streets of Bombay where multiple smuggler ganglords coexisted in relative peace, became bloody. The entire decade of the 1980s witnessed bloody battles on the streets between rival gangs run by Dawood Ibrahim, the Pathan gang, the Rajan gang and the Arun Gawli gang, among others. The decade also saw the decline of smuggling dons like Karim Lala, Haji Mastan and Varadarajan Mudaliar.

By the mid-1980s, increasing pressure from the Mumbai Police forced Dawood to flee the country. He fled to Dubai in 1986 and started running his gang from there. His stranglehold over the crime world continued remotely. His close aides like Chhota Shakeel and

Chhota Rajan moved to Dubai a few years later and were running the Mumbai underworld from there.

As the business of smuggling, extortion, kidnapping for ransom, land-grabbing and murder became more lucrative, the rivalry among gangs became more intense. All of them wanted their share of money from this *Maya Nagari* and hence waged bloody wars against each other. By the 1990s, the underworld had become a big bad world of money, power and lawlessness.

At the same time, industrialisation and liberalisation had ensured that the Indian economy was booming. This resulted in several new businesses coming up, which in turn meant new opportunities for the underworld to exploit. Also, the faces of the criminals were changing.

Till the late 1980s, most of the gangsters were from Mumbai and neighbouring districts of Maharashtra. For instance, Dawood's family hailed from the coastal village of Khed, in the Ratnagiri district of Maharashtra.

Over the next decade, most of the gangsters were roped in from outside the state, especially from Uttar Pradesh and Bihar. This was done primarily to hoodwink the police. Gangsters who belonged to Mumbai or neighbouring areas were easily identified by the police and arrested. But those recruited from UP and Bihar were difficult to keep track of because they did not have any criminal records, and no history sheets in Mumbai or Maharashtra. They had no background or family based in Mumbai or Maharashtra either. They would simply come to Mumbai, do their job and go back home, making it near impossible for the police to trace or track them.

There was another advantage to hiring hitmen from different states – they would bring their famous *kattas*, or country-made firearms, locally produced in their hometowns. These were sold in the black market for paltry sums and were almost always impossible to trace back, as they did not have any registration or embossed identification marks.

While gangsters and weapons were being sourced via illegitimate means from different states, the underworld was also figuring out ways to move money. It led to the formation of an entirely new and different type of crime: *hawala*.

The transnational and international network formed by these criminals ensured that the *hawala* network became quickly operational and successful. This was another business which the organised crime syndicates ventured into quite successfully and continue to use even today.

The Government of India, which was aware of the rampant smuggling of gold, silver and other valuables by the underworld in the 1970s and 1980s, had by the 1990s made major changes in its economic policies. Several stringent laws had been enacted, including COFEPOSA, making it extremely difficult for gangs to conduct smuggling activities with ease. With the illegal passage of gold, silver and valuables not being lucrative anymore, the underworld shifted its focus elsewhere.

Extortion, kidnapping, abduction, drugs, arms trafficking, film financing and real estate had started raking in the big bucks. Gangs which had the money and muscle power started grabbing prime real estate at throwaway prices, using force if necessary.

There was more. Gangsters like Dawood Ibrahim, Chota Shakeel, Abu Salem and Anees Ibrahim (Dawood Ibrahim's younger brother) had recognised the money-making potential of Bollywood. Instead of making extortion calls to filmmakers and risking being exposed, they slyly infiltrated the film industry and through the people they placed inside, started financing films with big budgets.

This proved to be a masterstroke – it not only yielded huge profits for the criminals but also gave them a chance to get close to the film stars, especially the actresses.

The infamous case of the Hindi film *Chori Chori Chupke Chupke,* in which high profile producer Bharat Shah, director Nazeem Rizvi and his assistant Abdul Rahim Allah Baksh Khan were arrested is part of underworld history. The special MCOCA court in Mumbai convicted and sentenced Bharat Shah to one-year's rigorous imprisonment (Shah was convicted for having deliberately concealed information from the police about extortion plans between Shakeel and Rizvi), while Rizvi and Khan were sentenced to undergo six years of rigorous imprisonment. ***(Read about the entire case in detail in Chapter 7 on page no. 140.)***

It is well known that famous Bollywood stars made a beeline to Dubai to mark their presence at lavish parties thrown by Dawood in the 1990s. Several actors have been photographed and videographed watching cricket matches in Sharjah sitting beside Dawood, Chhota Shakeel and other gangsters.

In the mythological epic *Ramayana*, we learn that the demon Maricha took the form of a golden deer and made Lord Ram chase after him through the jungles of Panchavati. Immediately after that, the demon Ravana disguised as a sage abducted Sita and took her to Lanka. And in the *Mahabharata*, we learn that the demon Putna came in the disguise of a beautiful woman to poison Lord Krishna.

In the same manner, the demons of our world – i.e., the criminals – disguised themselves as businessmen and started doing legitimate business in different industries. These include:

- Real estate and construction
- Hotels
- Films
- Cable TV
- Money laundering
- *Hawala* transactions
- Other business fronts

• Real Estate and Construction Industry

Some builders are themselves responsible for the entry of gangs into the construction industry. They took the help of the criminals to get the flats or plots of land vacated and to settle property-related disputes. They paid protection money to gangs, who reinvested this money with the builders.

The nexus between the real estate developers (or builders, as they were called then) resulted in a reign of terror for the ordinary citizens of Mumbai and Maharashtra. Through their gang connections the builders spread terror and would force people to vacate their homes, and then forcibly take over land belonging to legitimate owners.

These atrocities resulted in the Government of Maharashtra enacting the Rent Control Act in 1999, which gave power to tenants, property owners, the police, the administration and the judiciary to ensure that no one was victimised by the gangsters or builders. However, the unholy nexus between builders and gangsters resulted in a war between rival builders. A fallout of these rivalries was that several builders were branded as being close to a particular gang and targeted and shot dead by rival gangs.

Details of builders killed by various gangs

Date	Victim	Gang responsible
07/03/1995	Pradeep Jain	Abu Salem
18/09/1995	Om Prakash Kukreja	Dawood Ibrahim
12/06/1996	Shantilal Patel	Chhota Rajan
17/04/1997	Vallabh Thakkar	Arun Gawli
19/08/1997	Natwarlal Desai	Arun Gawli
05/02/1998	Manish Shah Lala	Arun Gawli
20/10/1998	Sohail Sayyed	Chota Rajan
01/03/1999	Majid Khan Wahi Khan	Chota Rajan

Other killings of businessmen

- Sunit Khatau of Khatau Mills was helped by the Gawli gang to sort out labour problems. He was killed by the Amar Naik gang in 1994.
- Garment dealer Bharat Shah of Roopam store was shot dead on 8 October 1998, by members of the Chhota Shakeel gang.

• Hotel Industry

The hotel and restaurant industry in Mumbai has an annual turnover of several thousand crore rupees. It offers direct and indirect employment to more than a million people. The underworld had developed strong interest in this world, especially in restaurants and bars.

In the hotel industry, especially the infamous dance bars of Mumbai, more than 75,000 dancers were employed. They raked in huge moolah for hoteliers, as rich businessmen from Mumbai and Gujarat splurged lakhs of rupees (sometimes in just one night on a single girl) there. The exorbitant amount of money flowing, the glamour and the flesh trade involved, turned out to be a natural attraction for the underworld.

Hoteliers killed by criminal gangs

Sr. No	Date	Victim
1	13/06/1995	Harish Vallabhdas Bhatia
2	15/06/1995	Ramnath Payyade
3	18/12/1995	Aslam Patni
4	08/10/1996	D.N. Ghosh
5	07/10/1998	Deviprasad Narayan Hegde
6	07/10/1998	Balkrishna Gopal Kotiyan
7	13/10/1998	Amar Vasu Shetty
8	30/10/1998	Krishnadas and Haridas Kurup
9	01/06/1999	Leo Jainath Carvalho
10	20/01/2000	Jiyauddin Naimul Haq
11	04/04/2001	Shafiq Ahmed Khan
12	04/05/2001	Jaya Shetty
13	21/12/2001	Ratnakar Shetty

- **Cable TV Industry**

Because of the multi-crore investment and introduction of the latest technology like fibre optics, gangsters had forcibly placed their relatives and contacts as local area distributors. Thus, their grip over the cable industry was established. And they strengthened that grip with blood.

Cable executive Ram Panjabi was killed on 11 September 1998 in Mumbai and soon thereafter P. Ramakrishna, Zee TV's regional director (south) and Siticable's resident director, was shot dead outside his home in Vijayawada.

Thus, by the mid-1990s, or the final years of the last decade of the previous century, the underworld's hold over Mumbai was a given. Organised crime had Mumbai in its stranglehold and was ruling the City of Dreams.

As the cases escalated in number, gravity and frequency, it was time for the Mumbai Police to do something about it, otherwise Mumbai would never be safe again.

◆◆◆◆◆◆

Chapter 3

VINTAGE GANGSTERS OF MUMBAI

There was a famous saying in the underworld in the 1970s: *Hum beimaani ka dhanda bhi imaandari se karte hai* (Our business may be dishonest, but we conduct it with utmost integrity). This used to be true of the three most famous gangsters of Mumbai in the 1960s and 1970s.

Haji Mastan, Varadarajan Mudaliar and Karim Lala built an empire out of smuggling, the *matka* business and illegal hooch, but within their criminal nexus they had set certain principles and ethics that they followed unequivocally. While this does not justify the crimes they engineered, in hindsight, compared to the reign that followed, they were the lesser of the evils that we had to deal with.

They built their empires based on trust and mutual respect. All three had their gangs in operation around the same time in Mumbai, from the 1960s to the late 1980s. Over time, they decided to split the city into three parts and promised not to encroach on each other's territory. Due to this, they were able to operate their syndicates smoothly without fear of interference by the others.

They were Mumbai's very own version of *The Godfather's* characters of Don Corleone and his sons.

- **Karim Lala**

Hailing from a small village called Samalam in the Shegal district of Kunar province in Afghanistan, Abdul Karim Sher Khan was born to a poor Pathan family. He was just nine years old when his extended family decided to migrate to India to escape poverty in Afghanistan.

Abdul Karim Sher Khan along with his extended family reached Mumbai in 1920 and settled in a small ghetto in the Bhendi Bazaar area. It was a time when the entire country was dealing with the deadly plague epidemic.

Having to support a large family, Abdul Karim Sher Khan started working as a porter in the docks. Being a heavily built, fair-skinned Pathan who spoke with a heavy Afghan accent, Khan immediately stood out in the crowd of porters who were thin, lanky and dark-skinned. He was soon noticed and approached by a local ethnic Pathan gang to work for them for a sizeable amount of money. This gang was employed by Gujarati and Marwari businessmen as recovery agents. Abdul Karim Sher Khan agreed and got immediate popularity as a recovery agent and gained a new moniker: 'Karim Lala'.

In no time Karim Lala rose through the ranks and became the head of the Pathan gang. He established his supremacy over the crime world in South Mumbai. The Pathan gang soon became notorious for contract killings, land grabbing, extortion, kidnappings, hooch smuggling and the *matka* business.

Lala ruled with a hand of terror for two decades. Along with Haji Mastan and Varadarajan Mudaliar he formed the troika of ganglords who ruled the Mumbai criminal world for most of the 1960s and 1970s. By the late 1970s, failing health forced Lala to take a step back. He handed over the reins of his gang and his empire to his nephew, Samad Khan.

But Lala had left his mark on the Mumbai crime world. It was noticed even by Bollywood and quite a few characters in the movies made during that time were based on Lala, his personality and his life.

The most famous of these was played by actor Pran Krishan Sikand Ahluwalia, better known by his mononym 'Pran', in the blockbuster movie *Zanjeer*. Pran's character was that of a Pathan from Kabul who came to Mumbai and became a gangster. He was named Sher Khan in the movie, taken from Karim Lala's real name: Abdul Karim Sher Khan.

Incidentally, this was the same movie which made superstar Amitabh Bachchan into a star overnight, with the title of 'Angry Young Man'. Bachchan portrayed the character of an upright police inspector in the film.

After having retired from the crime world, Pathan ran a legitimate business of hotels and a travel agency. He died in 2002 in Mumbai at the age of 90.

- **Haji Mastan**

Born Mastan Mirza in 1926 to a Tamil Muslim family in a small village in the Panaikulam area of Tamil Nadu, Haji Mastan migrated to Mumbai with his father. He was eight years old.

At a very young age Mastan began doing odd jobs in the Crawford Market area of South Mumbai and soon found his way into the docks. By the time he was in his twenties, Mastan had a strong foothold in the docks. It was during this time that the Government of India had put a heavy import duty on gold, which resulted in people choosing to smuggle the precious metal.

Post-Independence, the foreign exchange drain was accentuated in 1962 during the border dispute with China. Morarji Desai, then finance minister, passed the Gold Control Act, 1962, which recalled all gold loans given by banks and banned forward

trading in the metal. In 1963, the production of gold jewellery above 14 carat was banned. In 1965, a gold bond scheme was launched, with tax immunity for unaccounted wealth. All these steps failed to yield the desired result. Desai finally introduced the Gold Control Act on 24 August 1968, which prohibited citizens from owning gold in the form of bars and coins.

All existing holdings of gold coins and bars had to be converted to jewellery and declared to the authorities. Goldsmiths were not allowed to own more than 100 grams of gold. Licensed dealers were not supposed to own more than 2 kg of gold, depending upon the number of artisans employed by them. They were banned from trading with each other.

Desai believed that Indians would respond positively to these steps and stop buying gold and help conserve precious foreign exchange. New gold jewellery purchases were either recycled or smuggled gold. This legislation killed the official gold market, and a large unofficial trade sprang up, dealing in cash only. Gold was smuggled in and sold through the unofficial channels that involved many jewellers and bullion traders.

A huge black market developed for the precious metal. Goldsmiths were an unorganised labour force and could not cope with the new situation. *(Source: Wikipedia; JETIR, "Impact of gold trade on Indian economy", April 2019, Vol. 6, Issue 4.)*

Mastan sensed an opportunity in this and soon started smuggling gold using his network in the docks. He was a sharp young man who almost immediately started making big money. He joined hands with Sukkur Narayan Bakia, a notorious smuggler from the union territory of Daman. This was done to control the gold smuggling syndicate in Mumbai and in the seacoast of Maharashtra and Gujarat. The syndicate smuggled gold by the sea route from countries in the Persian Gulf.

Early in his crime career, Mastan realised the importance of money and power. He consciously cultivated an image of being powerful, hobnobbing with high-ranking police officers, bureaucrats, ministers, people in important posts in the government, industrialists and film personalities.

He was known for his extravagant taste and love for branded clothes, watches and other accessories. He would dress in white and ride in a white Mercedes, smoking a cigar. He did this deliberately to appear affluent and influential to the public.

Three prominent gangs ruling the underworld in Mumbai during this time: Mastan's gang, the Pathan gang and Vardarajan's gang. A shrewd man, Mastan realised that if the three groups kept fighting amongst themselves, it would benefit no one but cause losses to all. Therefore, with the help of a common friend, Jenabai Daruwali (another Mafia frontrunner engaged in illicit liquor business), Mastan arranged for a meeting between the three crime lords at his sprawling mansion situated by the seaside on Pedder Road.

At the meeting it was decided that the three gangs would split the areas and operate within the boundaries of their own territory and not encroach on each other's. Thus began a very successful underworld era of smuggling in Mumbai. It lasted for about two decades, from the 1960s to the late 1980s.

While smuggling operations were in full swing, the shrewd businessman Mastan branched out into other sectors like real estate and film financing. He eventually became a film producer himself.

In the early 1980s, Mastan became more interested in cultivating his own image and sourced out his criminal operations to those in his gang, and to Varadarajan. Mastan was close to Varadarajan; both hailed from the same area in Tamil Nadu. In fact, he became so close to Varadarajan that when Varadarajan died in Madras on 2 January 1988, Mastan chartered a special flight to bring his body to Mumbai so that his last rites could be conducted in the city, as Varadarajan had wished.

During the Emergency in 1977, Haji Mastan was jailed. While imprisoned, he claimed to have been influenced by Jaiprakash

Narayan's ideology. After being released he launched his own political party, the Dalit Muslim Suraksha Maha Sangh, in 1985.

However, neither his political career nor his stint as a film producer gained as much success as did his criminal activities. He died in 1994 in Mumbai following a cardiac arrest.

Bollywood's enchantment with these mafia dons continued – several characters in movies were based on Haji Mastan and his lifestyle, the most famous being played by superstar Amitabh Bachchan in the film *Deewar.* In more recent years, *Once Upon a Time in Mumbai* was based on Haji Mastan's life, the lead played by Ajay Devgn. Emraan Hashmi enacted the role based on Dawood Ibrahim's character.

- **Varadarajan Mudaliar**

Born into a poor family in Tuticorin (now Thootukudi) district of Tamil Nadu, Varadarajan Muthusamy Mudaliar migrated to Mumbai in 1945 when he was 19 years old. He and his father settled in the Dharavi slums, which housed a massive population of South Indians, mainly from Andhra Pradesh and Tamil Nadu.

To make ends meet, Varadarajan started working as a porter (coolie) at the then Victoria Terminus (VT) railway station. He frequented the docks which were situated close to the station and soon got involved in smuggling goods to and from the dock area. He began earning well.

His business acumen was strong, and he soon realised that his strength was numbers. He started setting up his own empire in Asia's biggest slum, Dharavi. Varadarajan resorted to all sorts of crimes to establish his supremacy, from extortion and kidnapping to contract killing, land grabbing, illegal gambling and liquor dens, manufacturing illicit liquor and bootlegging. Within no time he became the undisputed king of illegal manufacture and smuggling of illicit liquor (hooch) in Mumbai.

Varadarajan also developed a Robin Hood kind of personality – he started helping poor South Indians in Dharavi in every way possible.

He would settle disputes, give money to the needy, etc., and soon developed a cult-like following in the Dharavi-Sion-Matunga area. The Ganapati festival celebration he hosted became the talk of the town and was visited by top personalities from the film industry and other prominent people.

Varadarajan joined hands with Haji Mastan and Karim Lala, making a triumvirate that ruled the entire Mumbai underworld for close to two decades. For a brief period in the early 1980s Vardhabhai, as he was fondly called by his followers, was the undisputed king of the Mumbai underworld, because Haji Mastan had retired from his crime business and Karim Lala had handed over the reins of his empire to his nephew, Samad Khan.

However, Varadarajan's rein at the top was short-lived. Soon afterwards, the Mumbai Police started specifically targeting him and his gang members. The police registered and filed multiple cases against Varadarajan and his people across many police stations in the city. They even stopped him hosting his Ganapati festival celebration, which was a huge blow to him and his reputation. Frustrated and angry, Varadarajan decided to leave the city and fled to Chennai.

He lived his last years in obscurity and finally died of a heart attack in Chennai on 2 January 1988. His last wish was to be cremated in Mumbai. His close friend Haji Mastan chartered a private plane to bring his body from Chennai to Mumbai for his last rites.

Just like with the other dons, the Indian film industry was fascinated by Vardhabhai. His character too was portrayed in many films, the most famous being *Nayakan*, directed by Mani Ratnam with Kamal Hassan playing the main role. The same movie was later remade in Hindi – called *Dayavan*, it starred Vinod Khanna in the lead.

◆◆◆◆◆◆

Chapter 4

BLOODY AND MESSY UNDERWORLD – THE DAWOOD ERA

A lot has been written, read and seen about India's most wanted man, global terrorist Dawood Ibrahim Kaskar. What is not known widely is that Dawood was singlehandedly responsible for changing the narrative of Mumbai's crime trajectory when he made an entry into the Mumbai underworld.

As the undisputed kings of the crime world in Mumbai, Haji Mastan, Mudaliar Varadarajan and Karim Lala abided by the rules they had set for the gangs and their operations. They would not encroach on each other's area of operations; they would not steal from each other; they would not indulge in violence against each other; and rival gang members' families would not be targeted. Therefore, the three gangsters operated their teams without many skirmishes.

However, Dawood broke all the rules and converted the Mumbai underworld into a bloody and messy realm.

Ironically, Dawood Ibrahim was born into the family of a Mumbai policeman. His father, Ibrahim Kaskar, was a head constable in the

Detection Crime Branch (DCB), Criminal Investigation Department (CID) of the Mumbai Police.

Born on 27 December 1955, Dawood was one of 12 siblings (seven brothers and five sisters):

Brothers:

1. Shabbir Ibrahim Kaskar (eldest brother) – Dead. He was killed by rival gangster Samad Khan on 12 February 1981, in one of the most daring underworld shootouts at a petrol pump in Prabhadevi in Mumbai.
2. Iqbal Ibrahim Kaskar – Alive. He fled the country in the 1990s. Kaskar was deported from UAE in 2003 and arrested in a murder and conspiracy case. He was later acquitted in both cases. He is currently in Mumbai and is reportedly looking after the remaining operations and businesses of Dawood in the city.
3. Noora Ibrahim – Dead. He died in 2011 after both his kidneys failed.
4. Anees Ibrahim – Alive. He lives in Pakistan and is currently believed to be handling all operations of the D-Company, along with gangster Chota Shakeel.
5. Mustaqeen Ali – Alive. Lives with Dawood in Karachi, Pakistan.
6. Mohammad Humayun – Dead. On 23 June 2016, Dawood's youngest brother died after fighting a losing battle with cancer. He was 40 years old and had left Dawood and his criminal activities and was leading a normal life in Karachi, Pakistan.

Sisters:

1. Shaheeda Hasan Miya Wagle – Dead.
2. Zaitun Hamid Antulay – Alive. Resides in London.
3. Farzana Saud Tungekar – Alive. Reportedly stays in the western suburbs of Mumbai.

4. Mumtaz Rahim Faki – Alive. Reportedly resides in Karachi.
5. Haseena Parkar – Dead. When she was alive, she handled all gangland-related activities of Dawood in Mumbai.

The family lived at 33/36, Pakmodia Street, Haji Ismail Musafirkhana in Dongri, South Mumbai. During Dawood's early years, home was in the Zadgaon area of Dongri. He went to the Ahmed Sailor High School in Nagpada but dropped out when he was just 12 years old.

Working as a police constable and supporting a family of 14 people was not easy for Ibrahim Kaskar. Given the situation, Dawood became a street urchin from a very young age.

Dawood rarely attended school, choosing instead to roam the streets of Mumbai with his elder brother Shabbir, also a drop-out from the same school. Both children would look for odd jobs to make money. The mean streets of the city quickly taught Dawood invaluable lessons that helped him run his own gang in later years. Money was an important and powerful tool, he discovered.

Another lesson he learned was that loyalty and trust were hard to come by, and that it was good business sense to hold on to someone once you found them to be loyal and trustworthy. Dawood followed this mantra through his life of crime, according to underworld folklore. He was known to handsomely reward loyalty and always treasured trustworthy people, keeping them in his close circle of friends.

Dawood and Shabbir took to small-time theft and fraud in the Mohammad Ali Road and Bhendi Bazaar area of South Mumbai. The Pathan gang and the Haji Mastan gang had an iron grip over the crime world in South Mumbai at the time. Samad Khan, the eccentric nephew of ganglord Karim Lala, was head of the Pathan gang, while Haji Mastan himself was lording it over his smuggling operations.

Both Dawood and Shabbir realised that they were the smaller fish in this dangerous ocean and had to obey the *jungle raj* if they had to survive. In fact, to get access and exposure to their style of working, they even took up small-time jobs for both gangs – they would do recovery (*vasuli*) from businessmen, offloading smuggled goods and transporting them to hideouts.

They were mentored by a local goon named Baashu Dada, who taught them the tricks of the trade and how to be street-smart.

Both indulged in fraud in and around Manish Market. A modus operandi they called *'Adla Badli'* (bait and switch) was the norm – they would show potential customers electronic equipment like a watch, radio, transistor or video player, and once the buyer paid for it, they would switch the device with a rock or rags and take the money. Immediately after this one of them would start blowing the police whistle they had stolen from their father, to create the impression that the cops were raiding the area. They would create chaos and confusion and flee with the money. If the buyer found out about the fraud and confronted the brothers, they would employ the services of burly goons from the Pathan gang and scare the buyer away.

Even though the local police received a lot of complaints against Dawood and Shabbir, they rarely acted upon it, since they knew that both were sons of a constable of their own force. As a precaution or punishment, they would inform their father, who would summon the brothers to the crime branch to make them sit there for the whole day.

The brothers were making money through such petty crimes, but Dawood was ambitious. He had seen the wealth and power of the Pathan gang and the Haji Mastan gang and had dreams of becoming as big as them or even bigger.

Dawood was always on the lookout for bigger fish to fry to get as much money as possible. Things changed for him forever on 4 November 1974. Interestingly, he was still a teenager at the time. Dawood got a tip from one of his cronies that an *angadia* (a traditional courier who charges commission for transferring cash and valuables from one place to another, also called *hawaladar*) was scheduled to carry a large amount of cash on a particular day at a specific time. The information was solid, and Dawood decided to make his move. But he wanted to do it flamboyantly, in *filmi* style. He and three of his cronies got into an ambassador car (registration number MRX 5552) and lay in wait.

Dawood had the entire sequence planned. When the *angadia's* car was crossing Carnac Bunder bridge in the Masjid Bunder area, Dawood sped towards it in his car and ambushed him. It was a narrow-lane bridge and the *angadia* had no escape. Dawood got out of his car and confronted the businessman at knifepoint. He then snatched the *angadia's* bag, walked back to his vehicle and sped away. The bag contained ₹ 4.75 lakh in cash, a huge sum in those days.

Carnac Bunder bridge was then under the jurisdiction of the Pydhonie Police Station – the *angadia* rushed there and informed the police. A case was registered, and Police Sub-inspector (PSI) T.B. Gaud was given the responsibility as Investigating Officer (IO).

Investigations revealed a startling fact that even Dawood was not aware of. The money that was stolen did not belong to the *angadia*, but to the Metropolitan Bank in Bombay. This disclosure sent shockwaves not only through the police department, but also the crime world, because in those days, gangsters were not known to target banks and loot them. Everyone took notice and Dawood became a name to reckon with.

However, Dawood's act of daredevilry had not gone unnoticed. Samad Khan, the leader of the Pathan gang was furious when he learned that such a big robbery had taken place in his area. Like all gangsters who nurse huge egos he was furious that somebody else had committed this kind of crime on his turf without his knowledge or help. He made Dawood and Shabbir his sworn enemies and decided to teach them a lesson and re-establish his supremacy in the process. Samad Khan's revenge was to eventually change the Mumbai underworld and Mumbai forever.

Meanwhile, PSI Gaud conducted a thorough investigation and arrested Dawood and his buddies. The arrest generated a lot of interest in police and crime circles because the perpetrator was the son of a policeman – it was uncommon for family members of policemen to be detained for such serious crimes in those days.

The crime world too kept a close watch on developments, especially because everyone had learned of Samad Khan's sworn vengeance against the Kaskar brothers.

After a few months of investigation Gaud filed a robust chargesheet against Dawood. The case was tried in the Sessions Court and after almost five years the then Sessions Judge R.V. Joshi found Dawood guilty and sentenced him to four years in prison. Incidentally, this happens to be the only case in which Dawood has been put on trial in a court of law in India and has been convicted for his crime.

Immediately after the verdict, Dawood appealed against the Sessions Court order in the Bombay High Court. He also filed a bail application during the pendency of hearing in the High Court. He was granted relief and was out on bail in no time. He never went back – he jumped bail and never went to prison. In fact, Dawood has never gone to jail for any of his crimes in India. Once he was free, he unleashed a reign of terror in Mumbai and India like never before. His reign over Mumbai's underworld had begun.

Even though Dawood knew that the Pathan gang was out to eliminate him and his brother, he continued to operate in South Mumbai, albeit more carefully. Then a national development that had ramifications across the country changed India's history forever. It was a dark chapter for almost everyone in the country, but it turned out to be a blessing in disguise for Dawood.

For two years – 1975 to 1977 – Emergency was declared in India, and everything stopped. All note-worthy gangsters – Haji Mastan, Karim Lala, Varadarajan Mudaliar, Yusuf Patel, Samad Khan, Amir Zada, Alam Zeb, Bada Rajan and Rama Naik – were put behind bars. Dawood, who was not yet a convicted felon, luckily escaped this incarceration. He capitalised on this opportunity immediately and filled the void created by the absence of the big gangsters and slowly started taking over all their operations.

Dawood and Shabbir took over smuggling operations and started suppling the grey market with goods. They even did *vasuli* (recovery) for Gujarati businessmen who had earlier employed the Pathan gang for the same work.

Dawood's operations grew exponentially and he was astute enough to ensure that he captured the gangsters' markets in a way that on their return from jail, they would find it difficult to restart their businesses.

By the late 1970s, when most of the gangsters were freed, they learned that Dawood had become a big name in the crime world. He had formed his own gang called 'D-Company', which controlled most of the criminal operations in Mumbai. The gang had taken over gold and silver smuggling, extortion, kidnapping, abduction, *matka*, illegal liquor, land grabbing, drug trafficking and murder for hire.

The ganglords also realised that Dawood had changed the nature of the game into a business of bloodbath. It was something the yesteryear dons were neither equipped to deal with, nor willing to do.

As the 1980s began, Dawood had established his supremacy and was handling a majority of the operations. His gang was increasing, and he was making a lot of money.

However, an old enemy loomed over Dawood's escalation to the top of the Mumbai underworld. The leader of the Pathan gang, Samad Khan, was still nursing old wounds and looking for an opportunity to teach Dawood a lesson. Samad also wanted to take back all the operations that Dawood had usurped while he was in jail.

Along with Alamzeb and Amirzada (members of the Pathan gang), Samad Khan started keeping a close watch on Dawood, Shabbir and their other gang members. They even had informers who would tip them off about Dawood's whereabouts on a day-to-day basis.

Dawood and Shabbir were slowly taking over most of the operations of the Pathan gang. They called themselves the 'Young Company'. Since they belonged to a Konkani Muslim family from the Khed area of Ratnagiri district in western Maharashtra, they could speak Marathi fluently. Being the sons of a policeman also helped.

They were used by some police officers to get back at the Pathan gang. Both would often tip off the authorities about the gang's operations and whereabouts, resulting in tremendous loss to the group. Even though Haji Mastan had warned both sides not to indulge in violence against each other, the situation was soon out of control and Samad Khan was baying for the Kaskar siblings' blood.

Knowing the strength and ruthlessness of the Pathan gang, both Dawood and Shabbir were careful and protected themselves. They had a team of bodyguards protecting their building in Pakmodia Street in the Bhendi Bazaar area of Mumbai. Dawood had huge iron doors installed at the entrance to ensure that no one could enter without their knowledge.

However, there was a chink in their armour. Shabbir, who was married, began frequently visiting a sex worker in Congress House situated in the red-light area of South Mumbai. Samad Khan got wind of it and decided to exploit this weakness.

On 12 February 1981, late at night after meeting the sex worker, Shabbir left from Kamathipura in his car and drove in the direction of Haji Ali. A source tipped off Samad Khan about Shabbir's whereabouts. A team comprising Samad Khan, Alamzeb, Amirzada and Jangrez Khan got into another car and rushed to try and cut Shabbir.

Shabbir was headed towards the petrol pump near Siddhivinayak temple – a routine refuelling stop for him. Samad Khan and his cronies managed to pick up Shabbir's trail at Haji Ali and followed him. Around midnight Shabbir reached the petrol pump and got out of his car. He was stunned to see Samad Khan and his gang waiting. Shabbir immediately realised what was happening and lunged towards them to fight. But they overpowered him and stabbed him repeatedly, relentlessly. When Shabbir fell to the ground, they pumped several bullets into him and left. Shabbir died on the spot.

Samad Khan was not done with his revenge. He and his gang sped towards Pakmodia Street. His plan was to take Dawood by surprise and kill him that night, before he got news of his brother's murder.

Samad's plan would have worked, because when the gang reached Pakmodia Street, things were normal, nobody aware of Shabbir's death. However, Dawood's close aide Khalid Pehelwan, who was present inside the building, saw the car and recognised it as one belonging to the Pathan gang.

He immediately warned Dawood and closed the iron gates to the building in the nick of time, before Samad and his gang could enter.

The Pathan gang could not break the iron gates and started firing indiscriminately at the building. Dawood and his gang members responded by firing back. This went on for a long time. Eventually, the Pathan gang had to leave, as the police had been alerted.

Shabbir's death shattered Dawood. He swore to avenge his brother's death and not stop till the entire Pathan gang was eliminated. Even though he was heartbroken, Dawood was intelligent enough to understand that he alone could not take on the might of the Pathan gang. He hired the services of the Bada Rajan (Rajan Nair) gang and gave them the *supari* (murder contract) to kill Samad Khan, Alamzeb and Amirzada.

Revenge is a dish best served cold. It took a while for the Bada Rajan gang to avenge Shabbir's death, but when they did so, it was done in quick succession. More than two and a half years after Shabbir was murdered, on 6 September 1983, Amirzada was shot dead in a daring attack inside the Sessions Court by David Pardesi, a member of the Bada Rajan gang. Pardesi, dressed as a naval officer, shot Amirzada in a crowded courtroom. In 1985, Alamzeb was shot dead in an encounter in the premises of the Gujarat Housing Board near Palampur Patia in Surat.

A year later, on 4 October 1984, Samad Khan was shot dead by members of the Rama Naik gang in South Mumbai. (Rama Naik was a well-known gangster and was the mentor of Arun Gawli.) Interestingly, exactly five days after Samad Khan was murdered, David Pardesi escaped from the Arthur Road Jail in an operation that was straight out of a movie plot. Pardesi sawed through the bars of the window of his jail cell, used a rope to climb down and fled. This he reportedly did with the help of jail employees.

The killing of Shabbir Ibrahim Kaskar and the revenge killing of Samad Khan are the bloodiest killings recorded in the saga of the Mumbai underworld.

Even as he nursed the desire to avenge his brother's murder, Dawood had become a high-profile gangster wanted for murder. The police were hot on his trail, and he was finding it increasingly difficult to move freely in Mumbai without fear of being arrested or being murdered by rival gang members.

With the killing of Samad Khan, Alamzeb and Amirzada, Dawood had effectively eliminated the dangerous Pathan gang from the city – the police were happy that there was one less group to deal with. But Samad's killing had catapulted Dawood to the *numero uno* position in the Mumbai underworld, and Dawood was one who didn't shy away from causing violent havoc that could spill on to the streets of the city. He had become the undisputed king and was extremely dangerous and powerful.

The police could not afford to have him on the loose. The Mumbai Police force was tasked with nabbing Dawood. They even named him in the killing of Samad Khan and made him an accused in the case. This meant that Dawood was now a wanted criminal who was on the run from the law. It therefore also gave the police powers to investigate him and his gang activities.

In 1986, Dawood fled Mumbai to the Middle East, settling in Dubai, and would 'remote control' operations in the Mumbai underworld from there. He quickly established his empire in the Gulf and became even more powerful, since he no longer had to fear being tracked by Indian law enforcement agencies or rival gangs. This meant that he was no longer confined to the city of Mumbai, but able to spread his criminal network across the Indian subcontinent, the Gulf states, the African continent and around the world. Dawood was out of the Mumbai Police's reach, because India did not have an extradition treaty with the United Arab Emirates (UAE).

It was much later in 1999 that India and the UAE signed an extradition treaty. It was ratified on 24 May 2000.

After the signing of the treaty, India, in collaboration with the UAE, has managed to extradite and deport several criminals wanted in India, including Dawood's brother Iqbal Kaskar.

In Mumbai, Dawood's operations had been limited to smuggling, looting, extortion, kidnapping and murder for hire, but after moving to Dubai, his realm expanded to include narcotics, arms dealing, match-fixing and a betting syndicate, *hawala* operations, counterfeiting currency and film financing. The D-Company had gone global very quickly.

Dawood's supremacy over the Mumbai underworld held strong through the 1980s. While he ran his gang from Dubai, his close aides Chhota Shakeel (Mohammad Shakeel Babu Miya Shaikh) and Chhota Rajan (Rajan Sadashiv Nikhalje) handled ground operations in Mumbai. Both rapidly made a name for themselves in Mumbai's crime world. That meant that both were very soon on the Mumbai Police radar. By the late 1980s, both Shakeel and Rajan too had fled the city and joined their boss in Dubai.

The era of Dawood's rivalry with Rajan and Arun Gawli was yet to begin.

Dawood was living a king's life. He would throw lavish parties in the Middle East, attended by top celebrities from Bollywood and big industrialists and businessmen from India. In fact, it was almost a diktat to celebrities to present themselves whenever summoned by Dawood. Some obliged happily, while others went because they were afraid or did not have an option.

Dawood was even seen at several cricket matches at the Sharjah cricket ground during the India-Pakistan One Day International matches. There have been several reports about his interacting with Indian and Pakistani cricket players. And Junaid, the son of one of Pakistan's most famous cricketers, Javed Miandad, even married Dawood's daughter Mahrukh.

By the early 1990s Dawood was running the most successful criminal empire east of the Suez Canal. His operations ranged from India to South Africa, the Middle East, Pakistan, Afghanistan, Nepal and Southeast Asia.

While much of his activity spread across the globe, Dawood maintained a close watch on his gang's operations in Mumbai. The city where he and his business were born held special meaning for him. He would personally oversee most of what happened in the city and would even decide on who would do a particular operation.

He had some of the most dreaded and lethal gunmen and gangsters working for him – Subhash Singh Thakur, Firoz Konkani, Dilip Buwa, Maya Dolas, and Abu Salem, to name a few.

Dawood would take matters into his own hands when something went wrong in Mumbai. In one incident that was a personal attack on him, politician-criminal Ashok Joshi, who was heading the Joshi gang and operated in the Bhandup area in the eastern suburbs of the city, killed Satish Raje, one of Dawood's closest aides. Raje looked after all the financial operations of the D-gang. His killing was a personal loss to Dawood, who immediately decided to avenge his death.

Dawood asked Chhota Rajan to eliminate Ashok Joshi. On 3 December 1988, Chhota Rajan led a 15-men hit squad to conduct an operation that was among the most daring killings in the history of the Mumbai underworld. Chhota Rajan and his gang ambushed Joshi as he was travelling in his car near Panvel. Joshi and his close aides were killed in a flurry of bullets fired by Rajan and his gang. The incident sent shivers down the spine of the Mumbai underworld. Now, no one dared to cross swords with Dawood or his D-Company. (Read in detail the story of Ashok Joshi's killing in Chapter 8 on page no. 162.)

Dilip Buwa was a sought-after sharpshooter in the underworld. After Joshi's killing, Dawood asked Buwa to take over gang activities and the area of operation in Bhandup. Buwa and Maya Dolas went to Bhandup on 17 September 1989, and shot dead five of Joshi's gang members in broad daylight and took over the gang.

However, reports and rumours that Dilip Buwa and Maya Dolas were trying to take over the D-Company's operations in Mumbai were increasing. Dawood was informed that Dilip and Maya were planning to split the gang on communal lines and form a Hindu team to take on the might of the D-Company.

By sheer coincidence, on 16 November 1991, Dawood's close aide Gopal Rajwani managed to learn the whereabouts of Dilip Buwa, Maya Dolas, Anil Pawar and four other gangsters who were holed up in an apartment in Lokhandwala Complex in the Andheri suburbs of Mumbai.

The Special Task Force (STF) of the Mumbai Police, headed by Aftab Ahmed Khan, a daredevil IPS officer from the 1965-batch, got a tip-off about the whereabouts of these men, and immediately laid siege to the area. The police soon learned that they were in flat no. 002/003, A-wing of Swati building in the posh residential complex.

When the gangsters realised that they had been surrounded by the police, they started firing. The police officers appealed to them several times to surrender – a team of three officers even entered the building and tried to talk to them, but they retaliated with more gunfire. An exchange of fire, of the kind never seen before in a public residential place in Mumbai, ensued.

Another coincidence: that day a team of filmmakers from the BBC was shooting nearby. They heard about the siege at Lokhandwala and immediately diverted the crew to the spot. The entire shootout was captured live on television and seen across the world.

After several hours of the gun battle in which several hundred rounds of ammunition were fired, the police team finally managed to kill Maya Dolas, Dilip Buwa, Anil Pawar, Raju Pujari and Ashok Nadkarni. Two others who were killed were passers-by and not part of the gang. It was a much-needed success for the Mumbai Police in the fight against the underworld.

After the shootout there were allegations and rumours that it was Dawood who gave away the location of his trusted gangsters. However, this was never proved to be true. Even today, the shootout at Lokhandwala is considered among the most successful operations of the Mumbai Police.

Some years ago, a movie titled *Shootout at Lokhandwala* starring Sanjay Dutt, Vivek Oberoi and others was made and became an instant hit.

Even while his operations in Mumbai were affected, Dawood was busy building a global criminal empire. By the early 1990s, he had spread his activities across the globe. More importantly, he started developing deep connections in Pakistan, also with their controversial Inter-Services Intelligence (ISI) agency.

December 1992 is a watershed month in India's history. The demolition of the Babri Masjid on 6 December that year and the massive riots that followed in December 1992 and January 1993, changed India's political and communal landscape forever.

What it also did change was Dawood's image, permanently. Before March 1993, he was known as a fugitive mafia boss who was wanted in murders, smuggling, kidnapping and other activities; basically, just a gangster. After March 1993 he became a wanted global terrorist. Things had changed drastically and permanently for Dawood. He realised it too, and fled to Pakistan, where he has reportedly been under the ISI's protection ever since.

Along with smuggler Tiger Memon, the ISI and 23 of his close aides, Dawood planned and executed the serial bomb blasts in Mumbai as revenge for the demolition of the mosque and the riots that followed. On the fateful day – 12 March 1993 – between 1.30 p.m. and 3 p.m., as many as 13 powerful RDX-laden bombs ripped through the city of Mumbai, striking important and strategic locations, including the Bombay Stock Exchange (BSE) and the Air India building at Nariman Point. Such was the audacity of the attacks that within minutes 257 innocent people had lost their lives and more than 1,400 were injured.

An immediate investigation by the Mumbai Police exposed the plot – it was clear that Dawood had planned the terror attack with the help and backing of the ISI. After this, Dawood shot to global infamy and was declared a 'global terrorist' by the US in 2003.

In 2011, after his links with the Taliban – and especially with Osama Bin Laden – had been established, the premier American agency Federal Bureau of Investigation (FBI), ranked him Number 3 on the list of the 'World's 10 Most Wanted Fugitives'.

These actions from the Government of India, the Mumbai Police, the Central Bureau of Investigations (CBI), Interpol, the FBI, and the U.S. government ensured that Dawood and his criminal activities were restricted, to a large extent. In fact, after the 1993 serial bomb blasts, the Mumbai Police went into mission mode against the underworld, especially the D-Company. Such was the force and impact of the

Mumbai Police that the D-gang was almost eliminated from Mumbai by the end of the decade.

Most of Dawood's close associates either left him, were killed by rival gangs or in police operations, or are languishing in jails across the country. Only Chota Shakeel, Anees Ibrahim and a few others are still with him. After the 1993 blasts, Chhota Rajan split with Dawood. Though they separated due to problems in their gang and business operations, Rajan used the opportunity to announce that the divide was because of Dawood's anti-national activities. Rajan tried to anoint himself as a patriotic don, to no avail.

The bitter rivalry between the two men spilled over onto the streets of Mumbai, with each targeting the other's gang members and killing them. Most of Dawood's and Rajan's gangsters were killed by inter-gang rivalry.

Despite all this, Dawood continues to live a lavish lifestyle under the protective and watchful eye of the Pakistan government and the ISI. He has changed his official identity and has become a Pakistani citizen.

Even though at the time of the 1993 bomb blasts Dawood's favoured haven was Dubai, it was no longer safe for him after his name as a mastermind of the bomb blasts was confirmed and a notice against him was issued by Interpol. With the help of the ISI, Dawood immediately fled to Pakistan and was soon joined by his wife, four daughters, one son, brothers and a few close associates.

In 2006, Dawood's daughter Mahrukh married Pakistani cricketer Javed Miandad's son Junaid in a glittering ceremony in Dubai and Pakistan.

Even though Pakistan and the ISI have always denied that Dawood is in their country, there is ample evidence to indicate that he is indeed living in Karachi as a wealthy businessman. As per reports, he lives like a king in a palatial house situated in the posh Clifton area of Karachi city.

The house is spread over several acres. It has a swimming pool, state-of-the-art gymnasium, tennis courts and a snooker/ billiards room. A fleet of luxury cars includes top brands like Mercedes, BMW and Audi.

Dawood has a fetish for wearing expensive watches. He is known for throwing lavish parties at which money and alcohol flow like water. His guests are reportedly treated to a feast of beautiful models, escort girls and sex workers regularly.

- **Dawood and Bollywood**

The Indian film industry has been smitten by Dawood and his life of crime. Several movies have been made on the ganglord.

Some of them are:

- *Company*
- *D*
- *D-Day*
- *Shootout at Lokhandwala*
- *Once Upon a Time in Mumbai*
- *Haseena Parkar* (this movie is based on Dawood's sister)
- A video-game – *Hitman 2*, released in 2018, featured a Mumbai-based crime lord who is named 'Dawood Rangan'.

In the 1980s and 1990s, Dawood had a stranglehold on Bollywood and is believed to have financed several movies. Top Bollywood celebrities have been known to throng Dawood's lavish parties in Dubai and the Middle East at the time.

- **Dawood and Cricket**

Dawood and his cronies like Sharad Shetty and Chhota Shakeel have been involved in match-fixing and cricket betting. The entire match-fixing and betting syndicate was run by the D-gang from Sharjah in the 1980s and 1990s. In 2013, former India captain Dilip Vengsarkar claimed that in 1986, just before the Sharjah Cup final, Dawood Ibrahim came to the Indian team's dressing room and offered a car to each player if they beat Pakistan in the final match that day.

- **Dawood Ibrahim – Convergence of Crime and Terrorism** *(Source:https://www.efsas.org/publications/articles-by-efsas/dawood-ibrahim-convergence-of-crime-and-terrorism/)*

On 9 July 2019, the United Nations Security Council (UNSC) addressed the issue of the links between organised crime and terrorism. During the open debate, India's permanent representative to the UN, Syed Akbaruddin, recognised the relevance of the nexus between terrorism and organised crime, stating: *"Terrorism and organised crime are both manifestly malicious organisms drawing sustenance from the same deadly swamp. At times, they coexist; at other times, they cooperate; and in instances, they converge."* He then identified one of the most well-known examples of such a convergence: Dawood Ibrahim and his crime syndicate-turned-terrorist network, the D-Company.

Mr. Akbaruddin alluded to the whereabouts of Dawood Ibrahim, who has been on the run since March 1993 and is wanted for his involvement in a series of bombings in Mumbai that killed more than 250 people. In his statement, he declared that Dawood Ibrahim is operating *"from a safe haven that declines to acknowledge even his existence"*. As diplomatically as this sentence was phrased, the identity of the accused *"safe haven"* is blatantly obvious: Pakistan.

Pakistan has continuously denied India's allegations that Dawood Ibrahim is operating from its territory. While the D-Company network extends to all corners of the world, it appears that Dawood has established a base in Pakistan, more specifically in the port city of Karachi.

• Shift to a Religiously Motivated Terror Network

In the aftermath of the 1993 Mumbai serial bomb blasts, Dawood shifted his operations from Dubai to Karachi and is widely believed to have received protection from the Pakistani ISI. By orchestrating the bombings and using his smuggling routes to provide the weapons used in the blasts, Dawood condemned himself to be branded a 'terrorist', thus stepping away from the 'mafia don' label that he had worn with pride for two decades.

Aside from being wanted in India on charges of murder, extortion and terrorism, the United States identified him as a Specially Designated Global Terrorist in 2003 and a Significant Foreign Narcotics Trafficker in 2006. Dawood was listed on the UNSC Consolidated List in 2003 pursuant to paragraphs 1 and 2 of Resolution 1390 (2002) as being associated with Al Qaeda, Osama bin Laden or the Taliban for *"participating in the financing, planning, facilitating, preparing or perpetrating of acts or activities by, in conjunction with, under the name of, on behalf or in support of ... supplying, selling or transferring arms and related material to"* or *"otherwise supporting acts or activities of"* Osama bin Laden, Al Qaeda and the Taliban.

Earlier, in 2002, evidence revealed that the D-Company had financial links to Lashkar-e-Taiba (LeT) and that Dawood had financed attacks in Gujarat, India.

Adhering to the ideology of such radical Islamic groups and engaging in the planning and logistics of terrorist attacks provides some evidence as to how Dawood's organisation shifted from a financially motivated crime syndicate to a politically motivated terror network.

While the D-Company itself has not claimed credit for any terrorist attacks, there is evidence which links its provision of financial and logistical support that sponsored the execution of such attacks. This transition of the D-Company also created a schism within the syndicate; the organisation had previously been secular, but the new alignment with radical Islamist ideologies caused Hindu members of the syndicate to leave and join a gang formed by Dawood's former right-hand man, Chhota Rajan.

Scholars have argued that the convergence of organised crime groups and terrorist outfits and their evolution towards hybrid forms can be explained by resource dependence theory, as well as inter-organisational structures.

For example, Wu and Knoke (2017) explain that the resources required for terror groups to carry out their operations are often controlled by organised crime syndicates, as in the case of D-Company controlling smuggling routes. Hence, a collaboration between both the terror organisation and crime syndicate is a logical business agreement.

Yet, the fee extracted by the crime syndicate cuts back on the terrorist organisation's profit and operating revenue, because of which some terror organisations may choose to concentrate more efforts directed at organised crime, in order to cut out *'the middleman'*.

In the event this happens, it would also show a transformation in the aims of the terror group, depending on the extent to which its activities become profit motivated. Regarding inter-organisational structures, Wu and Knoke suggest that terrorist organisations develop a structure like organised crime syndicates in order to escape detection and counter-terrorism measures.

This evolutionary path can be observed in Al Qaeda's change from a central command structure – which is more effective in terms of conducting complex operations and communications, yet more vulnerable to detection and disruption from counter-terrorism measures – to a *'franchise-based system'*, which loses communication effectiveness but gains in security.

While decentralised cells gain independence by managing their own logistics and selecting their own targets, this could disrupt the *'political'* aims of the organisation. While experts have regularly used the example of the D-Company to illustrate the organised crime-terror nexus, some critics believe that organised crime groups are unlikely to completely merge with terror groups. In this case, the D-Company seems to share the ideology of certain terror groups, but has not declared itself publicly as an organisation that would challenge the political and social system of a territory and obtain full control over it; contrary to Al Qaeda or the Taliban.

The D-Company uses its criminal expertise to aid in the operations of terror organisations, as it has gained notoriety due to its smuggling, trafficking and counterfeiting activities that can be considered essential to the survival of a terrorist organisation. Indeed, the D-Company's network is capable of smuggling terrorists across borders, trafficking narcotics and laundering money for a terror organisation. It is speculated that the boat used by the perpetrators of the 2008 Mumbai terror attacks to sail from Karachi to Mumbai was provided by the D-Company.

Based on academic theories and what we know about the D-Company's operations, it does remain unlikely that the D-Company operates fully as a terror organisation. Dawood's involvement in the 1993 Mumbai bombings led to him being branded an internationally designated terrorist, but the D-Company in itself has not been designated a terrorist organisation by either India, the United States, or the UN.

While the extent to which the D-Company has become a terror organisation in the traditional sense of the term can be questioned, the current alliance between an extensive criminal organisation and various terror groups is an undeniable threat to international security.

If states and international organisations hope to adopt effective measures to combat terrorism financing, all the facets of organisations such as D-Company must be thoroughly observed and analysed. Designating Dawood Ibrahim as an international terrorist does not take away from the fact that he is, first and foremost, a mafia don and thus operates as such.

What must be understood from the story of Dawood Ibrahim and the D-Company is that the lines between terror organisations and crime syndicates are becoming increasingly blurred, and that the two threats must not be treated as mutually exclusive.

International crime syndicates have continuously shown an ability to adapt to their environments in order to elude capture and detection, and their aptitude for forming short- or long-term alliances with terrorist organisations must essentially be seen for what they are: profit- and power-centric business enterprises.

What is different about Dawood Ibrahim's case is his close relationship with terror organisations such as Al Qaeda and the Taliban. He is believed to have travelled to Afghanistan under the protection of the Taliban and met with Osama bin Laden. Evidence suggests that he has shared smuggling routes spanning from Africa and the Middle East to South Asia with Al Qaeda. However, due to the mystery shrouding the D-Company and the extent to which it operates with terrorist organisations, it remains unclear what exactly the formal agreement between these organisations consists of.

• Conclusion

The crime-terror nexus has become an apparent reality of today's world, which flourishes in politically unstable regions such as South Asia. States have recognised the symbiotic relationship between terror groups and crime syndicates and can no longer hope to abolish one without tackling the other.

In 2017, the Washington DC-based NGO Global Financial Integrity released a report estimating that transnational organised crime generated approximately $2.2 trillion per year. Taking into account the proliferation of terrorist and militant groups, it is inevitable that these forms of consortiums that "*draw sustenance from the same deadly swamp*" will find ways to cooperate and/or converge.

The story of Dawood Ibrahim and his D-Company, and the consolidated influence it has over the South Asian region, is one that is constantly evolving and requires a comprehensive approach tackling various facets – crime syndicate and terror network included – in order to find the best methods to address such issues.

As the problem is transnational in nature and not exclusive to South Asia, greater cooperation and intelligence sharing between states is paramount, which remains challenging when states such as Pakistan continue refusing to recognise their own complicity.

It further remains to be seen if China will be able to exert enough pressure on Pakistan's military establishment and force a crack-down on terrorist groups and their associates in order to protect its BRI or continue tacitly supporting Pakistan-based terrorist organisations as long as these groups focus on India, Jammu & Kashmir and Afghanistan, and thereby ignore the plight of their Muslim brethren in Xinjiang and not expand their operations or otherwise bridge their presence into China.

With India, the United States and the international community at large continuously providing evidence against Pakistan, Islamabad may eventually be pushed into a corner and be forced to change its foreign policy based on using criminals like Dawood Ibrahim and terrorist organisations as strategic assets. Much of this will also depend on the results of its review by the Financial Action Task Force (FATF).

(Source: https://www.efsas.org/publications/articles-by-efsas/dawood-ibrahim-convergence-of-crime-and-terrorism/)

◆◆◆◆◆◆

Chapter 5

GANGSTERS AND THEIR GENEALOGY – EVOLUTION OF THE MUMBAI MAFIA

Profiling the gangsters of the Mumbai underworld is a voluminous task. There have been hundreds of criminals from the 1960s to the early 2000s. In this chapter, I have profiled a few who were considered well-known and were quite active during their time. Readers will get an idea of the kind of people who were operating during those times and how dreaded they were, as well as the crimes perpetrated during that day and age, and how tough it was for the police to deal with them.

Dawood Ibrahim, the most prominent among them, was profiled in the previous chapter. Such has been his villainous reign that an entire chapter had to be dedicated to his misdeeds.

• Abu Salem

The story of Abu Salem Qayum Ansari aka Abu Salem is a classic story about how youngsters were smitten by the underworld in the 1980s and 1990s and made it a career choice. A rags to riches tale of the criminal world which has few parallels.

Abu Salem is a native of Sarai Mir village situated in the Azamgarh district of Uttar Pradesh. At a young age he left home for Mumbai to stay with a relative and make ends meet. He tried his luck in various odd jobs, like running a telephone booth, selling cutlery, and tailoring. He married a 17-year-old girl, Samira Jumani from Jogeshwari situated in the western suburbs of Mumbai.

In the early 1990s he ran a small tailoring shop in a shopping complex in Andheri (West). During that time, Salem had an altercation with local criminals over *hafta* (protection money). This led to a fight amongst them, and a case was registered against Salem in the Andheri police station.

It was the first case registered against Salem in Mumbai. In fact, at that time it might have seemed innocuous. Even Salem may not have given it too much attention, as he was out on bail in no time and back to leading a normal life.

This was the very case that was used years later against Salem by the Government of India in the Portuguese court to identify him. By that time Salem had changed his identity, acquired a fake passport (no. C811677, issued by Pakistan on 8/9/1998) with a new name – Arsalan.

He had changed his looks and appearance extensively, which made him virtually unrecognisable. It was almost impossible to identify him. However, the fingerprints taken when that first case was registered proved to be of major help to the authorities, because they were an exact and undisputable match to his latest avatar.

Salem's cousin, Akhtar, worked for a member of the Dawood gang. Salem was attracted to the crime world and offered his help. He was a very good driver and was hired to be one. From 1988 to 1993 he drove for the D-gang. It was during this stint that he delivered illegal arms – AK-47s and hand grenades – to actor Sanjay Dutt at his residence in Bandra, a few days before the 1993 serial bomb blasts.

Incidentally, after the 12 March 1993, blasts in Mumbai, a majority of Dawood gang members fled the city. Some went to Dubai – Salem was one of them. In Dubai, he very soon became a trusted aide of Anees Ibrahim and started doing important jobs for him.

Salem was extremely good at making extortion calls and creating terror in the mind of the person he was calling. He took over the responsibility of making those calls on behalf of Anees Ibrahim and Chota Shakeel. He climbed the ladder within the gang very quickly and soon he was making extortion calls to Bollywood stars, filmmakers and industrialists in Mumbai. He was also involved in smuggling, arms sales, *hawala*, counterfeit currency and other crimes of the Dawood gang.

From 1993 to 1998, Salem rose from lieutenant to key operative in the Dawood gang and was extremely close to Anees Ibrahim. In fact, Anees had so much faith in Salem's functioning and abilities that he was given free rein to conduct operations from anywhere. Salem had a fake Pakistani passport and was travelling across the Middle East and Africa, conducting various operations for the D-Company. His run came to a halt when, in December 1997, he was arrested by the Dubai police on charges of fraud. He, however, managed to escape by showing his Pakistani passport with its fake identity.

A few days later, things began to sour between Anees and Salem. They started having monetary disputes over the extortion calls made to Bollywood stars. Salem complained that he was being underpaid by Anees and believed that he should get a larger share as the money was being paid to the gang purely on Salem's ability to create terror in the minds of the victims. Salem felt that as it was his talent that was earning them the income, he should be adequately compensated for it. However, Anees did not agree, and Salem decided to part ways with him.

His first decision after the fallout was to flee Pakistan for the

Middle East. There he changed his identity again and got himself a new passport. Soon he realised that the Middle East was not safe for him either, since it was still Dawood's backyard. So, he moved to the US and started buying property there.

Salem soon started his own gang, with operations conducted in Mumbai. He would make extortion calls and use youngsters lured from his native town of Azamgarh, UP, to threaten victims or kill them, or at least collect money from them.

Salem announced his arrival in the crime world with a bang, quite literally. On 12 August 1997, he had music baron Gulshan Kumar shot dead. This incident created such a sensation in the film world and underworld that almost overnight he became a name to reckon with. Salem had allegedly taken money from music producer Nadeem Akhtar Saifi to murder Gulshan Kumar, Nadeem's rival in the Hindi film music industry. Following these allegations becoming public, Nadeem reportedly flew to London and, despite repeated attempts by the Mumbai Police, has not been deported to India till date.

Even to date, Gulshan Kumar's killing is among the most daring shootouts carried out by the Mumbai underworld in the city. This single incident catapulted Salem to infamy in the Mumbai film industry and money started pouring in. Those who refused to pay were dealt with severely.

In January 2000, Rakesh Roshan, film producer and father of superstar Hrithik Roshan escaped a near fatal shooting when Salem's men (Sunil Vitthal Gaikwad and Sachin Kamble) opened fire on him in Mumbai. Roshan had reportedly refused to give Salem money or film distribution rights of his movies.

Between 1998 and 2002 Salem targeted some of the most prominent personalities in Bollywood. These included:

- Film actress Manisha Koirala's secretary, Ajit Dewani
- Film producer and director JP Dutta
- Film actress Preity Zinta
- Film director Rajiv Rai

- Actor Aamir Khan
- Director and producer Ashutosh Gowarikar
- Director and producer Jhamu Sughandh
- Director and producer Lawrence D'Souza
- Director and producer Manmohan Shetty

During this time, Indian law enforcement agencies informed Interpol about Salem, his activities and his whereabouts. Interpol in turn informed the Federal Bureau of Investigation (FBI), the premier law enforcement agency in the United States, about Salem.

After the 9/11 terror attacks in the US by Osama Bin Laden and his terror outfit Al Qaeda, authorities began a massive crackdown on criminals in the country. Salem realised that if he continued to stay in the US he would be caught, as he was a known associate of Dawood Ibrahim. By then, Dawood had already been branded a global terrorist.

Along with his girlfriend, film actress Monica Bedi, Salem fled to Portugal. It was clear that Salem chose that country because it did not have an extradition treaty with India. However, Salem did not know that Interpol was watching him and had informed Indian authorities that he was in Portugal.

Based on the information given by Interpol and India, Salem and Monica Bedi were arrested by the Portuguese authorities in Lisbon in September 2002. It was a huge victory for the Indian law enforcement agencies, especially the CBI, their first with regard to having a fugitive arrested in a foreign country, especially one with which India did not have an extradition treaty.

Despite the arrest, India had to fight a long legal battle in Portugal's highest court. Salem alleged that as a Muslim, he would be victimised in India. He told the Portuguese court that he feared that he would be given the death sentence by India – this was a major concern for Portugal's apex court. Following this, India gave a written assurance to the court that Salem would not be given capital punishment and would get a fair trial.

It took a legal battle of three years before Salem and Bedi were eventually extradited to India in 2005 and handed over to the CBI. The long legal battle fought by CBI was headed by IPS officer Vijay Shankar Tiwari, who later went on to become CBI Director. While Tiwari was in Portugal, I was holding the post of Joint Director of CBI in Mumbai. Tiwari and I were in constant touch during the legal battle; whenever Tiwari and his team needed any assistance from Mumbai, my team and I would provide it.

Salem was booked in as many as 25 cases, prominent among them being the *1993 Mumbai Serial Bomb Blasts* case and the *Pradeep Jain Murder* case. He was convicted and sentenced to life imprisonment in the *Pradeep Jain Murder* case and later to life imprisonment in the *1993 Mumbai Serial Bomb Blasts* case as well.

Trials are ongoing in the other cases, while Salem is lodged in the Taloja Jail in Navi Mumbai. A few years ago, there was an attempt on his life by Mustafa Majnu (accused in the 1993 serial bomb blasts case and lodged in the same jail as Salem), who attacked Salem with a sharp-edged weapon.

Abu Salem and Monica Bedi

The sordid saga of Abu Salem and Monica Bedi's love story is stuff that, ironically, Bollywood movies are made of. One was a career criminal and gangster, hailing from a small town, who made it big in the underworld; the other, a young Oxford University graduate in English Literature, trying to make a name for herself in tinsel-town.

In the history of the Mumbai underworld, there are several cases of dons having affairs with actresses, but there aren't many in which marriage was intended. Salem's was one: he was so smitten by Monica Bedi that he wanted to make her his wife.

Monica was born in Chabbewal, a small town in the district of Hoshiarpur, Punjab, in 1975. Shortly afterwards, her parents moved to Norway, where she spent 16 years of her life. Monica loved dancing, and during one of her visits to India at the age of 20, she decided to stay back to learn Kathak. It was in her dance class that she met veteran actor Manoj Kumar, who offered her a film opposite his son, Kunal.

The film never took off, but her acting career did.

Monica Bedi first heard about Abu Salem in 1998 when he called her over the phone from Dubai and invited her to a lavish Bollywood party. She went and met Salem. There was instant chemistry between the two – Salem fell in love with her. He never shied away from expressing his feelings. In fact, Bedi has spoken openly about how Salem was smitten by her.

Even though there is no official record of this, immediately after the party Bedi started getting film offers from top directors and producers. It is believed that Salem called and threatened them with dire consequences if they didn't sign Monica for their movies. In a span of two or three years she did several films with top actors and directors of the time.

In 2000-2001 Monica left India to join Salem, using a fake passport she had obtained with his help. They started their life in Portugal under false identities. But their love story ended abruptly in 2002, when they were arrested by the Portuguese authorities for having forged documents. It is not yet clear if they were married, but their love story has reportedly gone down in history in the underworld and Bollywood. They were eventually extradited to India.

In 2006, Monica Bedi was convicted for carrying a fake passport and sentenced to imprisonment. The Supreme Court later upheld her conviction but reduced her prison sentence to the time she had already served – following which she did not have to serve any jail time. She later participated in *Big Boss 2* and a few other TV shows. Salem continues to languish in Taloja Jail serving a life term and facing trial for his pending cases.

- **Rajendra Sadashiv Nikhalje, a.k.a. Chhota Rajan**

His ancestral roots are in Patan town in Satara district of western Maharashtra but he was born on 5 December 1959, in a small tenement in the Vikhroli area of the eastern suburbs of Mumbai.

Rajendra Sadashiv Nikhalje, as he was named, was introduced to the crime world when he was a mere teenager, by his mentor Rajan Mahadev Nair aka Bada Rajan. It was a few years later, when Bada Rajan was killed by the Pathan gang, that Rajendra Sadashiv Nikhalje became his natural successor and took on the moniker 'Chhota Rajan' to take his mentor's work and gang forward.

As a youngster, Rajan dropped out of school since his family could not afford to have him continue his education. He did odd jobs for a living. In 1974, when Rajan was only 15 years old, Bada Rajan took him under his wing and gave him the responsibility of selling cinema tickets in black in Chembur.

Incidentally, it was around the same time – though neither of them knew it then – that Dawood had entered the criminal world in South Mumbai. Years later, they became very close friends and committed some of the biggest crimes in the city. Much later they became staunch enemies, which they remain till date.

In the late 1970s, Bada Rajan had become an important member of the Dawood gang. His position in the gang smoothened Chhota Rajan's entry into the Dawood gang. Meanwhile, as a ticket black-marketeer, Chhota Rajan had quickly made a name for himself in the Chembur area. His success encouraged him to graduate to more serious crimes and he began engaging in smuggling, extortion, kidnapping and other serious crimes for Bada Rajan. It was evident that Chhota Rajan was good at his work, and he soon rose in rank within the gang, second only to Bada Rajan.

It was then that Dawood Ibrahim, Chhota Rajan and Arun Gawli were working together as part of the same gang. While Dawood handled the overall operations of the gang and concentrated on South Mumbai, Gawli ran the gang activities in Central Mumbai, while Rajan was in-charge of the eastern suburbs. The trio formed the Mumbai underworld's deadliest killing machine. Rajan and Gawli were known to be ruthless killers, while Dawood did most of the planning.

In 1985, on Dawood's orders, Rajan, along with Gawli, Rama Naik and Babu Reshim, murdered a gangster, Parasnath Pande, at Mumbai Central. All four were arrested and jailed and were out on bail almost a year later.

According to underworld folklore, Dawood was so impressed with their work that he gave all four of them brand new revolvers worth lakhs of rupees as a reward.

A few months later, Gawli split from the gang because he found that his brother Kishore alias Papa Gawli was murdered on Dawood's instructions on 22 February 1990. Gawli swore revenge and thus took on the might of Dawood and Rajan. After Gawli's departure, Rajan and Dawood became a formidable pair.

However, after Dawood fled Mumbai and went to the Middle East, it was Rajan who was in-charge of operations in Mumbai. During this time, he committed some of the most dreaded operations of the Mumbai underworld. Prominent among them was the execution of gangster Ashok Joshi on 3 December 1988: (Read more about this in Chapter 8 on page no. 162.) This killing skyrocketed Rajan to the top of the criminal ladder.

But Rajan was facing the heat of the law, as the number of cases against him increased. The police were constantly at his heels, and he was finding it difficult to run operations without being targeted by the authorities.

In 1989 he went to Dubai to attend the wedding of Noora (Dawood's younger brother) and never returned to India.

From 1989 till 1993 Rajan and Dawood worked together and conducted operations in Mumbai from Dubai. During this time, they eliminated all their rivals in Mumbai, except for Arun Gawli, who was giving them a tough time. After separating from them, Gawli built his own gang and was operating from his base in Dagdi Chawl in the Agripada area of South Mumbai. Fierce rivalry raged between Gawli and the combined force of Dawood and Rajan between 1989 and 1993.

However, things changed permanently in 1993, when Chhota Rajan split from Dawood and formed his own gang. Rajan claimed that the 1993 serial bomb blasts in Mumbai were planned and executed by Dawood without his knowledge. He also took the opportunity to claim that he was a patriot and not an enemy of India, and that he did not approve of the bomb blasts that Dawood had engineered. Using this as an excuse, Rajan split from Dawood and fled Pakistan and the Middle East, moving to South-East Asia. A few of his very close associates also left with him and Rajan formed his own gang.

Heralding a new era in bitter rivalry, Rajan publicly made a statement claiming that he would take revenge on Dawood for having waged war against India. He portrayed himself as a patriotic gangster and decided to eliminate all Dawood gang members who were part of the 1993 serial bomb blasts conspiracy. Rajan killed six members of the Dawood gang for their alleged involvement in the case.

Salim Kurla was the first one to be killed by Rajan, on 21 April 1998, in Andheri. Next to be targeted was Mohammad Jindran, a real estate developer who was killed on 29 June 1998. Then came the turn of property developer Majid Khan (brother of Yakub Yeda, a close aide of Dawood) on 1 March 1999. On 7 February 2001, Hanif Kadawala, a hotelier and an accused in the blasts, was shot dead in his office in Bandra. In April 2021, a special CBI court acquitted Rajan and his close aide Jagannath Jaiswal in the murder of Kadawala for want of evidence.

On 2 April 2001, Akbar Abu Sama Khan was shot dead by two unidentified assailants in South Mumbai. Sama was accused of helping Tiger Memon and assisting in loading the cars and scooters with RDX in Memon's garage in Mahim just before the blasts. Sama Khan had allegedly participated in the landing of RDX at Shekhadi near Shrivardhan in Raigad district in early 1993.

As per underworld sources, there is another reason – which some believe is the real one – why Rajan split with Dawood.

On 23 April 1992, Khim Bahadur Thapa, a Shiv Sena corporator from Bhandup, was shot dead outside Hotel Ashok near the Mangatram petrol pump in Bhandup (West). The killing sent shockwaves across the political spectrum in Maharashtra, as well as through the underworld. Rajan had reportedly ordered the killing without informing Dawood or seeking his permission. He allegedly got Thapa killed because

he had apparently informed the police of the whereabouts of a close associate. This angered Rajan and he decided to teach Thapa a lesson.

Dawood was furious at this and asked his close associates, Subhash Singh Thakur and Sunil Sawant alias Sautya, to kill Rajan. They hatched a plot in Dubai, but it failed. Rajan got a whiff of the plan and fled Dubai, severing ties with Dawood.

After Rajan was arrested and deported to India in 2015, the CBI took over investigations into all the 72 cases registered against him in India. One was the murder of Thapa. The CBI registered an FIR in the case on 27 November 2019. After conducting investigations, a closure report was filed in the court in December 2020, citing no evidence or witness to conduct a trial. The court accepted the CBI's closure report and closed the case against Rajan.

What was to follow was a fierce and gruesome street war in Mumbai, which would see some of the bloodiest encounters ever witnessed in the city.

After Rajan started targeting D-Company members in Mumbai and killing them, in retaliation Dawood and Shakeel began targeting and killing Rajan's men, as well as Shiv Sena and BJP leaders who had taken active part in the December 1992 and January 1993 communal riots in which several hundred Muslims and Hindus had been killed. The riots were a repercussion of the Babri Masjid demolition in Ayodhya, Uttar Pradesh, on 6 December 1992, by Kar Sevaks belonging to the BJP, Shiv Sena and other Hindutva political outfits.

The Bangkok shootout

Things had come to such a head between Dawood and Rajan that they were baying for each other's blood. Rajan was at a slight advantage, as he knew almost all of Dawood's associates, his businesses, even his residences and offices in Dubai and Pakistan.

In fact, in 1998, Rajan sent his top lieutenants to Karachi in Pakistan to eliminate Dawood. The hit squad included Vicky Malhotra, Fareed

Tanasha, Balu Dokre, Ejaz Lakdawala, Vinod Matkar, Sanjay Ghate and Baba Reddy. Their plan was to reach Karachi and kill Dawood when he was scheduled to visit a *dargah* after his daughter Maria's death.

However, the shooters had to abandon the plan because Dawood arrived at the *dargah* with heavy security; and the team had no chance to get anywhere close to him. As per initial information, Dawood was tipped off about the operation to eliminate him and changed his escort from the usual two bodyguards to a larger, heavily armed team of bodyguards.

The squad then decided to stay in Karachi to try one more attempt on Dawood's life, but Rajan asked them to leave Pakistan immediately. He had learned that Dawood had been tipped off and would now seek revenge.

Rajan had been on the run ever since he split with Dawood and fled Dubai in 1993. Initially he hopped from one country to another in Southeast Asia but soon realised that Dawood had a strong network across the region through his drug cartel connections. Rajan then started working out of a yacht moored off the coast of Malaysia and Cambodia.

But this too was short-lived, as the Malaysian Coast Guard and other authorities kept interfering. Rajan finally settled in Sydney, Australia – one of the few places where Dawood did not have much of a network. He began his extortion, murder, kidnapping, arms supply and smuggling activities. He had his men in Mumbai, who would do his dirty work, while Rajan oversaw operations.

Things changed for Rajan in 2000, when the Mumbai Police tipped their counterparts in Australia about Rajan's suspected whereabouts in their country and his criminal antecedents. Australian authorities began investigating him and started cracking down on his activities. Sensing that he could be caught and arrested by the Australian police, Rajan fled Sydney and went to Bangkok.

His close aide and long-time partner, Rohit Verma, was residing in Bangkok. He had married a local girl and was living under an assumed name as a businessman. Verma arranged for Rajan to stay with him, under an alias.

But Rajan's luck ran out when, through his strong network, Dawood got tipped off about his whereabouts. Dawood immediately decided to carry out a hit on Rajan. It was August 2000 when he asked his trusted aide, Chota Shakeel, to execute his plan to have Rajan eliminated in September 2000.

Shakeel immediately called Rashid Hussain Shaikh alias Rashid Malabari, and Sayyad Muzakkir Mudassar Hussain alias Munna Jhingada. The prime reason for Shakeel choosing Malabari was because Rajan had orchestrated his brother Sajid's killing in 1997, in what was one of the most gruesome underworld murders of the time.

Munna Jhingada was arrested in Bangkok by the Thai police in 2000 after the attempted assassination of Chota Rajan. They decided to deport him to his home country. Since Jhingada was in possession of a (fake) Pakistani passport, the police decided to deport him to Pakistan. Jhingada and his boss Chota Shakeel also wanted him to be deported to Pakistan. However, the Indian authorities got information about this arrest and immediately informed the Thai authorities that Jhingada was an Indian national wanted in India for several crime-related cases.

The Government of India decided to send a delegation to Thailand to speak to the authorities there and convince them to deport Jhingada to India. I was tasked by the Government of India to be part of the delegation that travelled to Thailand. Our team met with top officials from the Thai government and explained to them about Jhingada's nationality and his long criminal history in India.

The primary court where the case was being tried gave its judgement in favour of India and ordered the deportation of Jhingada to India. Jhingada immediately appealed to the higher court against the primary court's order.

After a prolonged legal battle, the superior Thai court decided to deport Jhingada to Pakistan. Following this, Jhingada was deported to Pakistan in October 2019. It is believed that Jhingada

continues to live in Pakistan under Dawood's patronage.

Originally a resident of Jogeshwari in Mumbai, Jhingada has more than 60 criminal cases registered against him in Mumbai and other parts of the country. Jhingada was a sharpshooter in the D-Company. He was called to Karachi by Dawood in 1997 and continues to live there.

Malabari, who was looking to avenge his brother's death, jumped at the opportunity and along with Jhingada, assembled a crack team. A total of 11 people – 4 Pakistanis, 6 Indians and 1 local Thai Muslim who was to provide logistical support to the team – reached Bangkok on 14 September. Arrangements had been made for their stay and food. Dawood had also ensured that the required weapons along with a massive cache of ammunition were waiting for them when they reached their hideout. 15 September was decided as the day on which they would kill Rajan.

On the fateful day at around 9 p.m., when a sleek and stylish black limousine pulled up outside the lavish Sawan Court apartments in the tony Sukhumvit area of Bangkok, no one including the security guard suspected anything. Before he realised what was happening, seven armed men got out of the car – two of them held a gun to his head and asked him to keep quiet and not raise an alarm. The other five rushed to the second-floor apartment – Flat C3. The surprised security guard said the flat belonged to an Indian jeweller named Michael D'Souza, who lived there with his wife Sikandi Hama and their daughter.

On reaching the apartment Jhingada rang the doorbell, which was answered by D'Souza. The moment he opened the door, he realised something was wrong and tried to shut it, but Jhingada, Malabari and the other gunners opened fire and entered the house. D'Souza was killed instantly and his wife, who tried to intervene, was severely injured.

Rajan, who was in one of the rooms, heard gunshots and locked himself in with D'Souza's young daughter. The shooters tried to enter but couldn't, so they started shooting indiscriminately at the door. Two bullets hit Rajan, one in the leg and the other in the stomach. He realised that if he stayed in the room he would eventually be found and killed, so he took D'Souza's daughter and jumped from the second-floor window.

Rajan landed on his feet but fractured an ankle. He could not move and lay there. Meanwhile, the shooters desperately tried to open the door, to no avail. Eventually they decided to leave, fearing that the residents would alert the police, and they would be caught. They got in their limo and sped away. Unaware of what was going on, the residents rushed Rajan to nearby Sukhumvit Hospital.

The police started investigations. Even though gang wars, rivalries and violence were not uncommon in Thailand, the rule about no killings or murders in Bangkok was strictly enforced. Also, they couldn't understand why a well-established Indian jeweller residing in a posh locality had become a target of a gang war killing. The authorities were shocked to find that as many as 50 rounds had been fired.

As the mystery began to unravel, they realised that Michael D'Souza was none other than Rohit Verma, a well-known Indian gangster.

Rohit Verma was wanted in several cases in India, prominent among them the murder of Thakiyudeen Abdul Wahid, the owner of the now defunct East West Airline, on 13 November 1995.

Wahid was travelling in his car from his office in Bandra to his home in Andheri. At around 9.30 p.m., a team of killers comprising Rohit Verma, Joseph John D'Souza, Sunil Malgorkar, Bunty Pandey and Ejaz Lakdawala ambushed Wahid's car on SV Road in Santacruz (West).

They broke the windshield of Wahid's car with a hammer and then fired as many as 30 bullets at Wahid and fled from the spot. Wahid succumbed to his injuries almost instantly.

Rohit Verma and the others fled the country immediately after the killing.

When the Bangkok police reached the hospital and tried to speak to Rajan, he was unable to talk due to his injuries. His passport identified him as Vijay Daman, a businessman visiting his friend in the city.

However, the nature of the crime led the police to investigate further. With the assistance of the foreign office, they got in touch with their counterparts in India, since the murdered businessman was from India.

The Indian authorities responded almost immediately and identified the injured Vijay Daman as Rajendra Sadashiv Nikhalje alias Chhota Rajan, a fugitive gangster and mob boss from Mumbai, wanted for several heinous crimes in India. The murdered man was identified as Rajan's close aide and ace shooter Rohit Verma, who was also wanted in India.

The Bangkok police soon realised the importance of the situation and placed armed security around Rajan and the hospital. They anticipated that since the actual target was Rajan, there was a possibility that the shooters would try again once they learned that their target was still alive.

Meanwhile, the gunmen returned to their hideout, unsure if they had killed Rajan.

The Bangkok police was issuing conflicting reports to the media saying that two persons were killed, and one woman was injured. Other reports said all three were killed. Another reported that one was killed and two injured. However, their identities were not revealed.

By the next morning it was clear that Rajan had survived the attack and was in the hospital under intense security from the Bangkok police. Malabari called up Dawood in Karachi and informed him about what had happened. He even assured Dawood that he would make another attempt to kill Rajan. Dawood asked him to drop the plan and escape Bangkok.

However, the Bangkok police managed to apprehend four of the men, including the local Thai and three Pakistani shooters. They later told the police that they were paid USD 1 million by Shakeel to kill Rajan.

Even though Rajan escaped the near-fatal attack, he was in a lot of trouble. He was severely injured, unable to move, and in the custody of the Thai police. It was only a matter of time before he was arrested and tried in Bangkok for breaking Thai laws, and then extradited to India where he would be arrested for much more severe cases like murder, kidnapping, extortion, etc.

He was operated upon and the bullet from his stomach was removed by the Thai doctors. Even though he was out of danger, Rajan lay comatose in a hospital bed. His days were numbered. And, after realising who he was, the Bangkok police increased the security blanket around him in the Sukhumvit Hospital.

The great escape

Immediately after the news of the attack on Rajan reached India, a team of police officers from the Mumbai Crime Branch, led by the then Assistant Commissioner of Police (ACP) Shankar Kamble rushed to Bangkok to liaise with the Thai police. They informed the local authorities who Rajan really was and how dangerous, warning them that they should take the incident extremely seriously.

While ACP Shankar Kamble and his team rushed to Bangkok, under my supervision a team of Crime Branch officials prepared the extradition treaty document. A delegation headed by the then Deputy Chief Minister Chhagan Bhujbal, Additional Chief Secretary (Home) M.R. Patil, Mumbai Police Commissioner M.N. Singh and myself rushed to Delhi to meet and brief the then Union Home Minister L.K. Advani.

Advani heard us patiently and assured us that the Government of India would put its best efforts into deporting Rajan back to India.

ACP Shankar Kamble stayed in Bangkok for two months working with the Thai authorities to try and get Rajan back to India, but it did not yield any results.

Another murder attempt could not be ruled out, so the security cover around Rajan and the Sukhumvit Hospital was increased manifold. The Mumbai Police insisted that Rajan be shifted to a government hospital so that the security blanket around him could be strengthened. But the Thai Police continued to have him treated at the private facility.

Unknown to the Mumbai Police, it was Santosh Shetty, a close aide of Rajan, who had convinced the doctor who was treating Rajan to not allow him to be moved. At the time of the attack, three of his closest associates were with him in Bangkok – Rohit Verma, who was killed in the attack, Bharat Nepali and Shetty. When the shooting happened, Nepali and Shetty were not in the house but were in Bangkok.

On hearing about the attack on Rajan, they rushed to the Sukhumvit Hospital. They soon arranged for Rajan's wife Sujata Nikhalje to travel to Bangkok from Mumbai to be with him during treatment. They also asked Rajan gang members Fareed Tanasha and Bunty Pandey to come to Bangkok.

Rajan was under intense medical care. He was not able to move and was finding it difficult to speak. The biggest concern for Nepali, Shetty, Tanasha and Pandey was to ensure that he was not handed over to the Indian authorities by the Thai police. They had to do something quickly, but Rajan was not in any condition to be moved. Also, the security on the third floor of the hospital was impenetrable. So, they decided to wait and convinced the doctors treating Rajan to deliberately slow down the treatment so that the local authorities would be unable to move the patient, which would buy them time to ideate an escape plan.

Almost two months went by. The security cordon had been lulled into a routine. Over the two months, on the pretext of Sujata Nikhalje wanting to spend time in privacy with her husband, gang members pressured the police detail to move to the adjacent room. It was soon a situation where Rajan's wife and one visitor (always a gang member) would be allowed in Rajan's room, while the four policemen guarding him would be stationed in the adjacent room.

By November, the doctors were running out of excuses to keep Rajan hospitalised and soon he would be fit for discharge. The gang was under great pressure and given the desperate situation, they devised an audacious escape plan (there has never been any official confirmation of the escape plan, but it was reported by the media based on information from Rajan's men).

As per media reports from that time, for two weeks Shetty and Nepali trained in rappelling, reportedly by a Chinese girl named Pun, who was believed to be Shetty's girlfriend and a rappelling professional. After training was complete, they decided to implement their daring plan in November 2000. One late evening, Fareed Tanasha offered drinks to the security detail. It had become a routine by then and they had no reason to believe anything was amiss. However, they didn't know that Tanasha had laced their drinks with mild sedatives. By midnight, the four security guards were fast asleep.

At around 2.30 a.m., Shetty and Nepali walked up to Rajan's room, where Rajan and his wife were waiting. They were nervous because the plan was risky, and they were unsure how it would be implemented. Shetty and Nepali lowered a rope from the window to the ground floor, where Tanasha and Pandey were waiting. They tied a haversack full of rappelling equipment to the rope, which was pulled up into Rajan's room. It was decided that Nepali, who was the strongest man in the team, would heft Rajan on his shoulders like a sack and rappel down three floors, while Shetty and Rajan's wife would simply walk down the stairs and out of the hospital.

Nepali strapped the ropes and equipment around himself, lifted Rajan on his back and slowly started climbing down from the third-floor window, while Tanasha and Pandey waited with bated breath as they watched from below. The few minutes that Nepali took to reach the ground seemed like an eternity. Finally, the men reached the ground without incident. The first part of the plan had been successful. It was time to put in motion the next part, which was equally difficult.

Shetty reportedly used his local contacts and managed to get an army car as their escape vehicle. This was done so that they would not be stopped en route by local policeman. They boarded the car and sped towards the shipyard, where they reportedly boarded a helicopter and air-dashed to Cambodia. Cambodia was chosen because of Shetty's contacts there who would help in getting further medical treatment for Rajan.

The operation was executed like clockwork and before the break of dawn, Rajan and his men were out of the country. It was not until 8 a.m. the next morning that hospital authorities and the police realised that their patient had escaped.

Rajan's movie-style escape generated a lot of media attention. The Thai police, however, dismissed the story, saying that Rajan and his men had simply walked out of the hospital after lacing the security detail's drinks. Nevertheless, the escape was a huge embarrassment for the authorities.

Chhota Rajan's gang members continued to stay with Rajan in Cambodia during his treatment, which lasted a few months. After it was completed, Rajan once again went into hiding and was believed to be operating from a yacht off the coast of Cambodia. Shetty and Nepali returned to Bangkok, while Tanasha and Pandey went back to India.

After spending time in and around Cambodia, Rajan once again led a vagabond lifestyle, hopping from one country to another. All the while he was conducting his crime operations in Mumbai and other parts of India over the phone and other means of long-distance communication. His lieutenants in Mumbai during that time were Fareed Tanasha, D.K. Rao, his wife Sujata Nikhalje and a few others.

Eventually, Rajan once again settled in the suburbs of Sydney in Australia and started running his gang from there. He was involved in several cases of extortion, land grabbing and murder during this time. He also got a fresh passport from India with a fake name, once again changing his identity.

Rajan's luck ran out once more in 2015, when Chota Shakeel located him in Australia and sent out a crack team to kill him. That operation failed because the team was not able to identify Rajan's house. Rajan got a whiff of the plan and knew that it was no longer safe for him to stay in Australia. However, the Australian authorities learned about the failed attempt on his life. Rajan tried to flee Australia – he took a flight to Indonesia and from there, planned to hide in some Southeast Asian country. As soon as the flight took off, Australian authorities tipped off the Indonesian police about him and he was arrested the minute he landed in Indonesia on 25 October 2015.

His arrest instantly created international news, and Indian authorities sprang into action immediately. A team of top officials from the Ministry of External Affairs (MEA), Ministry of Home Affairs (MHA) and the Central Bureau of Investigation (CBI) was assembled, and it rushed to Indonesia to ensure that this time Rajan did not escape but was held in Indian custody.

After a court battle, Rajan was finally deported to India and arrested immediately after he landed in Delhi. There were as many as 72 cases registered against him in Mumbai, Maharashtra, and other parts of the country. Considering the sensitivity of the situation, the MHA decided to hand over all the cases to the CBI and gave orders to investigate and prosecute Rajan in each one.

Rajan was lodged in Tihar Jail in Delhi after he was brought back to India in 2015. Trials are ongoing in most of the cases. In May 2018, the special (Maharashtra Control of Organised Crime Act, 1999) court in Mumbai sentenced Rajan to life imprisonment for his involvement in the sensational murder of journalist Jyotirmoy Dey.

On 25 April 2017, the special CBI court in New Delhi sentenced Rajan and three others to seven years' rigorous imprisonment in a fake passport case.

- **Arun Gawli, a.k.a. Daddy**

Arun Gulab Ahir, a.k.a. Arun Gawli aka Daddy, once among the most dreaded gangsters in Mumbai, today languishes in a jail in Nagpur, serving a life sentence. He and 11 others were convicted in the murder of Shiv Sena corporator Kamlakar Jamsandekar by the special MCOCA court in Mumbai on 27 August 2012.

On 2 March 2007, two men barged into Jamsandekar's house in

Asalpha village in Ghatkopar and shot him dead. Investigations by the Mumbai Crime Branch revealed that Jamsandekar's rival had given a *supari* (contract to kill) to Arun Gawli to eliminate three-time corporator Jamsandekar following a land dispute. The court observed that Gawli had been paid ₹ 30 lakh for the job.

Gawli was a ruthless killer and an arch-rival of Dawood Ibrahim and Chhota Rajan. He had dominated the Mumbai underworld in the late 1990s. Born in a small tenement (714-E, room number 37) in Dagdi Chawl in the Agripada area of South Mumbai, Arun Gawli was the oldest of six siblings. His father, Gulab Puran Gawli was a worker in Simplex Mills in Lower Parel. He became unemployed because of the mill workers' strike, after which he started selling milk in the Agripada area. He died in 1977 at the age of 50, leaving behind his wife and six children. Arun's mother Laxmibai worked in a textile mill near Nair Hospital in Bombay Central. After her husband's death, she had to struggle to take care of her six children.

Arun Gawli studied till Std. VII in the Municipal School in Bakri Adda near Byculla, after which he joined City High School, Thakurdwar in Girgaon, till Std. IX. At the time, still in school, he started working as a temporary labourer in Shakti Mills in Mahalaxmi. Gawli dropped out of school that year and started doing various odd jobs to support his mother and siblings.

In 1973 he joined Godrej & Boyce Co., in Vikhroli as a worker in their dye-casting department. Barely a year in, Gawli was forced out of his job due to the strike announced by trade union leader Dr. Datta Samant. He then spent a year in the transformer department of Crompton in Kanjurmarg. However, this time, he himself quit because he had become too involved in criminal activities and was making a lot more money.

As a criminal and a vagabond, Gawli started moving around in his area to establish his network. He got in touch with his schoolmate Bablya Sawant, who lived in the Lal Vitachi Chawl (red brick chawl). Coincidentally, Rama Naik resided in the same building. Naik was from the same school as Gawli, a year junior to him.

Gawli soon developed a close friendship with Rama Naik, and

they formed their own gang, which included Ashok Chowdhary alias Chota Babu and Bablya Sawant.

At that time, the Byculla area already had two gangs that were involved in a power struggle, with street fights and violence against each other. The two gangs were the Byculla Club and the S-Bridge gang. The Byculla Club was owned and run by Mohan Chowdhary, father of Ashok Chowdhary. He ran a *matka* club and liquor business in the area. The S-Bridge gang was led by Mohan Sarmalkar, who was in the same business in the area near the S-Bridge which connects Byculla (West) to Byculla (East) and is operational even today. Local gangsters like Parasnath Pandey, Kundan Dubey, Raja Dubey, Shiva Ghati and Appa Ram Patil were part of the team.

To strengthen his Byculla Club against the S-Bridge gang, Mohan Chowdhary asked his son Ashok and his friends to join him. Following this, Rama Naik, Ashok Chowdhary, Arun Gawli, Vilas Chougule, Bablya Sawant, Babu Reshim and others joined the Byculla Club and formed their own group. This sparked a constant battle of superiority between the two gangs and among the gangsters of both. They indulged in regular rioting and violence against each other.

Things took an ugly turn for both sides when Rama Naik's brother Arvind fell in love with Kundan Dubey's sister. Dubey did not approve of the affair. One day, Dubey slapped Arvind over a quarrel that ensued apropos the love affair. Arvind's younger brother Umakant, who was present there, intervened and tried to ward off Kundan's blow. In the fight that ensued, Kundan stabbed Umakant to death. The year was 1976.

Even though Kundan was arrested by the Agripada police, Rama Naik was furious and swore to avenge his brother's murder. After a few months Kundan was out on bail, and he started pressurising the police and witnesses to withdraw the case against him. Rama Naik heard about this and offered his full support to the witnesses and ensured that the case went to trial. Kundan was found guilty and sentenced to life imprisonment. When he was in jail, he made friends with Shashi Rasam, son of a policeman and a gangster from Grant Road. Rasam was head of the Cobra gang. Hearing about Kundan's life imprisonment, Rasam was furious and decided to kill Rama Naik in revenge.

Rasam attempted to kill Naik a couple of times, but on both occasions a violent fight occurred between Rasam's men and Naik's gang on the streets of Byculla. In 1977, both were arrested and jailed. They were released on bail in early 1978.

During that time, Arun Gawli got information that Rasam was going to meet Kundan's sister Pushpa in X-lane, Byculla. Gawli, Rama Naik, Chhota Babu and Harvard (nickname as per police records) decided to target and attack Rasam on that day.

They lay in wait near X-lane. At the given time Rasam arrived in a taxi and went to Kundan's house. However, Pushpa was not there. So Rasam hailed a taxi and left. Naik's gang decided to follow him. They got into a taxi. When his cab reached the Bombay Central railway station bridge, Rasam got out to buy paan from a nearby shop. This was the opportunity Naik and his gang were waiting for. They got out of their taxi and rushed towards Rasam. Gawli and Harvard stabbed Rasam several times in the back and legs. After severely injuring him, Gawli and his gang members fled from the spot. Rasam managed to walk into the Bombay Central railway station and died there.

Interestingly, when the case was registered by the Nagpada police, everyone from Rama Naik's gang other than Arun Gawli were named as accused in the case and arrested. It is a mystery how Gawli's name did not figure in that case.

When Emergency was declared in 1975, because of his criminal record, Rama Naik was detained under the Maintenance of Internal Security Act (MISA) and jailed. He was lodged in Kalyan jail during this time. He met Rajan Nair alias Bada Rajan, who was also jailed under MISA. Around the same time, Naik also met then underworld don Varadarajan Mudaliar; he too had been jailed under MISA. Bada Rajan was a trusted aide of Varadarajan. In fact, Bada Rajan had even committed a murder on Varadarajan's orders, after which the two became very close.

After his release, Bada Rajan started frequenting Naik's den in Byculla. His gang members were with him, including Chhota Rajan,

Romesh Sharma, Ganesh Singh Bisht alias Danny, Ashok Kunder and others. The camaraderie between the Bada Rajan gang and the Rama Naik gang increased to a level where they would frequent each other's areas.

However, later in 1978, Rama Naik, Babu Reshim and Arun Gawli were externed from Mumbai for a period of two years. Rama Naik approached Bada Rajan, who harboured him in the Tilak Nagar area. Arun Gawli and Babu Reshim stayed out of Mumbai for a month and later joined Rama Naik. After a few days, they risked moving back to Byculla and hid in Dagdi Chawl.

Though they were supposed to be outside Mumbai, Arun Gawli and his associates Babu Reshim, Vilas Chougule, Motiram Mahadik, Chota Babu and Vinayak Shetty planned to kill Parasnath Pandey, since his nefarious activities had increased in the area. Gawli had developed a contact with a man called Ramesh Kharat, who had an illicit relationship with Parasnath Pandey's wife. Kharat tipped off Gawli about Pandey's whereabouts.

As per reports, Pandey was supposed to come to Tambat Naka near Transit Camp in Byculla. Gawli and his gang laid a trap there and when Pandey arrived, they attacked him and stabbed him to death.

Since they were officially externed from Mumbai, Gawli and his men rushed to Pune and surrendered to the police there. Following this, the Agripada police arrested them and brought them to Mumbai, where they were sent to jail. Gawli, Rama Naik, Babu Reshim and others involved in the Parasnath Pandey murder case were found guilty and sentenced to life imprisonment. They, however, appealed in the higher court and were out on bail during the pendency of their hearing.

In March 1983, Gawli and his associate Taraman Ghatkar stabbed to death a man called Shridhar Shetty inside Dagdi Chawl. The killing was over a petty quarrel. Shetty was the owner of a beer bar in Byculla. His murder became a serious issue and instead of the local police, the Mumbai Crime Branch was asked to investigate. Gawli, Ghatkar and their associate Razak Shaikh were arrested and put in the Crime

Branch lock-up.

Coincidentally, Ashok Joshi, a high-profile gangster from Kanjurmarg, and his men – Sada Pawle, Kiran Walawalkar, Keshav Uchil, Dilip Kohak alias Dilip Buwa, Gurunath Walawalkar and Ashok Asthana – were lodged in the same place, accused in the murder case of Nanji Shah of Kanjurmarg. At the same time, Chhota Rajan, Danny, Romesh Sharma alias Guna, Shrikant Desai alias Shri Mama, Bastav and Robert were also there, arrested in the murder case of John Ferreira at Juhu Chowpatty.

After a few weeks in the lock-up all the gangsters were moved to Arthur Road Jail in judicial custody. It was a time when almost every notable gangster seemed to be in the same prison together. Instead of being a jail, it became a place where the camaraderie between these gangsters increased. During this time, Arun Gawli became very close to Ashok Joshi. They decided to work together once they were out.

Lodged in the Arthur Road Jail at the same time were Gawli's rivals from the Pothya Bhatkar gang. Prominent among them was Amar Naik.

In a short span of time, Naik had made a name for himself in the underworld. The Gawli gang had been in a constant fight with the Pothya Bhaskar men over extortion money, protection money and territory in the Dadar, Parel, Lalbaugh and other areas of Central Mumbai. When Gawli found that Amar Naik was also in Arthur Road jail, he decided to take the opportunity to show him who was superior. One day, when Naik was walking around, Gawli stabbed him with a blade several times. This was Gawli's first encounter with Naik.

After being in jail for almost two years, Arun Gawli was acquitted in the murder case of Shridhar Shetty and released. However, Shetty's brothers Jayanta Shetty and Appu Shetty decided to avenge their brother Shridhar's death. They first targeted Arun Gawli's right-hand man Babu Reshim. Unknown to the Gawli gang, the Shetty brothers persuaded Vijay Kanjari alias Vijay Utekar and forced him to turn on his team.

On the orders of the brothers and Arvind Dholakia, Vijay Kanjari and his brother, Ravi fired at Babu Reshim when he had come to the

X-lane in Byculla. However, Babu Reshim survived and escaped. This happened in January 1987. An enraged Babu Reshim along with his friend and Gawli gang member Vijay Tandel stabbed Raja Karmarkar, who was a friend of Vijay Kanjari and Jayanta Shetty. Karmarkar survived the attack, but Babu Reshim was arrested by the Agripada police for attempted murder. He was lodged in the police lock-up at Jacob Circle, Saat Rasta.

The Shetty brothers got information about Reshim being at the Jacob Circle lock-up. They decided that it was the best opportunity to target him and get revenge for the killing of their brother. They once again gave the *supari* (contract to kill) to Vijay Kanjari, who immediately formed a team of close associates – Rajesh Utekar, Raju Bhaiya, Mahesh Maskarm, Kishore Kanjari, Ravi Kanjari and others. Sharad Shetty, a close aide of Dawood Ibrahim, was also part of this team. The killing of Babu Reshim has gone down in the annals of underworld folklore as one of the most gruesome and heartless killings ever known.

At that time, Iqbal Mirchi, who was smuggling gold and drugs for Dawood Ibrahim, was running Hotel Fisherman in Worli in partnership with businessman Mahesh Dholakia. However, they split after a dispute; Mirchi went to Dubai and complained to Dawood about Dholakia.

Dawood used the killing of Babu Reshim as an opportunity to settle scores with Dholakia. In a cunning way he informed Rama Naik that Reshim was murdered at the instance of Dholakia. Reshim was Naik's blue-eyed boy, so overcome by emotion, without verifying the information, Naik decided to kill Dholakia. He planned and formed a team of gangsters – Dilip Buwa, Anil Parab, Jaspal Singh Chouhan alias MLA, Sopan, Ganesh Bhosale alias Vakil, Dilip Kulkarni alias DK, Naresh Awtoo alias Jukkar and Sanjay Raggad.

The team stalked Dholakia for a few days and when they got an opportunity, they shot him dead near his residence in Pedder Road on 30 March 1987, barely a month after the killing of Reshim.

A month later, Raggad was stopped by the police during a *nakabandi* and found in possession of an unlicensed revolver. The police immediately took him into custody and interrogated him, during which he told them about the Dholakia killing. When they asked where his accomplices were, he said that they were holed up in Dagdi Chawl.

Following this, the Mumbai Police team raided Dagdi Chawl and arrested Ganesh Bhosale alias Vakil, Dilip Kulkarni alias DK and ace shooter Tanya Koli from inside the building. Arun Gawli was also arrested, even though he claimed that he was not involved in the killing of Dholakia. The police team also recovered a huge cache of arms from the tenement.

Gawli's mentor Rama Naik was shot dead in a police encounter by the then Police Sub-inspector Rajan Katdare in Chembur in 1988. After his death, his gang split into two. Gawli became the head of one gang. At that time, the prominent criminals with him were Sunil Ghate, Ashok Chowdhary, Ganesh Bhosale alias Vakil and Dilip Kulkarni alias DK.

Following Gawli's elevation as the head of the gang, the dreaded gangster from Kanjurmarg Ashok Joshi joined hands with Gawli, along with his gang members Sada Pawle, Keshav Uchil, Kiran Walawalkar, Vinay Karanjekar, Pandurang Madvi, Yogesh Paradkar and Gurunath Walawalkar. Two of Ashok Joshi's close aides, Dilip Buwa and Anil Parab refused to join hands with Gawli; they tied up with Chhota Rajan instead and started working with his gang.

This churning of power in the underworld was putting a new dynamic into place. Dawood, Shakeel and Rajan were in one team, pitted against their arch-rivals Arun Gawli and Ashok Joshi in the other. This new order was about to play out in the bloodiest battles on the streets of Mumbai.

Immediately after, on the instructions of Chhota Shakeel and Chota Rajan, gangster Anil Parab planned an attack on Ashok Joshi in Kanjurmarg. On 8 October 1988, Joshi was travelling in a car along with his friend Ramakant Naghave and two other associates when Anil Parab, Pakya Shetty and a gang of young college boys fired indiscriminately on the vehicle. Joshi took evasive steps in the nick of time and was saved, but the other three, including Naghave, were killed in the shooting.

The attack on Joshi was a clear indication that the battle was on – Gawli chose to take it forward. He, along with Joshi, decided to hit Dawood where it would hurt most. Gawli decided to target Satish Laxman Raje, who was an extremely important part of the Dawood gang, a man who managed the finances of the D-Company. Raje knew where all of Dawood's money and accounts were. Gawli understood that targeting Raje would financially cripple Dawood and company operations for a long time.

Gawli formed a team comprising himself, Ashok Joshi, Paul Neuman Patricks, Vijay Tandel, Dilip Landge and Karunakar Hegde for the job. For a few days they kept a close watch on Raje's movements to understand his routine. When they surmised his daily routine, they decided to target him.

It was the morning of Monday, 21 November 1988. Satish Raje left his home in Parel village, got into his white air-conditioned Honda Accord and started his journey towards South Mumbai – this was his routine every Monday morning. Unknown to him, a taxi started tailing him from the time he left home. When Raje reached the bustling Sir J.J. Hospital junction signal, the taxi behind him overtook his car and intercepted it.

Raje was caught unawares and had to brake suddenly. Gawli and his aides sprang out of the taxi and started attacking the Honda with hammers. They shattered all the windows of the car and started shooting at Raje from both sides with their .32 revolvers. After using all the bullets from the two guns, the shooters didn't stop – they rained heavy blows with hammers on Raje's head. (Use of hammers was Gawli's way of sending a message to Dawood that it was revenge for Babu Reshim's murder. Reshim's killers had used a hammer to kill him.)

Raje died on the spot and his killers fled.

Raje's murder sent a shiver down the collective spine of the D-Company, especially Dawood. He was shattered and full of rage. He wanted not just revenge, but a reprisal that would send a message of who was the real boss of the underworld.

And if Raje's killing wasn't enough, a week later Gawli and his associates killed Manu Prakash Karamchandani, another close associate of Dawood.

Arun Gawli takes the D-Company head-on

Ashok Joshi's murder on 3 December 1988, was a shock to the Gawli gang. Arun Gawli himself was shocked at the way Joshi was targeted. Furious, he swore revenge and decided to eliminate all the top members of the Dawood gang, wherever and whenever they were found.

He had a meeting with Sunil Ghate, Sada Pawle and Vijay Tandel, told them about his plans and asked them to start tracing senior members of the D-Company. They also decided to target well-wishers, supporters and financiers of Dawood's team.

Gawli, who was hiding in Khopoli after Joshi's murder, came to Mumbai and stayed in Dagdi Chawl. A few days later, a team of police officials from the Mumbai Crime Branch raided Dagdi Chawl and arrested Ashok Chowdhary alias Chota Babu, Sada Pawle, Ganesh Bhosale alias Vakil, Vijay Tandel, Dilip Kulkarni, and Arun Gawli for the murder of Satish Raje.

The men were in jail for seven or eight months before being released on bail. During that time, his gang members killed a man named Jayant Chheda who ran a *matka* den near Hindmata Cinema in Parel and black-marketed cinema tickets. Chheda was a known supporter of Dawood's gang. One day, Gawli's men Kiran Walawalkar, Suresh Patil, Namdeo Patil and Ramchandra Patil spotted Chheda in the red-light area of Kamathipura in Grant Road.

They started chasing him. Seeing them, Chheda started running. From the red-light area of Kamathipura, he ran all the way to the BEST bus depot in Tardeo, where his assailants caught up with him. Suresh Patil fired several shots at Chheda and severely injured him. Kiran Walawalkar and Namdeo Patil stabbed him several times. Chheda died on the spot. Suresh Patil was arrested on the spot, while

Namdeo Patil and Ramchandra Mahadik surrendered at the Tardeo police station, while Kiran Walawalkar absconded and remained a wanted man.

A few days after Chheda's murder, Gawli was released on bail on the condition that he would stay out of Mumbai until further orders. He moved to Pune near the Deccan Gymkhana with a friend but visited Mumbai secretly.

During one such trip to Dagdi Chawl, he plotted the killing of Jayanta Shetty, owner of Pingara Bar in Byculla. Shetty had provided logistical support to Vijay Kanjari, during the killing of Babu Reshim. Gawli was looking for revenge. Sunil Ghate, Sada Pawle, Dilip Buwa, Sambhaji Patil and a couple of others executed Gawli's plan and killed Jayanta Shetty in December 1989.

As per the information gathered by Gawli, Ashok Joshi's driver Shyam Nair was called by Chhota Rajan for a meeting at Worli to a bungalow belonging to businessman Mahendra Chordia. This was where Rajan had bribed Nair to switch sides and made him his informer. It was Nair who eventually gave information about Joshi's journey on the night of 3 December 1988.

Based on that information, Chhota Rajan had killed Ashok Joshi. Gawli knew that Chordia was associated with the Dawood gang. He discovered information which revealed that Chordia was a business partner of Dawood in most of his smuggling activities and would handle a majority of his *hawala* operations.

Gawli decided to target Chordia. One of Gawli's gang members was a man called Shrimali, who sold *Cole* books (the pocketbook guide for racegoers) outside the Mahalaxmi Race Course. He knew Chordia, who was a regular at the races. One afternoon, Shrimali came to Dagdi Chawl with information that both Chordia and Dawood Ibrahim's younger brother Iqbal Kaskar were at the racecourse.

Based on this information, Gawli sent his trusted aides Stalin, Raju Shirsat and Shrimali to the racecourse to bring Chordia and Kaskar to Dagdi Chawl. However, when they reached Mahalaxmi, only Chordia was present. Kaskar was nowhere to be seen.

They picked up Chordia and took him to the under-construction Devi Sadan building near Dagdi Chawl. Arun Gawli and Sunil Ghate joined the others and started interrogating Chordia. When they were convinced that Chordia was indeed a close associate of Dawood, Raju Shirsat, Kiran Walawalkar and Shrimali stabbed him to death.

Gawli had once again dealt a severe blow to Dawood with Chordia's killing. But this also meant that Dawood would seek revenge against Gawli.

The vengeance did not take long. On 22 February 1990, Dawood gang members Sunil Sawant, Anil Parab, Shrikant Desai alias Shri Mama, Ramesh Sharma alias Gunga, Avdhoot Bonde, Shirish Parab and Ashok Parab killed Kishore Gulab Gawli alias Papa. He was Arun Gawli's brother.

Dawood had got his revenge for the killing of Chordia. Not only was Gawli saddened by the murder of his brother, but he was also enraged that Dawood had attacked and killed his younger sibling who was not involved in any gang related activities and was not part of the underworld.

Around the same time, the Amar Naik gang, through their gangster Dashrath Rahane, met Arun Gawli. They joined hands to take on the Dawood Ibrahim gang. They also entered into a mutual agreement that they would not encroach on each other's territories and scavenge each other's businesses.

As a goodwill gesture of this new bond, Rahane and his close aide Francis D'Souza killed Narsimha Shetty and Trimurti Seth to avenge the killing of Papa Gawli. Both Shetty and Seth were involved in smuggling activities for the D-Company in South Mumbai.

The pendulum of revenge killings continued in the Mumbai underworld, marking the bloodiest time in this violent history, with both gangs targeting rival members.

To avenge Shetty and Seth's killing, their partners Ashok Shetty alias Ashok Anna and Dinesh Shetty alias Dinesh Anna gave a *supari* to Dawood gang members Sunil Sawant and Viju Shetty. In March 1990 Sunil Sawant shot dead Francis D'Souza in Tardeo.

A few days after Papa Gawli was murdered, Arun Gawli's associates from Dadar came to meet him at Dagdi Chawl. They informed Gawli that the D-gang's active member Anil Mambulkar had distributed sweets in his area, celebrating Papa Gawli's death. This information made Gawli furious, and he immediately ordered his associates Ajay Ahire and Appa Rane alas Kachcha Papad to kill Mambulkar. Following Gawli's instructions, Ahire, Rane and Kauda Babu shot Mambulkar dead in the Naigaon area of Dadar.

Around the same time, Gawli also planned the killing of Rajesh and Suresh Kanjari. He had them on his radar soon after they killed his close friend and aide Babu Reshim in the police lock-up at Jacob Circle. Gawli formed a crack team of his associates: Rafiq Patni, Nandu Palav, Ashok Paradkar and Salim.

As per the plan, they stalked Rajesh and Suresh Kanjari for a few days and then one day cornered them. There was an exchange of fire, and the brothers were shot dead. Rajesh managed to injure Salim, who died later in hospital. With this killing Gawli had avenged the gruesome murder of Babu Reshim.

By May 1990, Gawli was getting restless; his brother had died in February and even after three months he didn't know the identity of his killers. Even though he had always suspected Sunil Sawant, Gawli wanted to be sure.

In desperation, he ordered his gang members to pick up a man called Kamti from the Kranti Nagar area of Kandivali. He was a known associate of Sunil Sawant. Kamti was brought to Dagdi Chawl, where Gawli and his gang members tortured him for information. Kamti finally informed Gawli that it was Sunil Sawant, Manoj Kulkarni, Anil Parab and Shrirang Pawar who had killed Papa Gawli.

Following this revelation, Gawli kept a lookout for the four killers. He had instructed his gang to locate them. In late May 1990, Gawli got a tip-off that Manoj Kulkarni, who had been on the run after Papa Gawli's killing, was at his residence in Girgaon.

Gawli immediately formed a team comprising Vijay Tandel, Prakash Joglekar (reportedly a police constable), Raja Jadhav and

Shekhar Talli. They dressed as Crime Branch officers, got into a white Ambassador (the type used by senior Mumbai Police officials during those years) and drove to Girgaon.

They reached Kulkarni's residence and, on the pretext of arresting him and taking him to the Crime Branch, forced him into the car and sped towards Dagdi Chawl, where he was brought to Gawli. Kulkarni almost immediately confessed to having been part of the team that killed Papa Gawli. Hearing this, Gawli ordered his men to kill him. They took him outside the jurisdiction of the Agripada police station and shot Manoj Kulkarni dead inside the Tardeo bus depot.

Gawli was on a killing spree and there was increasing pressure on the Mumbai Police to stop him and his gang's activities. In fact, officially, Gawli was externed from Mumbai and was operating from outside the city. However, he would often visit Dagdi Chawl secretly to supervise his gang's operations.

On 19 July 1990, the Crime Branch conducted a surprise raid on Dagdi Chawl. The police rounded up several members of the Gawli gang. They had information that Gawli too was inside the building, even though he was not supposed to be in Mumbai. They searched the premises and found that there were several hiding places in the walls, rooms and floors of many flats in the chawl. In one such space they found a loaded carbine and other arms and ammunition. They discovered a small hole in the floor under a bed in one of the rooms. When they opened it, they saw Gawli hiding there, lying in a foetal position. He was immediately arrested.

Others who were arrested that day were Dilip Kulkarni, Neelam Walawalkar, Sonu Walawalkar, Raja Jadhav and Tanya Koli. All of them were indicted in the Manoj Kulkarni murder case and put behind bars.

Gawli remained in jail for a long time, but his gang continued with its activities, targeting members of the Dawood Ibrahim gang. Gawli masterminded most of the killings from jail, while his associates implemented his plans.

Killings by Arun Gawli gang

- **Amin Lambu and Yusuf Lamba:**
  Both were part of the gang which allegedly gave information to the police about Rama Naik's location, leading to his death in a police operation in Chembur. Naik was Gawli's mentor and to avenge his killing, Gawli had his team-members kill both Lambu and Lamba. They were attacked in Pakmodia Street in Nagpada and shot dead.

- **Rajji Mehendi:**
  He was believed to be a close associate of Dawood and looked after the smuggling activities of D-Company in Mumbai. In 1991, while still in jail, Gawli decided to target him. One day when Mehendi was travelling in his car, he was intercepted near the Kala Nagar junction in Bandra (East) by Tanya Koli, Mohan Mali, Ganesh Bhosale alias Vakil, Namdeo Patil, Vijay Tandel and Bandya Adilkar. The moment Mehendi stopped his car, they fired indiscriminately at him with an AK-47 assault rifle and other guns. Mehendi fired back and one of his bullets hit Vijay Tandel who was injured. However, Mehendi was no match for the sophisticated firearms used against him and died on the spot.
  An injured Vijay Tandel was rushed to KEM Hospital by Tanya Koli and the others. He was arrested by the police after he was discharged. The police raided Dagdi Chawl and arrested Tanya Koli, Mohan Mali, Bandya Adilkar, Namdeo Patil, Keshav Uchil, Ganesh Bhosale alias Vakil and others.

- **Salim Gardwala:**
  Arun Gawli had information that Salim was a close associate of Dawood. Gawli's henchmen Guru Walawalkar and Rajan Shirsat shot Salim dead in Dhobi Ghat near the Mahalaxmi area of Central Mumbai.

- **Mamya Pandit:**
  He used to collect money for the Dawood gang from the Hindu Colony area of Dadar. Gawli wanted him dead. His gang members Sudhakar Mirgal and Prakash Mudras shot him in his area of operation.

- **Ibrahim Parkar:**
  He was Dawood's brother-in-law (Haseena Parkar's husband) and had settled a lot of scores and disputes in the Nagpada area using Dawood's name. He had an office in Pakmodia Street where he sat every day. Gawli's men Vijay Narsale, Raju Bhatatia, Sharad Bhandale and Shailesh Haldankar stormed into his office one day and shot him dead on 16 March 1991.

- **Nitin Gawande:**
  He belonged to the Thapa gang in Bhandup and had reportedly taken part in the operation in which Ashok Joshi was shot at but survived. Gawli still wanted to teach him a lesson. In 1993, Gawli's aides Vinayak Karanjekar, Pandurang Madvi, and Yogesh Paradkar shot him dead in Kanjurmarg.

- **Panchand Dedhia:**
  He was a grain shop owner from Kanjurmarg. He was also an eyewitness in the murder of Nanji Shah, in which Ashok Joshi was the main accused. Dedhia had refused to pay protection money to Gawli, following which the latter decided to kill him. Pandurang Madvi and Yogesh Paradkar, two of Gawli's close aides, shot Dedhia dead in Kanjurmarg.

- **Ziauddin Bukhari:**
  He was a Congress MLA from South Mumbai and was allegedly close to the Dawood gang. He used his political weight to do the work of Dawood and settle several disputes in Dawood's name. Gawli got information that Dawood had also planned to attack Dagdi Chawl during the 1993 serial bomb blasts in Mumbai.

Gawli learned that Bukhari had played a key role in helping Dawood to execute the 1993 serial bomb blasts. Gawli decided to eliminate Bukhari. Gawli's accomplices Ashok Chowdhary alias Chota Babu, Vijay Narsale, Raju Philips, Sudhakar Mirashi and Daya Pujari shot Bukhari dead near Byculla bridge on 23 April 1993.

- **Gendya Mama:**
  He was a close aide of Amar Naik and after relations between Gawli and Naik soured to the point of no return, Gawli decided to target Naik's gang members as well. Gendya Mama was shot dead by Kiran Walawalkar, Vijay Burma Kamble alias Muchwa and Ganesh Bhosale alias Vakil at the BIT Chawl in Bombay Central.

- **Prabhakar Kakade:**
  He was a cousin of Chhota Rajan and handled a lot of the monetary transactions for the Rajan gang. He was murdered in 1993 in the Tilak Nagar area by Gurunath Walawalkar, Vijay Kamble alias Muchwa, Vinayak Karanjekar, Vijay Bapu Salve alias Narsale and others.

- **MTNL linesman, Salim:**
  In his effort to find everyone who was involved in the killing of his brother, Arun Gawli discovered that an MTNL linesman by the name of Salim had provided information about Papa Gawli to D-gang members. Salim had tapped the telephone lines in the chawl, and one day overheard Papa Gawli talking to his girlfriend, telling her about his whereabouts.

  Salim promptly gave this information to D-gang members who were easily able to track Papa Gawli and kill him. After Gawli learned this, he immediately ordered the killing of Salim. In 1992 Vijay Narsale, Baban Raghav and others picked Salim up from the Parel area and after ascertaining that he was indeed the one who had given information about Papa Gawli, shot him dead.

- **Suresh Patil:**
  He was Arun Gawli's own man. However, Gawli learned that Patil had misappropriated gang money to the tune of ₹ 50 lakhs, a huge amount in those days. Gawli interrogated Patil thoroughly but got unsatisfactory answers.

  Gawli was sure he had committed the fraud and had one of his men kill Patil in Dagdi Chawl. Gawli did this to send a signal to his men that betrayal would not be tolerated. This was the first time that Gawli had killed his own man.

The see-saw battle between Arun Gawli and the Naik brothers continued through the 1990s. Gawli's gang became stronger with the likes of Ashok Mohan Chowdhary alias Chota Babu, Sada Pawle, Sunil Ghate, Vijay Tandel and Kiran Walawalkar playing major roles. Even when Gawli was in jail, these men ensured that gang activities continued smoothly.

Gawli made sure that his people were adequately taken care of, even in his absence. He ensured that each member got a sizeable amount as salary each month. As and when any one of them was jailed, the others would ensure that home-cooked food would be provided to them.

Advocates would also be paid well to ensure that they kept fighting cases for the members whenever needed.

Gawli was in jail for most of the 1990s, released only late in the decade. After that he formed his own political party, the Akhil Bhartiya Sena (ABS), and won the elections to the state assembly, becoming a Member of the Legislative Assembly (MLA) of Maharashtra.

Most of the first decade of this century went by without Gawli being proved to be involved in various cases, and he remained out of jail. His luck ran out, however, when Kamlakar Jamsandekar, Shiv Sena Corporator from Saki Naka, was murdered at his residence near Saki Naka, Andheri (East) on 2 March 2007.

The Mumbai Police almost immediately unearthed the plot to kill Jamsandekar and found that it was the handiwork of Arun Gawli and his men. The Mumbai Crime Branch arrested Gawli under the stringent Maharashtra Control of Organised Crime Act (MCOCA), under which he was denied bail. The case put up by the Mumbai Police against Arun Gawli was solid and the court soon found him guilty and sentenced him to life imprisonment. He continues to languish in Nagpur jail and is unlikely to ever be released. The gang has been completely disbanded by the police. Even Dagdi Chawl is today a pale shadow of its former flamboyant self.

- **Chhota Shakeel**

Born Mohammed Shakeel Babu Miyan Shaikh on 31 December 1955, in the Khed taluka of Ratnagiri district, Maharashtra, Chhota Shakeel was brought up in the Dongri area of South Mumbai. A school dropout, he started a travel agency in Dongri in the 1980s. It was a dubious enterprise from the start. Shakeel met Dawood and his gang when he was working as a travel agent.

Over time, Shakeel grew close to Dawood and his operations. During one of his visits to Dubai in 1988, he formally joined hands with Dawood and his D-Company. Shakeel never came back to India. Along with him, three others – Bishal Cheetah, Johnny Akhawat and Liger Bhai alias Mushu Bhai – also joined hands with Dawood.

During that time, the functioning of the D-Company was split between three people: Dawood was overall in-charge of operations, Sunil Sawant alias Sautya looked after cricket betting and match-fixing, and Chhota Rajan controlled and oversaw all operations in Mumbai.

For about five years Shakeel remained in the shadows, working as a sidekick of Dawood. His time at the helm came in 1993 when, after the serial bomb blasts in Mumbai, Chhota Rajan split from Dawood to form his own gang. Dawood asked Chhota Shakeel to take over

Chhota Rajan's role in the gang. Shakeel did so successfully and soon became Dawood's closest confidant.

After the 1993 bomb blasts conspiracy was revealed and it was clear that Dawood had masterminded the entire operation along with Pakistan's Inter Service Intelligence (ISI) agency, there was increasing pressure on him to stay away from taking active part in crime-related activities.

Dawood could not leave Pakistan for fear of being arrested by Interpol. Nor could he speak on the telephone, which could be under surveillance by various law enforcement agencies across the world. Hence, all these responsibilities were given to Shakeel. He took over the gang's operations and even managed the work in Mumbai from Pakistan.

During that time, D-Company was fighting two enemies in Mumbai: on one side Chhota Rajan had sworn to target members of the gang, and on the other, Arun Gawli had decided to eliminate all Dawood's people in Mumbai after Papa Gawli was killed by D-gang members on the instructions of Chota Shakeel.

In 1995, Sunil Sawant alias Sautya was gunned down in Dubai by Chhota Rajan and his men. This left Dawood distraught, and he started depending on Shakeel even more, appointing him Chief Executive Officer (CEO) of the D-Company. Shakeel was not only a quick study but also was more far-sighted than Dawood or any of his rivals. Among the first things that he did after taking over as CEO was to create a proxy for himself. He worked with Rahim Merchant alias Dogla, a wealthy businessman from North Karachi in Pakistan, to create a substitute voice for himself (this information has officially never been confirmed, but it has been widely reported in the media).

The men worked closely for several weeks, until eventually Merchant managed to mimic Shakeel's voice perfectly. Once this was accomplished, in every phone call Shakeel made, Merchant would speak, impersonating him. Chota Shakeel would write down everything that was to be said and hand it over to Merchant, who would then replay it over the phone.

This con fooled almost all law enforcement agencies in India and across the world for a long time. In fact, the audacity of the con was such that Shakeel started calling anyone at any time, confusing law enforcement agencies, journalists and others for decades. They all wanted to know how Shakeel could talk to everyone without fear of being located by the police. His phone numbers were known to many journalists in India and abroad. Shakeel would call news channels and newspaper offices and speak to reporters about any news that had been published in favour or against Dawood Ibrahim or his gang.

Apart from dealing with underworld activities in Mumbai, Shakeel also began spreading D-Company operations internationally. He started international drug trafficking and tied up with suppliers in Afghanistan and Colombia. He bought mines in South Africa to start an illegal diamond mining business for the D-Company. As per reports, Shakeel smuggled diamonds for the Ukrainian crime organisation Odessa, in exchange for the latest weapons, arms and ammunition. To ensure that the gem smuggling business ran smoothly, Shakeel got himself two fake passports – one from Botswana and the other from Malawi.

Shakeel was instrumental in making Abu Salem a name to reckon with in the Mumbai underworld. Salem was first recruited as a driver in the D-Company. Immediately after the 1993 serial bomb blasts in Mumbai, Salem, along with several other members of the Dawood gang, fled to Dubai. He joined the D-Company there and started doing odd jobs. Shakeel used Salem for making extortion calls to Bollywood personalities, as well as to acquire film rights for international distribution.

However, Shakeel and Salem parted ways when, without Shakeel's approval, Salem had music baron Gulshan Kumar killed in a daring shooting in broad daylight. Shakeel was furious that he was not consulted before the killing. Salem, realising that his days were numbered, parted ways from Shakeel and fled.

Shakeel continued to target the film industry. He inserted his man Nazim Rizvi into the film industry and asked high profile producer

Bharat Shah to make *Chori Chori Chupke Chupke.* Both Rizvi and Shah were convicted by the Mumbai Crime Branch under MCOCA. Apart from this, Shakeel has claimed that he financed several films in Bollywood during the late 1990s and early 2000s.

In September 2000, Chhota Shakeel masterminded a near-fatal attack on Chhota Rajan in Bangkok, Thailand. (Read details in Chapter 5 on page no. 68.) Shakeel had been tracking Rajan ever since he split from the Dawood gang and had sworn to take revenge.

Immediately after the separation, Rajan started targeting members of the D-Company who were involved in the 1993 serial bomb blasts in Mumbai. In retaliation, Shakeel aimed at members of the Rajan gang in the city, as well as other Hindutva activists who were involved in the communal riots against the Muslims immediately after the demolition of Babri Masjid in December 1992.

Shakeel's plan almost worked, but Rajan managed to escape death. With the help of his gang members, Rajan fled the country and went to Cambodia. From there he went missing. Meanwhile, Shakeel kept an eye on Rajan and the whereabouts of his people.

Between 2000-2010, Shakeel cemented his place in the D-Company as the second in command. Dawood had placed utmost trust in him for all activities and Shakeel held the reins of almost every aspect of the gang's operations.

Dawood's younger brother, Anees Ibrahim, was getting increasingly restless about Shakeel's growing clout. He was not happy that his elder brother had given control of the gang to Shakeel, while Anees had to report to Shakeel.

Anees was looking for an opportunity to oust Shakeel and take over. He tried several times but failed because each time Dawood took Shakeel's side and refused to even consider Anees. This enraged Anees.

In 2016 Anees had a fallout with Shakeel over the gang's operations in Dubai. However, this time, Dawood did not show any bias. He did not want to let this incident affect his friendship with Shakeel; at the same time, he didn't want to strain his relationship with his younger brother.

The entire story hit a new low when, in 2017, Dawood's younger brother Iqbal Kaskar was arrested by the Thane police in an extortion case. Kaskar was reportedly working on Shakeel's instructions, which led to his arrest. This resulted in a major fallout between Anees and Shakeel; the former vowing never to work with the latter again.

After relations between Anees and Shakeel reached a point of no return, news came in one day that Shakeel had died. Two versions of the story were floated in the media. One: Shakeel died of a massive heart attack when he was in Dushanbe, Tajikistan, to seal an arms deal for D-Company. Two: Shakeel was targeted by an unknown group of people when he left his residence in Lahore, Pakistan. He was in his car when a grenade was hurled inside. A massive explosion followed and Shakeel was killed.

For a long time, it was unclear whether Shakeel was dead or alive.

As per media reports published in December 2017, Shakeel had died in January 2017. The first mention of this was through an audio clip – the voice purportedly that of Dawood himself. He is heard saying that Shakeel had died on 7 January 2017. Immediately after this audio clip went viral, another claimed that a man named Bilal, speaking to his relative, said that Shakeel had died of a heart attack and that Anees Ibrahim had taken over the gang and all Shakeel's finances, properties and position in the D-Company.

A letter written by the Royal Thai police to Interpol was leaked to the media which stated that Shakeel was dead and need no longer be tagged with an Interpol Red Corner Notice. This letter gave credence to the story that Shakeel had indeed died. However, it was revealed that the letter sent to Interpol was fake and the officer who had sent it did not work for the Thai police. Investigations by Thai authorities proved that. The Indian authorities later confirmed to the media that Shakeel was not dead.

Though there was no confirmation of Shakeel's death, reports suggested that Shakeel's close associates – Bilal, Mohammed Rashid, Iqbal Salim, Yusuf Raja and Parvez Khawaja – had quit the D-Company and left Pakistan. The media also surmised that Shakeel's bungalow at D-48, 15th Lane, Khayaban-Seher, DHA Colony, Lahore, Pakistan, wore a deserted look and had been taken over by the ISI. Reports indicated that the ISI had moved Shakeel's daughter, Zoya, out of Pakistan, while his second wife, Ayesha, was reportedly living in a house in Lahore cantonment area.

However, till date there is no solid confirmation about whether Shakeel is alive or dead. He had been shrewd enough not to use his own voice to speak to anyone over the phone for over two decades. Even today, if Shakeel talks to someone over the phone or the internet, it would be difficult to determine whether it is indeed him or his friend Rahim Merchant mimicking him.

- **Suresh Manchekar**

Suresh Manchekar, like Arun Gawli, was also a product of the shutdown of mills in Mumbai in the late 1970s and early 1980s. Manchekar was born in Parel in 1961; his parents were poor mill workers. After the mills shut down and there was no employment anywhere, Manchekar took to the streets to commit petty crimes and make money. His mother, Laxmi Dhanraj Manchekar, was his inspiration and always stood behind her son, no matter what he did. When Manchekar started becoming infamous and came under the police radar, he started moving to other states and cities.

Unlike Dawood Ibrahim, Chhota Shakeel and Chhota Rajan, Manchekar did not flee the country, but would leave the city and state to find safety elsewhere. He was active in Mumbai, Thane and other districts of Maharashtra, and his activities extended to Karnataka, Andhra Pradesh and Madhya Pradesh. By 1986 he had committed his first murder but achieved greater infamy in the underworld when, in 1989, he allegedly murdered Vinayak Wable, a Shiv Sena corporator from the Sewri area of Mumbai.

After this, Manchekar became a name to reckon with in the underworld and very soon had more than 70 cases of murder, extortion and kidnapping registered against him in Mumbai and elsewhere in Maharashtra.

By the 1990s and early 2000s Manchekar had created quite a reign of terror in Mumbai and its satellite townships. He extorted money from builders and businessmen and during his peak, had more than 200 people in his gang.

He was a cunning man. He built a house near the Maharashtra-Karnataka border, in Belgaum. Whenever he wanted to make a phone call or have a meeting with his gang members, he would drive into Karnataka to do so, thus avoiding attracting the attention of the Maharashtra police. In this way, he hoodwinked the authorities for a long time.

His luck finally ran out when the Thane Crime Branch got wind of his whereabouts and began an operation to nab him. On 15 August 2003, the Thane Police headed by Inspector Angre surrounded him in Kolhapur district as he was travelling to another area. He refused to surrender and shot at the police. In the ensuing exchange of fire, he was shot dead. He was 42 years old.

Interestingly, while Manchekar was moving from one state to another, his mother Laxmi had become a godmother of crime. She had established her own base and was running Manchekar's gang by herself. She was involved in the killing of builder Mahendra Khanvilkar in Mumbai on 22 March 2000 – she had demanded ₹ 15 lakh as extortion money, which Khanvilkar refused to pay.

Coincidentally, a few days before Manchekar was killed in the police operation, Laxmi was convicted and sentenced to life imprisonment for the killing of Mahendra Khanvilkar. Manchekar's wife, Supriya, was later arrested by the police for continuing the gang's activities after her husband's death.

- **Subhash Singh Thakur**

Subhash Singh Thakur alias Subhash Rai alias Baba is believed to be among the most dreaded and dare-devil gangsters of his time. Among the first imports from Uttar Pradesh by the Mumbai underworld to strengthen its gangs, he was recruited by Dawood Ibrahim as a hitman. Almost overnight he became a name to reckon with when he, along with Shyam Kishore Garikapatti and Jayant Suryarao, barged into the Sir J.J. Hospital on the night of 12 September 1992, carrying an AK-47 assault rifle and other sophisticated firearms.

They went to Ward No. 18 where Shailesh Haldankar was undergoing treatment and had 24-hour police protection around him. Haldankar, a member of the Arun Gawli gang, was accused of killing Dawood's elder brother Shabbir Ibrahim Kaskar and was arrested. He was admitted to the J.J. Hospital on medical grounds. Dawood, who wanted to avenge his brother's killing, saw this as a perfect opportunity to target Haldankar. He tasked Thakur and Garikapatti with the work and asked them to eliminate Haldankar.

Thakur planned the daring shoot-out. The moment they reached the ward in the middle of the night, they started firing indiscriminately in the direction of Haldankar. They even hurled hand grenades. The hospital ward soon turned into a war zone. In the shoot-out Haldankar and two constables – Chintaman Gajanan Jaiswal and Kewalsingh Bhanawat – who were guarding him, were killed. Thakur, Garikapatti and Suryarao fled.

The incident shocked the city of Mumbai, especially the rank and file of the Mumbai Police. An immediate operation was launched to nab the killers and within a few days all three – Thakur, Garikapatti and Suryarao – and a few others were arrested.

Thakur was charged with the planning and killing of Haldankar and two constables. The trial took eight years, and in March 2000 a special court convicted Thakur and sentenced him to death. He has been in jail ever since. Garikapatti and Suryarao were sentenced to ten years' rigorous imprisonment.

A couple of years after he was arrested Thakur decided to sever ties with Dawood and form his own gang. He felt that Dawood did not help him while he was in jail and started his own operations while he was still imprisoned. He tried to hoodwink the system by getting himself transferred to a jail in Uttar Pradesh for his involvement in a local case there. It was easier for him to run his gang from his home state (Uttar Pradesh) than from Maharashtra.

He would regularly summon builders and businessmen from Mumbai to UP and threaten them, demanding money. He managed to create a strong presence in the eastern and western suburbs of Thane district, all the way to Ahmedabad in Gujarat. Thakur managed to stay in UP for a long time. However, the Maharashtra police finally managed to bring him back to Mumbai in 2016.

Mumbai Police ran a successful trial in court against Subhash Singh Thakur for his role in the J.J. Hospital shoot-out case. He was convicted and sentenced to death by the Sessions Court. However, he appealed to the Supreme Court, where his death sentenced was commuted to life imprisonment.

While he was serving his jail sentence in Maharashtra, Thakur created a false narrative that his life was in danger in Maharashtra and the D-Company was planning to target him and eliminate him. Following this, he was transferred to a jail in Uttar Pradesh. In 2019, he claimed that he was suffering from a serious kidney ailment. Following this claim, he was admitted to a special ward in the BHU Hospital in Varanasi.

For five years, Thakur stayed in the hospital ward enjoying a life of comfort away from the struggles of a jail life. However, after five years the jail and police administration grew suspicious of Thakur's ailment and a 12-member panel was constituted to check and report on his medical condition. The panel reported that Thakur was fit and healthy and no longer needed to be in a hospital. Following this, on 27 January 2025, Thakur was sent to the Fatehgarh jail and is currently lodged there to serve his life imprisonment.

- **O.P. Shrivastava, a.k.a. Babloo Shrivastava**

Om Prakash Shrivastava aka Babloo Srivastava is a native of Ghazipur district in Uttar Pradesh. He is believed to be among the most cunning and vicious criminals operating in the country. He is a law graduate from Lucknow University and specialises in abducting rich businessmen across the country and extorting money from them. He is notorious for going to any extent to ensure the success of his criminal operations, even resorting to murder if need be. He became known as the kidnapping kingpin of the criminal world, and a direct competitor to Dawood Ibrahim.

In his rise to cross-border clout, Babloo started as a small-time ruffian in UP. He was known to the local police as a law student who would regularly disturb the peace and disrupt law and order at the DAV College.

In 1988, backed by the then Congress (I), he was elected as the general secretary of the students' union in U.P. However, in 1990, when the BJP came to power in the state, they tried to arrest him under the Terrorist and Disruptive Activities (Prevention) Act (TADA). It was then that Babloo decided to flee the state. He moved to Bombay, set-up his own gang and started abducting businessmen in exchange for huge ransom amounts.

On 2 August 1992, a businessman from Delhi named Lalit Suneja was abducted and later found murdered. It was evident that it was the work of Babloo Shrivastava. Sensing that the police was on his trail, Babloo decided to flee the country. He obtained a fake Nepalese passport under the name of Arun Kumar Agarwal and fled the country to settle in Dubai. He had left his gang behind in Bombay, to continue carrying out abductions and kidnappings of rich businessmen and industrialists and making money.

When the 1993 blasts rocked the city of Mumbai, an Additional Commissioner of Customs by the name of L.D. Arora was transferred to Allahabad under mysterious circumstances. It was alleged that Arora had vital clues about the whereabout of the RDX that was brought into the country for the blasts. But before he could work on this information, he was transferred.

Incidentally, a few days before the blasts, Arora was instrumental in a huge drug bust in which a massive haul of ₹ 1,000 crores (a huge amount in those days) was seized, the contraband reportedly belonging to Mohammad Dossa. After this Arora was under the radar of the Mumbai underworld. Once he was transferred to Allahabad, he was killed by Babloo Shrivastava in the same month, March 1993. It is also widely believed that Srivastav demanded a pay-off of ₹ 5 crore to eliminate Arora.

Babloo Shrivastava is thought to have met Dawood in Dubai in October 1993. However, they soon had a fall out because of Babloo's growing clout in the *Satta Bazaar* (betting market) of Dubai.

Babloo Shrivastava and his gang were also instrumental in the sensational kidnapping of Mumbai-based businessman Vishwanath Mittal. However, the attempt failed, and Mittal was rescued in the nick of time.

On 21 June 1994, at around 11.30 a.m., Mittal was heading towards his office in Nariman Point in a Maruti 1000 car driven by his nephew Arun. As they cruised along Marine Drive, their car was ambushed by a Maruti 800 which overtook them at high speed. Arun had to brake suddenly as the Maruti 800 swerved in front of his car. As both cars screeched to a halt, four men jumped out of the Maruti 800 brandishing 9mm pistols. They fired in the air. Seeing the armed assailants shooting, Mittal and Arun were shocked. Before they realised what was happening, the gangsters forced Mittal out of the car, shoved him into their own vehicle and fled.

It would have been a clean operation, except for the fact that even in the highly volatile situation Arun had the presence of mind to note down the getaway car's license plate number. As luck would have it, it was the day of Moharram and there was heavy police presence on the streets of Mumbai. Arun ran to the nearest police team and gave them the information.

The main control room was immediately alerted and the police rapidly set up check points and *nakabandi* across the city. Forty-five minutes after the abduction the getaway car was stopped by a police patrol and Mittal was rescued. Two gangsters were arrested on the spot, while the other three managed to flee. One of the three who escaped – Ashok Tiwari – was shot dead in an encounter a few days later near the Gulistan Hotel situated close to the Minerva Theatre in Lamington Road area of South Mumbai. The other two remained elusive for a long time. One of them, K.P. Contractor alias Kali, was arrested almost 15 years later in April 2009 in Lonavala.

Babloo's luck finally ran out after he was detained at Singapore airport in April 1995 when he was travelling on a fake Nepalese passport in the name of Arun Kumar Agarwal. Authorities in Singapore notified Interpol and the CBI fought a long and hard legal battle to have Babloo extradited to India.

Finally, in September 1995, Babloo was extradited and brought back to India. He was tried in four cases and was convicted and sentenced to life imprisonment for the murder of L.D. Arora. He is currently in a jail in Uttar Pradesh.

• The Pujaris – Ravi and Hemant

By the first decade of this century, a majority of gangsters and criminals of the Mumbai underworld had either fled the country or were killed in police encounters or were behind bars. There was a vacuum in the underworld. The Pujari brothers tried to fill the vacuum and take over the underworld. The most prominent among them is Ravi Pujari.

Ravi Suliya Pujari:

Born in the Malpe area of Udupi district in Karnataka on 25 January 1961 (date recorded as per his latest passport) Ravi Pujari moved to Mumbai as a teenager in the late 1970s after he dropped out of school. He started working at a tea stall in Andheri to make ends meet.

However, the money he earned was not enough and because he was uneducated, his career options were limited. So, he soon took to a life of crime with petty theft, pickpocketing and robbery. He operated across Mumbai and its far suburbs like Dombivli and Kalyan.

In the early 1980s, Pujari allegedly killed a rival gangster named Bala Zalte. This immediately brought him into the underworld spotlight – Chhota Rajan noticed him and asked him to join his gang.

At the time Rajan was working with Dawood Ibrahim, so Pujari also started working for the D-Company. Thus started Pujari's association with the Mumbai underworld.

However, after Dawood and Rajan split after the 1993 Mumbai blasts, Pujari decided to join ranks with Rajan and split with Dawood. The entire decade of 1990s saw the two collaborating; Rajan had taken a special liking to Pujari. With Rajan's backing Pujari had committed serious offences like murder, extortion and kidnapping in Mumbai and surrounding areas. Unlike Dawood, Rajan and other gangsters of those times, Pujari decided not to leave the country and continued his criminal operations in Mumbai. In 1994 he was arrested in a murder case but was soon released on bail. His crime spree continued with cases in Mumbai, Mangalore and elsewhere.

When the heat on him increased, Pujari fled the country via Nepal. From there he went to Bangkok to join Rajan and shunted between Bangkok, Australia, Iran and Uganda. Things between Rajan and Pujari changed after the near-fatal attack on Rajan in Bangkok in 2000. At the time of the attack, Pujari was not in Bangkok with Rajan, but in another country.

Rajan's close aides somehow convinced him that Pujari could not be trusted and should be removed from the gang. Getting a whiff of this, Pujari himself split from Rajan and formed his own gang. Taking a cue from his former boss, he also tried to portray himself as a 'Hindu Don' and started targeting anti-Hindu elements in India.

For the last two decades Pujari has targeted several businessmen, politicians, industrialists and Bollywood personalities for extortion. Some of his targets have been top actors like Shahrukh Khan, Salman Khan and Akshay Kumar. He has even threatened social activists such as Shehla Rashid, Umar Khalid and Jignesh Mevani. Former Karnataka education minister Tanveer Sait filed a police complaint alleging Pujari had demanded ₹ 10 crore from him.

In India, Pujari reportedly has over 200 criminal cases against him, including for murder, extortion and more, with 97 extortion cases in Karnataka, 39 in Bangalore, 36 in Mangalore and more than a dozen each in Maharashtra, Kerala, Gujarat and elsewhere.

Through the 2000s and 2010s, Pujari hopped from one country to another – from Australia to Vietnam, Iran to Cambodia and Europe. He finally decided to settle down in Burkina Faso, a land-locked nation in West Africa, under a fake name: Anthony Fernandes. From there he moved to Dakar in Senegal and started living a life of a philanthropist there, doing social service and humanitarian activities.

He reportedly started a restaurant chain called *Namaste India*, with nine outlets across several West African countries. Pujari also provided drinking water pumps in rural areas affected by water scarcity. During Navratri, he would give clothes to the poor. He tried to create an image of a philanthropist in Senegal and was even featured in local newspapers for his charitable deeds.

But even while he was in Burkina Faso and Senegal, Pujari was involved in underworld activities in Maharashtra, Karnataka, Kerala, Gujarat and other states. Indian intelligence officials first traced Pujari to Burkina Faso and then to Senegal.

On 31 December 2018, Indian intelligence agencies learned that Ravi Pujari had been hosting cricket tournaments in Africa – they had photographs to prove it. He was finally detained at a barber's shop in Dakar, the capital of Senegal, by the local police.

Indian authorities were informed of the detention in January 2019, along with a request for documents to facilitate his extradition. In the absence of a bilateral extradition treaty with Senegal, the Government of India moved for extradition under the United Nations Convention Against Transnational Organized Crime (UNCTOC) adopted in 2000 as "the main international instrument in the fight against transnational organized crime". Pujari had cases against him under the Maharashtra Control of Organised Crime Act (MCOCA), which enables extradition under the UNCTOC.

His identity was established through fingerprints that the Mumbai Police had taken way back in 1994 when he was first arrested. Local judicial authorities were convinced that he was the man in question, even though he had changed his name, and approved Pujari's extradition to India.

After being a fugitive for more than two decades, he was finally brought to India in February 2020. The Karnataka police, who took custody of Pujari in Senegal, moved him to Bangalore, where he is currently being tried for several cases. At the time of his arrest, he was wanted in more than 150 cases and had 13 Red Corner notices against him.

Hemant Pujari:

Hemant Pujari started out in the world of crime as a crony of Chhota Rajan in the 1990s. He was working as a waiter in Ghatkopar when he got involved in a murder case. He managed to escape and joined forces with the Rajan gang. Born in 1973, he grew up in the Ghatkopar area of Mumbai.

He was a small-time gangster operating in Ghatkopar and Bandra (East), following Rajan's orders and conducting criminal operations in Mumbai and other parts of the country. Pujari shot to fame in the underworld after he murdered builder Shaukat Sarkar in November 1999 in Mumbai.

After the near fatal attack on Rajan in Bangkok in 2000, the gang broke into several parts. Hemant Pujari took this opportunity to start his own gang. Initially he tried to work on his own but success in the world of crime was elusive.

In 2006 he reportedly sought Chhota Shakeel's help, joining his gang. This apparently angered a lot of his men, who owed allegiance to Rajan. They were also not happy that Pujari was not helping gang members who had been arrested and were in jail. So many of them broke away from Hemant Pujari and joined the Rajan gang.

Before this, several of Pujari's close aides – like Kundan Singh Rawat, Pravin Shetty, Roshan Seth and Navin Shetty – had been killed in encounters with the Mumbai Police. Pujari was left almost alone and used the services of hire-to-kill gangsters from Azamgarh in UP. Very soon, he fled the country and made Cambodia his base.

He suffered a major blow when, in 2007, his ace shooter and close aide Ajay Mohite was gunned down in an encounter by the Mumbai Police. After this jolt, Pujari once again started making attempts to make amends with Rajan. However, after the Bangkok attack, Rajan suspected Pujari of giving information about him to rivals, so he never entertained Pujari again.

Hemant Pujari's name once again popped up when a hotelier was shot dead in Goregaon in March 2011. The hotelier, Angara Pujari, had received extortion threats from Hemant Pujari but refused to pay and was killed.

Pujari is currently wanted and absconding. There are reports that he is operating from Malaysia, while some believe that he is still in India and uses SIM cards from foreign countries to hoodwink the police. The CBI, through Interpol, has issued a Red Corner Notice against him.

- **D.K. Rao**

Ravi Mallesh Bora, better known as D.K. Rao, is a native of North Karnataka. He came to Mumbai in 1994 and started working as a security guard in Dharavi. Not happy with his job, Rao soon formed a small gang of his own by recruiting young boys from Dharavi who focused on small-time robberies and pickpocketing.

In 1996 he met a close aide of Chhota Rajan who put him in touch with Rajan, who immediately recruited Rao. After joining the Rajan gang, Rao had access to more gang members and entered a world of bigger crimes like extortion and kidnapping. He even took charge of recruiting people to join the Rajan gang.

He made a name for himself when he successfully planned the execution of Dawood's men who were involved in the 1993 serial bomb blasts in Mumbai.

On 11 November 1998, the Mumbai Crime Branch got a tip-off about a bunch of gangsters belonging to the Chhota Rajan gang, who would be coming to Senapati Bapat Marg in Dadar (West) for conducting an operation. The police immediately laid a trap at the spot. After waiting for some time, they saw that five gangsters had assembled.

The police immediately surrounded them and asked them to surrender. However, they opened fire at the police, and the police also retaliated with firing at the gangsters. In the cross-firing that ensued, four gangsters, viz., Raju Gore, Bipin Khandapal, Jairam Shetty and Ramesh Pujare were killed in the police operation. The fifth gangster was D.K. Rao, who was severely injured and was rushed to hospital. He was instantly operated upon and was saved in the nick of time.

After his medical treatment was over and he was released from the hospital, he was arrested by the Mumbai Police for his various offences including murders of D-Company gang members at the behest of Chhota Rajan.

A few months after his arrest, he was convicted and sentenced to ten years' rigorous imprisonment in an attempt to murder case. He was acquitted after a few years by the Bombay High Court. While he was in jail, he was implicated in the murder of Dawood gang member O.P. Singh who was killed inside Nashik jail in 2002. In December 2005 he was arrested by the Mumbai Crime Branch under MCOCA for trying to run his gang from inside prison.

In 2010, he was acquitted in all cases and released. However, in August 2011 he was arrested for his role in the killing of Arif Bael, driver of Iqbal Kaskar in Dongri. He is currently out on bail and has started a small political outfit with his brother in Dharavi.

• Ejaz Lakdawala

Ejaz Lakdawala has more than 50 cases of extortion, kidnapping and attempt to murder registered against him in various cities across India. Most of the cases are registered in Mumbai.

Born in the Pydhonie area of South Mumbai, Lakdawala and his family shifted to Mahim after a few years. His family admitted him into the prestigious St. Stanislaus School in Bandra (West). After completing his schooling, he moved to Jogeshwari, where he got acquainted with associates of Anees Ibrahim.

Anees Ibrahim immediately took Lakdawala under his wing and asked him to get inside information from the film industry for extortion purposes. Lakdawala was first arrested for the murder of Haren Mehta in 1993 – he reportedly killed Mehta during a spat while playing cricket. He was acquitted in the case in 1995.

While he was in jail, Lakdawala met Sunil Madgaonkar, a Chhota Rajan henchman. Madgaonkar, also known as Madya, roped in Lakdawala for the murder of Dawood gang member Farid Rajji. Lakdawala shot Rajji dead on busy Mohammad Ali Road but was hit in the leg when Rajji fired back. Injured, Lakdawala couldn't flee and was arrested. Rajji's brother was a close aide of Chota Shakeel and one of the main accused in the 1993 bomb blasts case.

After being arrested, Lakdawala was sent to Nashik Central Jail and in 1998, while being escorted to the Sir J.J. Hospital in Mumbai for a medical check-up, he seized the opportunity and escaped. He immediately left the city and then the country. Lakdawala went to Malaysia where he again started working for Rajan, taking over his extortion business. In 2000, after the attack on him, Rajan had to flee Bangkok and took shelter in Cambodia, where he was under medical treatment for a long time. In Rajan's absence Lakdawala took over the extortion operations of the gang, working out of Bangkok.

A couple of years later, Shakeel learned that Lakdawala was in Bangkok and working for Rajan and planned a full-scale operation to eliminate him. Shakeel was looking for revenge for the killing of Farid Rajji. He assembled a team of shooters that went to Bangkok in 2002 and attacked Lakdawala, who was reportedly hit by six bullets, but survived. However, this version has not been verified by any police report yet.

Lakdawala hid in Bangkok and underwent medical treatment. After recuperating completely, he fled to Canada and remained there, even when the Rajan gang was collapsing. Rajan's top lieutenants like

Bharat Nepali, Ravi Pujari, Santosh Shetty and others had already started working on their own.

In 2005, Lakdawala moved to Ghana, where he started his own gang with the help of his brother in Mumbai. They targeted builders using information provided by Lakdawala's foot soldiers in Mumbai. When threats didn't work, Lakdawala used shooters to scare people. After spending time in Ghana, he went to the United States and then to the United Kingdom.

For a few years Lakdawala lived in Kathmandu, Nepal, reportedly disguised as Mr. Chaudhary, also known as *Bhaijaan*. He operated his gang from a garment shop situated in a prime market in Kathmandu for around eight years.

His cousin Sameer Lakdawala, wanted in a 2012 extortion case of a Mumbai-based builder, was arrested in February 2019. It was Sameer's arrest that helped the Mumbai Police gather information about Lakdawala. Two months later, in April, Lakdawala's brother Aqeel Lakdawala was arrested in four cases of extortion. This helped police trace Lakdawala's daughter Soniya, who was married to Shahid Shaikh and had changed her name to Shifa Shaikh. The police kept a close eye on her movements. In December 2019, they received a tip-off that Soniya was travelling to Nepal using a fake passport and nabbed her on 28 December.

Under arrest in an extortion case, Soniya provided crucial details about Lakdawala and his whereabouts to the police during interrogation. She revealed that Lakdawala was expected to travel to Patna from Kathmandu on 8 January 2020.

Based on this information, the Mumbai Police, with the help of the Bihar Police, laid a trap at Jakhanpur Bus Stop. An unsuspecting Lakdawala, who had boarded the bus from Kathmandu, got off at the stop and the moment he set foot on Indian soil, was arrested. Lakdawala was thus finally caught, 20 years after he fled the country.

• Rohit Verma – The Hammer Man

The story of Rohit Verma is a classic story of a youngster from Mumbai who was lured into the underworld for money and who then stayed on, addicted to its power, fame and riches.

Born in 1966 in a lower middle-class family in the affluent area of Santacruz in the western suburbs of Mumbai, Verma grew up watching wealthy men and women splurging on expensive cars, clothes and restaurants. By the time he entered college, Rohit had nursed dreams of leading a lavish lifestyle.

Like any other youngster, he harboured dreams of getting rich quickly, without the effort of educating himself or finding a respectable job. Blessed with a sharp mind and inspired by fiction, Verma started his crime career with robbery. He would rob unsuspecting high society ladies of their handbags, purses and other valuables.

Over time, he stole valuables from people's cars by breaking windows with a hammer and taking whatever he could find. His little criminal enterprise netted him a lot of money, so he expanded his area of operation from Bandra to Andheri.

The local police soon became aware of a hammer thief operating in the western suburbs who was intelligent enough to not leave any trace of his crimes. He was, however, not sharp enough to avoid arrest, and was caught by the Khar police. Once out on bail, he continued with his crimes. His luck ran out in 1995 when he was arrested for the second time by Khar police, and this time could not get bail – he was sent to Arthur Road jail.

Soon, Verma's life changed forever; his career as a criminal took off. While he was in Arthur Road Jail, Verma had a chance encounter with Sunil Madgaonkar, alias Madya, Chhota Rajan's close aide and a top-rung leader of the Rajan gang. Madya, who was also in charge of recruitment for the gang, saw a spark in the 29-year-old Verma and offered him a job. Verma accepted.

Madya arranged for Verma's bail. After his release, Verma immediately started working for the Rajan gang. He became an overnight sensation in the underworld with his very first operation – the way he planned and executed it earned him visibility and respect.

In November 1995, Verma single-handedly planned and executed the ruthless killing of Thakiyudeen Wahid, Managing Director of East West Airline. Wahid was believed to be close to Dawood Ibrahim, and Chhota Rajan was eliminating all known associates of Dawood in Mumbai. Rajan decided to kill Wahid to send a strong message to Dawood and his gang. Both Rajan and Madya decided to give the new recruit Verma a chance to prove that he was ready for the underworld style of functioning.

Verma took on the challenge. He tracked Wahid for a few days to understand his routine. On 13 November 1995, when Wahid was travelling in his car near Nanavati hospital in Santacruz (West), Verma, who was waiting near the signal, threw a hammer at the vehicle. Such was the precision of the throw that the hammer shattered the windscreen of the car and hit Wahid's driver. Almost immediately after he flung the hammer, Verma whipped out his weapon and sprayed a volley of bullets at Wahid, even as his driver lost control of the car. In no time the car hit a divider and stopped with Wahid's lifeless, bullet-riddled body lying on the back seat.

Verma disappeared. When the police reached the spot, they were flabbergasted to see that the choice of weapon was a hammer. This was a new challenge for the police as they had no idea who was behind it. They never suspected that the much-evolved Mumbai underworld could use a hammer to kill.

The sensational way that Verma carried out his operation earned him the spotlight in the underworld. Both Rajan and Madya were extremely happy with him. Rajan then tasked Verma in the killing of more than half a dozen of his targets. Almost all of them were sensational murders.

After the death of Thakiyudeen Wahid, Verma killed Prakash Sinhasane, a close aide of Sharad Shetty who was a top lieutenant of Dawood Ibrahim. Verma was also the mastermind behind the murder of Dev Narayan Ghosh, owner of the Royal Security Group in Mumbai.

However, the most sensational killing by Verma was that of Mohan Kotian in Bangalore in 1998. Kotian's murder put Verma in the top league of underworld assassins. He became a name to reckon with.

Kotian, who was a longtime Rajan loyalist, had decided to break away and join hands with Dawood. Kotian called Verma to Bangalore to persuade him to join Dawood too. As per reports from the underworld, Verma sat before Kotian, listening quietly and intently to what he was saying. After Kotian finished speaking, Verma, without batting an eyelid, whipped out his .45 revolver and shot Kotian dead. In fact, he kept firing until the magazine was empty. Then he simply walked out.

The killing showcased a side of Verma that was cold and ruthless. People in the underworld had not only started noticing him but were now scared of him.

Another sensational murder Verma conducted was the high-profile killing of Mirza Dilshad Beg, a minister in the Nepal government who was very close to Dawood Ibrahim. The finesse with which Verma planned and executed the murder is often discussed as an American Mafia-style killing. Verma ambushed Beg in a lonely spot in Kathmandu and shot him dead. He then vanished without anyone realising who the shooter was.

His high-profile journey in the crime world was cut short at the age of 34, when he was shot dead by Chhota Shakeel's men in Bangkok. Chhota Rajan was staying in Rohit Verma's apartment in Bangkok when a hit squad of Shakeel barged into his apartment to kill Rajan. Rohit, who answered the door, could not take evasive action – he was the first to be killed by the volley of bullets from Shakeel's men as they entered the apartment looking for Rajan. Verma died on the spot, while his wife was severely injured.

- **Ashwin Naik**

An electronics engineer by qualification, Naik took over the gang run by his brother Amar Naik, who was gunned down by police in an encounter in the 1990s. While in jail, Naik was accused of plotting to kill his wife Neeta, a corporator, whom he suspected of having an extra-marital relationship with her police bodyguard, Laxman Ziman.

On 18 April 1994, Ashwin Naik was attacked by Ravindra Sawant, an associate of Arun Gawli in the premises of the Sessions Court in Kala Ghoda area of South Mumbai. Sawant, dressed as an advocate, opened fire at Ashwin Naik as he was being escorted to the court. However, Ashwin Naik survived the near-fatal attack on him, but a bullet fired at him got lodged in his forehead. This resulted in Naik suffering paralysis which rendered him permanently immobile and wheelchair-bound.

He had 16 cases of murder, extortion and criminal assault registered against him. During his early days as a criminal, Naik remained underground till he was first arrested by the West Bengal police on the Indo-Bangladesh border on 1 August 1999.

Over a period of ten years the former gangster was acquitted in all cases, including the murder of his wife. Although police suspected he had plotted to kill Neeta, he was exonerated due to lack of evidence, but three men known to be his loyalists were convicted for the murder in 2003.

Ashwin Naik's trial was held separately from the rest of the accused as a Delhi court trying him in a narcotics case did not grant the Mumbai Police his custody. Finally, he was brought to Mumbai from Tihar Jail in 2005 to stand trial for his wife's murder and, on 31 January 2009, the MCOCA court acquitted him.

After his acquittal Naik started living with his son and daughter in Chinchpokli in Central Mumbai. He started his own real estate company and became a builder.

In December 2015, Naik was arrested by the Mumbai Police for attempting to extort money from a builder. He is awaiting trial in this case.

◆◆◆◆◆◆

Chapter 6

THE UNDERWORLD–TERRORISM NEXUS

• The 1993 Serial Bomb Blasts in Mumbai

While Mumbai was already in the grip of the underworld, it became the victim of terrorism in the most horrific way. On 12 March 1993, serial bomb blasts ripped through the entire city targeting important installations like the Bombay Stock Exchange (BSE), Air India Building at Nariman Point, Passport Office in Worli, Shiv Sena Bhavan near Shivaji Park, among others.

Several hundred innocent Mumbaikars lost their lives and thousands were injured in what was the most blatant terror attack on Indian soil ever.

I was posted as the Deputy Director in the Intelligence Bureau (IB) in Mumbai when the attacks happened.

My office was situated next to the Century Bhavan in Worli. I distinctly remember, I was sitting in my office just around lunch time when an ear-shattering bang ripped through the afternoon calm and broke the windowpanes of my office.

Instantly I knew that this was not an ordinary noise like firecrackers or some tyre bursting. This was different. We soon learned that there were serial bomb blasts across the city and there was mayhem all around.

My team and I got to work; as part of the IB it was our job to get as much information and intelligence as possible on who could be behind the attacks and pass it on to our superiors and to the Mumbai Police.

A lot has already been written about the serial bomb blasts and investigations around it, so I will not delve too deep into the finer details.

As part of my investigation, I visited the Al Husseini building in Mahim, which was Tiger Memon's house and the nerve centre from where the bomb blasts were planned and executed. All the information that was gathered by us was passed on to Mumbai Police's Joint Commissioner of Police (Crime Branch) M.N. Singh, who was leading the investigations.

During the investigation, I personally inspected the site where keys to the scooters with unexploded bombs were discovered, revealing clues about the attackers' plans.

Another major breakthrough came when intelligence led us to Lido Cinema, where we uncovered weapons hidden in drainage systems – this discovery was based on my own intelligence inputs.

Eventually, all these findings contributed to the chargesheet in the 1993 bomb blasts case. The case also had connections to Lal Singh, also known as Manjit Singh, who was involved in the Kanishka plane bombing. He was subsequently arrested by the ATS of Mumbai Police led by Mr. A.A. Khan IPS and the entire operation of following Lal Singh alias Manjit Singh was done by the SIB (State Intelligence Bureau) of Mumbai. As a follow-up, weapons worth ₹ 2.65 crore hidden at Ahmedabad were recovered.

The investigation of the 1993 serial bomb blasts was not just about solving a crime, it was about unravelling a vast network of terror that had deeply impacted Mumbai. This was done with super efficiency by the Crime Branch of Mumbai, which I joined in August 1993 as Addl CP, Crime, on return from my deputation to IB.

• IC 814 Hijack – The Mumbai Angle

Mumbai experienced a terror attack when the city was rocked by serial bomb blasts in March 1993. It was later revealed that it was the handiwork of the Mumbai underworld, specifically Dawood Ibrahim and his gang. With the help of Pakistan's intelligence agency Inter-Services Intelligence (ISI), they had plotted and executed the blasts in Mumbai.

The next real terror case that India experienced was the audacious hijacking of Indian Airlines flight IC 814 in December 1999.

The flight, which was en route to Delhi from Kathmandu, was hijacked approximately 30 minutes after it took off from Nepal.

The situation was quite dramatic – just when the airline crew and the passengers were settling down for what was supposed to be an uneventful one-and-a-half-hour flight to Delhi, a young man armed with a pistol stood up in the aisle and shouted that the plane was being hijacked. Along with him, four other men, seated at various places in the aircraft, stood up, all of them masked and armed. Before the crew and passengers realised what was happening, the hijackers took up positions at strategic places in the plane.

One of the hijackers informed the pilot that the plane should be flown to Lahore, Pakistan. The pilot, 37-year-old Devi Saran, did as he was instructed. However, the authorities in Lahore refused permission for the aircraft to land. After circling the airport for a long time, the pilot had no choice but to change course and head for Amritsar because the plane was running low on fuel.

The aircraft landed at Amritsar airport, where the hijackers demanded that it be refuelled. However, Indian authorities did not agree to any of their demands. The hijackers threatened to kill the passengers one by one if their demands were not met.

Despite repeated commands from the hijackers to refuel the plane, the Indian authorities refused to agree. Angered by this, the hijackers identified seven passengers and took them to the executive class in front of the aircraft and tied them to the seats. They then called saying that if the refuelling process did not start within five minutes, they would start killing their hostages. And as they had threatened, after a few minutes, the hijackers stabbed two passengers in the chest – Rupin Katyal and Satnam Singh.

Katyal, a young businessman from Delhi, had gone to Kathmandu for his honeymoon, with his wife Rachna. Unknown to Rachna, Rupin soon bled to death in the executive class.

The Indian authorities still did not agree to meet the demands of the hijackers. The criminals were getting jittery, as they were on Indian soil and did not want to be ambushed by local security forces. So, they forced the pilot at gunpoint to take off and head for Lahore.

The then Prime Minister Atal Bihari Vajpayee was aboard a plane when IC814 was hijacked. When he landed in Delhi, National Security Adviser (NSA) Brajesh Mishra briefed him even before he deplaned. The Prime Minister along with the NSA rushed to where the crisis management team had assembled to deal with the situation.

When the flight reached Lahore, authorities shut down the airport and once again refused permission to land. The captain informed air traffic control that the plane would crash if it were not allowed to set down, as there was almost no fuel left. Despite reluctance from the airport authorities, the pilot force-landed the plane at Lahore airport.

The plane had to stay on the runway while the hijackers demanded fuel, food and water. The authorities at Lahore quickly provided what was needed. The pilot was then ordered to take off and set course for Kabul, Afghanistan.

However, by the time the plane reached Kabul it was late, and the airport was not equipped to handle night-time landings. The hijackers then diverted the flight to Muscat.

To the utter surprise and shock of the hijackers, authorities in Muscat refused permission for the plane to land. The aircraft was then diverted to Dubai, where they received the same response. The hijackers then ordered the pilot to take the plane to the Al-Minhar Air Base, a remote area near Dubai. The plane finally landed there.

Almost immediately, the hijackers demanded that the plane be refuelled, and they be provided with food. The authorities asked them to release the passengers. The hijackers were growing concerned and agitated that they were on the ground and could be attacked at any moment. They agreed to release 27 passengers, mostly the injured, sick and senior citizens. They also released Rupin Katyal's body – the only casualty of the hijacking.

After securing the release of 27 passengers, local authorities refuelled the plane and provided nourishments. Having got what they wanted, the hijackers once again asked the pilot to head for Kandahar airport in Afghanistan. The flight finally landed at Kandahar on 26 December. The hijackers must have heaved a sigh of relief, as they were now on their own turf and would soon be visited by their masters who would then take over the entire operation.

Almost immediately after landing, the flight was surrounded by armed Taliban fighters and the militia. They carried the latest weapons, which included rocket launchers and sophisticated AK-47s and other arms.

The hijackers soon made their demands. They wanted the Government of India to release Maulana Masood Azhar, leader of the Kashmiri militant outfit Harkat-Ul-Mujahideen. Azhar had been jailed in India for more than four years. Militants from his organisation had made several attempts to break him out of jail but had not succeeded. In one attempt he almost tasted freedom – his associates built a tunnel, but Azhar got stuck in it due to his heavy build. When he was caught and put back in a high security cell, he famously told one of the jail officers that they would not be able to keep him locked up for too long.

Azhar's arrest was a huge success for Indian security forces in their fight against terrorism, especially in Kashmir at the time. Releasing him would have a massive impact on the battle and, more importantly, he would once again start his reign of terror if he was set free.

The hijackers also demanded that 35 other terrorists in various jails in India be released. In addition, they wanted the body of terrorist Maqbool Bhatt to be handed over to them. Bhatt had been hanged to death in Tihar Jail after he was found guilty of terror charges and sentenced to death by the court.

Over and above this, they also demanded US $ 200 million in cash. It was a huge amount of money 25 years ago.

By then it had been revealed that the entire operation was planned by Azhar's younger brother, Abdul Rauf Asghar.

Abdul Rauf Asghar 'killed' in Operation Sindoor.

After the horrific Pahalgam Attack on 22 April 2025, in which 26 innocent tourists were killed by terrorists, the Government of India launched 'Operation Sindoor', a retaliatory strike on terror bases and camps inside Pakistan.

The Government of India has claimed that Abdul Rauf Asghar, younger brother of global terrorist and chief of Jaish-e-Mohammad (JeM) Maulana Masood Azhar, was killed during one of the strikes on JeM's headquarters in Bahawalpur in Pakistan.

It was also reported in the media (*The New Indian Express,* 10 May 2025) that Abdul Rauf Asghar was eliminated by Indian armed forces in Operation Sindoor on 7 May 2025.

Even though it was not confirmed by Pakistan, and they are not likely to confirm it either, Abdul Rauf Asghar's killing (if true) would be a major blow to the terror activities of JeM, especially its chief, Maulana Masood Azhar.

As part of India's response, the first to reach Kandahar was a young Indian Foreign Service (IFS) officer A.R. Ghanshyam. He was posted in Islamabad and had flown to Kandahar in a special United Nations (UN) aircraft. Joining him were N. Sandhu, a senior official from the Intelligence Bureau (IB), C.D. Sahay, Ajit Doval (current National

Security Adviser of India), Anand Arni from Research & Analysis Wing (R&AW) and Vivek Katju from the Ministry of External Affairs.

The negotiations began – it took a very long time, as the hijackers refused to give up on any of their demands.

The next day, a representative from the United Nations (UN) arrived in Kandahar to mediate between the Taliban and the Government of India. But nothing happened that day, as India had not responded to any of the demands made by the hijackers.

The militants were growing impatient and the very next day they issued a warning that if their demands were not met, they would start killing the passengers one by one.

Through the UN mediator, talks continued for a couple of days. The hijackers agreed to withdraw their demands for money and the release of other jailed terrorists.

Even though the situation was happening in faraway Afghanistan, and the central government in Delhi was handling it, the entire country was put on highest alert. It was the Christmas season and there was a generally festive atmosphere, since it was the last week of the twentieth century – the world was not only stepping into a new year, but into a new century.

The Mumbai angle...

Miles away in Mumbai on Christmas day, 25 December 1999, I was in my office, situated within the premises of the Mumbai Police Headquarters near Crawford Market in South Mumbai. I was posted as Joint Commissioner of Police (Crime Branch) on 29 June 1998, to head the elite Mumbai Crime Branch. Even though it was a holiday for Christmas, because of the hijacking all police forces across the country were put on high alert.

I was keenly following the broadcast of the hijacking on the television news channels. Little did I know that my day was going to change drastically very soon. At around 11 a.m., the intercom in my office rang – my personal assistant informed me that I had an unscheduled visitor. It was Hemant Karkare, an IPS officer from the Maharashtra cadre (1982 batch) who was posted in R&AW.

A soft-spoken and dedicated police officer, Hemant Karkare was primarily from the Maharashtra cadre and had served in Mumbai and Maharashtra before being sent on deputation to R&AW. Unfortunately, the fine officer, who was then the chief of ATS, was martyred during the 26/11 terror attacks in Mumbai in November 2008.

The moment I heard who it was, I asked my PA to send him in immediately since we shared an excellent relationship personally even though he was six years my junior in service. Karkare walked in with a sense of purpose and, after exchanging official pleasantries, immediately got down to business.

He informed me that R&AW had been closely monitoring the hijacking. Immediately after the news of the hijack came in, R&AW had started monitoring all telecommunication traffic in and out of India. They had pinpointed a mobile number that had been in constant touch with numbers in Pakistan and with the hijackers.

They had even managed to identify a mobile number which they had put under surveillance. This number was operational and in Mumbai, but R&AW had neither been able to locate the person who was using it, nor identify the individual.

Karkare told me that he had come to seek the Mumbai Police's help to track and trace the number and the person using it.

I could not believe that such a huge international conspiracy had a connection to Mumbai. I instantly called for an urgent meeting with my officers, apprised them of the situation, and we came up with a plan to trace the caller. I also informed then Commissioner of Police, Mumbai, R.H. Mendonca, about the development.

Teams were formed with specific tasks to ensure that the operation went smoothly and efficiently. Officials were warned about not talking to anybody about it, especially the media and the families of the (hijack) victims.

In the interest of national security and the passengers, it was extremely important that the operation be kept secret. Any leak of information could alarm the hijackers, and they could start killing the hostages.

Each of the teams was headed by an officer of the rank of Senior Police Inspector (Sr. PI). One team was dispatched to the mobile service provider to get details of the caller, the phone, the location of the cell towers, call logs and other details.

Another team was asked to put the mobile number under surveillance and monitor it around the clock. All other teams were entrusted with the responsibility of locating the caller.

As the officials waited with bated breath, the first bit of information came from the police team that had been dispatched to the mobile service provider. They reported that the number was being used between Juhu and Malad – the mobile towers between these locations were beaming the signals. They also got information that the caller was passing on crucial information about what the Government of India was doing and plans to deal with the situation.

Even though the information was useful, it was not as helpful, because in a crowded megapolis like Mumbai millions of people live between Juhu and Malad. There is also a vast moving population. Identifying anyone in the area with such minimal information was next to impossible.

Time was of the essence – the hijackers were getting impatient, and the Indian government was running out of options.

Technology-wise, not much help was forthcoming. These were the initial years of mobile phones in India and the technology to monitor calls, trace them and locate them was not as advanced as it is today. Apart from the ability to record phone conversations and getting an approximate location from where the last call was made, not much was possible. Even data indicating from which cell tower the last call was made was not available in real-time; there was a time lapse. After the call there was a time gap before authorities could identify the tower used. This resulted in a crucial delay for us.

Technology available to investigative agencies today is far superior to what it was over two and a half decades ago. Today, the exact location of the phone can be pinpointed through triangulation of mobile phone towers, GPS, Wi-Fi and other means within seconds. In 1999, the only technology available was to listen in to the telephone conversation and get the location after a delay of a few hours.

The first three days of our investigation yielded nothing. The authorities and officers were getting frustrated, and the government was losing vital time. The only information we had was that the team listening in on the phone conversations was able to hear the ambient sound of a cattle-shed in the background. During one call, the men could hear *azaan* being recited. We concluded the caller was near a cattle shed and a mosque.

Several Crime Branch teams led by senior officials combed the area from Juhu to Malad. They checked each cattle shed near a mosque, to no avail. As the day wore on, heads started drooping and legs became heavy. We still did not have any lead on the people in Mumbai who were in touch with the hijackers and passing on crucial information to them.

Just as the sun was setting at around 6 p.m., there came a ray of hope. The surveillance team monitoring the mobile number got an alert on their system that the phone was active. They immediately started listening in and recording the call.

They couldn't believe what they were hearing. They requested me and Police Commissioner Ronnie Mendonca to rush to the surveillance room. We ran there and listened to the call. We couldn't believe our ears and our luck. The Mumbai-based caller was talking to his handler in Pakistan to say that he was running low on cash and needed money urgently. The man on the other end told him to wait for 30 minutes for him to make arrangements and call back.

There was deathly silence in the room; everyone present knew that luck had finally turned their way. All of us waited to listen in to the crucial next phone call.

We waited for 30 minutes, but the call didn't come. The entire team stood there with bated breath and our palpitations increased with each passing minute. After an agonising wait of what seemed to be an eternity, the call finally came 45 minutes later at around 6.45 p.m.

It was a Jaish-e-Mohammad (JeM) terrorist calling from Pakistan. He asked the person in Mumbai his whereabouts. He was alert and did not give details or exact answers regarding his location but vaguely indicated that he was somewhere in Jogeshwari (East), a suburb in North-West Mumbai.

The JeM man then informed his colleague in Mumbai that they had managed to arrange ₹ 1 lakh, which would be delivered via a *hawala* transaction. The Mumbai contact was instructed to go to Shalimar Hotel at Mohammad Ali Road around 10 p.m. to collect the money. He was informed that a man dressed in blue jeans and a striped shirt would meet him there with the funds. Then the call was disconnected.

Once again there was silence in the surveillance room – all of us took a moment to realise the potential of the information we had just received. We couldn't believe our luck.

The Police Chief, myself and other senior officers rushed to the Commissioner's cabin so that we could update officials in the central government about the goldmine of information we had just received.

A conference call was put through and senior officials from the Ministry of Home Affairs, R&AW and the Intelligence Bureau (IB) in New Delhi had a tense 20-minute discussion with us on how to proceed.

Officials in Delhi felt that since negotiations between the Indian and Taliban delegates were underway in Kandahar, that should not be disturbed. Also, the terrorists still held the passengers hostage and if any news broke about the link in Mumbai having been exposed and arrested by the police, it may rattle them, and they may cause harm to the people they held captive.

It was eventually decided that officers of Mumbai Police would go to the rendezvous point and keep a watch on the person who would come there to collect money. They would neither confront nor apprehend him but would follow him stealthily and identify the place where he was based. In intelligence language it is called 'housing'.

Immediately after the conference I formed six teams, each comprising one senior and one junior police officer. They were instructed to go to Mohammad Ali Road and keep vigil around the Shalimar Hotel. Their instructions were clear: they were supposed to follow the person who would collect the money.

The teams reached the hotel at around 9.30 p.m. and waited at various strategic locations to ensure that they had a clear view of the hotel. At around 10 p.m., a man came there and was met at the entrance by a person in blue jeans and a striped shirt. The officers instantly knew that their intel was correct; the game was on.

After spending a few moments inside the hotel, both men came out – the person in blue jeans hailed a taxi and left in the direction of South Mumbai. Instructions to the officers were clear – they had to follow the person who had taken the money. They waited for him and after a few minutes, he too hailed a taxi and left. Immediately, the officers started tailing him in private cars, maintaining a safe distance to ensure that they did not raise an alarm.

The taxi reached Mumbai Central station, where the passenger alighted and walked into the railway terminus. The officers swiftly followed him to platform no. 1 and waited for the local train.

Unknown to him, he had at least a dozen shadows. A few minutes later the local train arrived, and he boarded it. The officers followed, some in the same compartment, others in adjacent ones.

After an uneventful journey, the train reached Jogeshwari, where the man alighted and walked out of the station. He got into an autorickshaw; the officers followed him in other autorickshaws.

When the autorickshaw reached the Bashir Baug area in Jogeshwari (West), it stopped and the man alighted, paying the driver. He started walking into the slums. This is where it got tricky for the officers. Bashir Baug slums are among the most densely populated in Mumbai, with a predominantly Muslim population. Anyone who is not a local can easily be identified and will be looked upon with suspicion.

Using all their experience and skill, the officers started following.

After walking for a few minutes through several criss-crossing bylanes, the man reached a small chawl and knocked on one of the doors. An unknown person opened it, and the man entered the room – the door was bolted behind him.

The officials heaved a sigh of relief. The place had been identified without any problems. They immediately informed me about the success of the operation and awaited further instructions. They were asked to maintain a strict yet stealthy surveillance on the room, till further orders.

A protocol was immediately set in place – a round-the-clock vigil was set up to keep a close watch on the place. Crime Branch officers dressed in local clothes took over strategic locations around the place to keep a close watch on activities in and around the room.

For two agonising days the officers maintained a strict vigil without raising suspicions. Finally, on 31 December 1999, the then chief of R&AW called Police Commissioner Mendonca and me to say that the negotiators had managed to get the hijackers to drop most of the demands, including the ransom and freeing of 35 militants held in various jails across India.

The Government of India finally agreed to the release of three terrorists – Maulana Masood Azhar, Ahmed Omar Saeed Sheikh and Mushtaq Ahmed Zargari – in exchange for the lives of 155 passengers and airline crew.

Passengers were freed after then Minister for External Affairs, Jaswant Singh, flew to Kandahar on a special aircraft, taking the three militants with him. The moment they landed in Kandahar and the hijackers got a green signal, they freed all the passengers. As soon as that happened, a team of highly trained commandoes of the Mumbai Police and senior officials of the Mumbai Crime Branch stormed into the room at Bashir Baug. Hemant Karkare and I too were there to oversee the operation.

The raid was done with such clinical precision that the terrorists did not get a moment to react. The team swooped down on them like an eagle grabs its prey and in no time four men were overpowered and arrested.

A total of four terrorists were taken. They were identified as:

- Rafiq Mohammad (Pakistani, aged 34)
- Mushtaq Ahmed Azami (Pakistani, aged 45)
- Mohammad Asif alias Babalu (Pakistani, aged 25)
- Gopal Singh Bahadur Mann (Nepali, aged 38)

To the utter shock of the Mumbai Police, a huge cache of arms and ammunitions that included two AK-56 assault rifles, five hand grenades, antitank TNT rocket launchers, shells and three detonators and explosives, six pistols, and ₹ 1,72,000 in cash was recovered from the room. It was as if the terrorists had planned to conduct a major attack in Mumbai.

Interestingly, a map of Matoshri was also recovered. Matoshri was the residence of Shiv Sena supremo Balasaheb Thackeray and continues to be current Shiv Sena (UBT) chief Uddhav Balasaheb Thackeray's residence even today.

Simultaneous raids were conducted in Jogeshwari and Malad. A flat rented by a Nepali couple was raided and live hand grenades, 2-3 Glock pistols and USD 10,000 in cash was recovered. With the discovery of American currency, it was clear that this was an international conspiracy.

The terrorists were arrested and, on interrogation, confessed to the hijacking and how they were part of it. The person who had gone to get the money and who was the caller was identified as Abdul Patel, a local Mumbai resident. He was the main conspirator in Mumbai who was leading the team.

Mohammad Asif alias Babalu and Rafiq Mohammad were found to be Pakistani nationals. Gopal Singh Mann was Nepali, while the others were terrorists belonging to the Harkat-ul-Ansar terror group working in Kashmir.

Their interrogation revealed that there were three other Pakistani nationals staying with them in the same room in Jogeshwari. Those men had gone out during the raid and were not arrested. The Mumbai

Police immediately went on the highest alert and started combing operations in Jogeshwari and Malad to nab them, but it was like finding a needle in a haystack.

During the prolonged interrogation of Abdul Latif Patel, it was revealed that the team, including the hijackers, had been in Mumbai since July 1999, preparing for the hijack.

The hijackers were identified as:

- Ibrahim Akhtar from Bahawalpur, Pakistan
- Syed Akhtar from Karachi, Pakistan
- Sumi Ahmed Qari from Karachi, Pakistan
- Mistry Zahoor Ibrahim from Karachi, Pakistan
- Shaqir from Sindh, Pakistan

They had come to Mumbai to plan and do a reconnaissance to choose which airport to target for their hijacking plan.

In Mumbai, they had rented a flat in Vaishali Nagar in Jogeshwari (West) and were staying there. They had joined a computer class to learn basic skills and managed to get fake Indian passports by paying a huge bribe.

In fact, the main operative, Abdul Latif Patel, had managed to procure two passports for Ibrahim Akhtar (brother of Maulana Masood Akhtar) using the same photo on two consecutive days by bribing officials in the passport office in Mumbai. Ibrahim Akhtar and the other Pak hijackers easily got their passports with Hindu names. After that, the terrorists got in touch with Seven Spice Travel Agency in Bombay Central. Through the agency they scoured the country to discover which airport would be best suited for their operation. When they were unable to identify any in India, they went to Nepal and chose Kathmandu. The five hijackers then stayed in Nepal and eventually put their plan into operation on 24 December 1999.

As per the directive from the Government of India, the Mumbai Police handed the men over to the Central Bureau of Investigation (CBI), who took them to Amritsar, where the case of hijacking was registered.

A separate case was registered against the travel agency. Incidentally, this was the only case (in the hijacking investigations) that eventually resulted in a conviction in the court of law which was later confirmed by the High Court of Punjab and Haryana.

This was one of the most high-profile cases ever investigated and solved by the Mumbai Police. The Mumbai Police could procure copies of the passports and disclose the real identities of the hijackers. In fact, the Dy. PM and Home Minister Shri L.K. Advani had appeared on television to reveal this. An international conspiracy was unearthed in Mumbai through genuine and thorough investigation. During the operation a cloak of secrecy was maintained, which was the primary reason for its success. Even a whiff of it leaked to the media would have produced a different outcome, since the whole operation would have been compromised.

I give the entire credit of this successful operation to those dedicated officers of the Mumbai Crime Branch who worked tirelessly on this case, and to the unwavering support of Police Commissioner R.H. Mendonca.

◆◆◆◆◆◆

Chapter 7

THE UNDERWORLD–BOLLYWOOD NEXUS

- **Film Industry**

The Mumbai film industry has been connected with the underworld since the days of Haji Mastan, Karim Lala and Yusuf Patel. The large amount of black money involved in film production attracted underworld criminals who readily financed films at outrageous interest rates.

As their clout increased, they started dictating terms to producers regarding the cast, production rights, video rights, overseas rights, et al. As a result, some film artistes started befriending gang leaders, particularly Dawood Ibrahim. The list included financiers, producers, directors, actors and actresses. Many artistes would visit Dubai as guests at Dawood's parties.

- Music director Nadeem was reportedly close to the D-gang. Allegedly at Nadeem's instance, Gulshan Kumar was shot dead on 12 August 1997, by Dawood's henchmen Abu Salem and others. The police had issued a Red Corner Notice against Nadeem for his alleged involvement in the Gulshan Kumar murder case, but he has never faced the law in India, successfully fighting every attempt by Indian law enforcement agencies to have him extradited to India from UK and Ireland.

- Producer Mukesh Duggal was shot dead on 8 March 1997, by D-gang men when he allegedly switched sides to the Rajan gang.
- Within a few days, in March 1997, Rajan's men shot dead Dara Munnavar Ali Davar, brother of actress and comedian Guddi Maruti.
- Samir Hingora and Hanif Kadawala of Magnum Videos were associated with the D-gang and involved in the serial bomb blasts. Both were released on bail. Kadawala was killed on 7 February 2001 by Chhota Rajan.
- Director Rakesh Roshan, father of superstar Hrithik Roshan, was shot at on 21 January 2000, because he refused to give in to extortion demands from the underworld.

Attacks on film personalities

Sr. No.	Date	Victim
1	07/06/1994	Javed Riyaz Siddiqui (Producer)
2	01/07/1994	Firoz Sarfraz Khan (Producer)
3	08/03/1997	Mukesh Nandsingh Duggal (Producer)
4	31/07/1997	Rajiv Rai (Producer)
5	12/08/1997	Gulshan Kumar (Producer)
6	15/10/1999	Munnalal Kesharwani (Worker in Gulshan Kumar's shop)
7	20/11/1999	Dhanraj Sonar (Watchman of Shri Sakseria, Film Producer)
8	15/12/1999	Anil Thadani (Distributor)
9	29/12/1999	Manmohan Shetty (Producer)
10	21/01/2000	Rakesh Roshan (Producer)

11	14/02/2001	Dinesh Anand (Actor)
12	30/06/2001	Ajit Dewani (Secretary, Manisha Koirala)
13	04/07/2002	Lawrence Baptist D'Souza, (Director)

• Mafia Connections in the Film Industry

Film producer Bharat Shah

Even though the Hindi film industry – popularly known as Bollywood – is more than 100 years old, it is widely accepted that the decade of the 1990s was its golden era in terms of commercial success and growth as a worldwide phenomenon.

The closing decade of the last century witnessed a boom in Bollywood in every aspect. For the first time a movie grossed over ₹ 100 crore. The years also saw the rise of some of the biggest stars of Indian cinema, actors who became global superstars. However, this exponential success came with its own Achilles heel – the Mumbai underworld.

With producers and financiers becoming millionaires almost overnight, more people started getting attracted to filmmaking. Since the field did not have industry status and was not considered to be part of the organised sector, banks and financial institutions stayed away from providing funds to filmmakers. Hence, filmmaking largely remained in the realm of a few wealthy honchos who had an easy flow of money or generational wealth – largely black money.

After some success at bootlegging, gold and electronics smuggling, extortion and looting, the allure of the film industry was too strong for the underworld to resist. Before the 1990s, Mumbai's crime lords had only been attracted to Bollywood for its dazzle and charm. Fugitive gangster and India's most wanted man, Dawood Ibrahim, had always been fascinated by Bollywood; he allegedly married a famous starlet. There are numerous instances of him throwing lavish parties in his palatial hideouts in Dubai and the Middle East, where top-notch film personalities would perform. They were all at Dawood's beck and call.

It was in the late 1990s that the underworld started taking a commercial interest in Bollywood. It was a union that was beneficial to both sides. While Bollywood needed hard cash, which the underworld had, the underworld could launder and hide its ill-gotten gains through films.

Soon it was an open secret that some filmmakers were taking money from smugglers and gangsters to make their movies. However, no one was taking note of this nor was anyone interested in taking action against these people. Law enforcement agencies had no idea how to act against them.

In 1999, a spot boy suddenly rose up the ranks and became a producer almost overnight. In fact, such was his meteoric rise that a top film star like Salman Khan (the lead actor of *Hum Aapke Hain Kaun,* Bollywood's first movie to gross ₹ 100 crore in India) had agreed to do his film. The film was titled *Chori Chori Chupke Chupke.* The spot-boy was Nazim Rizvi, a henchman of Karachi-based underworld fugitive Chota Shakeel. From being a complete nobody in Bollywood, Rizvi became a producer recruiting A-list actors.

In mid-1999, I received a tip-off through my network of sources in the underworld. The tip itself was shocking and would have far-reaching consequences if proven to be true. According to the confidential information I received, Shakeel was planning to produce a Hindi movie, entirely funded by money generated from terrorism. The information further revealed that the money was allegedly being transferred by *hawala* to a billionaire diamond merchant and business tycoon who in turn was reportedly passing it on through cheques to the film's producer.

It was soon revealed that the diamond merchant was Bharat Shah. A big name in business circles in India and an even bigger name in Bollywood, in the 1990s Shah had financed blockbusters in Hindi cinema and made the careers of several actors and actresses. The producer he was allegedly giving the ill-gotten money to was Nazim Rizvi, the former spot boy who was Shakeel's henchman in the industry.

This information was dynamite and something that would send shockwaves through the entire country, especially the Indian film industry and business community in Mumbai.

My sources had never let me down. All the information that was ever given to me had always proved to be authentic. In fact, during my stint as chief of the Mumbai Crime Branch, my fellow officers and I had dealt heavy blows to the underworld based on information from such sources.

I immediately assembled a team of my most trusted officers and got down to solving the case. It was going to be tough from the start because of several challenges that lay ahead. To start with, there was no complaint or complainant based on which the police could start their investigation. Another challenge was to get substantial and unquestionable evidence, otherwise the case would fall flat, and we would have egg on our faces.

Strategically, it was decided that the Crime Branch would gather irrefutable evidence by means of best available hi-tech electronic and forensic methods.

We approached the then Additional Chief Secretary (Home), for permission to put Rizvi's phone under surveillance and install an authorised wiretap on it. Understanding the sensitivity of the situation, permission was granted, and we were authorised to do the needful. Permission was obtained under section 5(2) of the Indian Telegraph Act, 1885, to intercept telephone conversations between Chota Shakeel and his henchmen in Mumbai.

How Mumbai Police played the hero for Bollywood

After we got the requisite permission, I walked into the Videsh Sanchar Nigam Limited (VSNL) office situated in the Fort area of South Mumbai to understand how interception works. Once I knew how it happens, I did something unusual that turned out to be a masterstroke. I asked the VSNL officials if they had the technology to tap a phone number that was making calls to India. They said they could. It was as if lightning had hit! I asked them to tap into Chhota Shakeel's number in Karachi.

VSNL instantly did so, and the Mumbai Crime Branch could thenceforth listen to all incoming and outgoing calls from Shakeel's phone. This was a huge win for us, especially because Shakeel knew nothing about it and kept using his phone without hesitation.

Following this, an additional line with the same number as that of Nazim Rizvi was set up in the Crime Branch. The mobile company gave us an extra connection to Rizvi's cell-phone number as well. Three of Shakeel's numbers were kept under observation. With everything in place, the Crime Branch began one of the most sophisticated state-of-the-art surveillance routines undertaken in the country during those times. A round-the-clock monitoring system was set in place to ensure that no phone call was missed. Every call was carefully scrutinised by a team of experts.

Police Inspector Sunil Temkar was given the responsibility of monitoring the calls, as he knew Shakeel's voice. Temkar had interrogated Shakeel in the past and could recognise his voice. Incidentally, Temkar also knew the voice of Faheem Mohammad Khan (alias Faheem Machmach), Shakeel's trusted aide, who was managing most of the crime syndicate over the phone from Karachi.

Over the next several days, thanks to the technology provided to us by VSNL, Temkar managed to intercept several calls between Shakeel, Faheem and Rizvi. What Temkar heard shocked not only him, but the entire police fraternity. We had stumbled upon a shocking plan by the underworld to spread a reign of terror in Bollywood and eventually take complete control of its operations. The conversations ranged from how to conduct criminal activities in Bollywood to extorting money from film personalities and forcing popular film personalities to work in their movies for a pittance.

Such was the sophistication of their modus operandi that they had even given code names to film stars. Bollywood's (then) latest heartthrob was Hrithik Roshan, who had become an overnight sensation with the superhit *Kaho Na Pyar Hai*. Hrithik was code named *'Chikna'* (a good-looking man). His father, yesteryear star Rakesh Roshan, was *'Takla'* (a bald man). Shah Rukh Khan, who was a huge star, was named *'Hakla'* (someone who stammers), after the character he played of a villain who stammers in the superhit movie *Darr.* High profile film producer Bharat Shah was called 'BS'.

It was clear that Shakeel was speaking with Rizvi almost every day. Sometimes the conversation would be over several phone calls in a day. They would discuss numerous matters, including monetary transactions beneficial to their crime syndicate to continue unlawful activities of contract killing, extortion and other misdeeds.

In one conversation, the police found a conversation that revolved around how money was recovered from film actor Sanjay Dutt on behalf of Mansoor.

Some of the calls focused on how Shakeel was planning to produce films by forming a production house that would be run by one of Rizvi's relatives. These men were oblivious to the fact that we were listening in to their conversations while tapping and recording each call.

Unaware, they spoke freely to each other about their plans. One plan involved targeting Rakesh Roshan, because he had not responded to Shakeel's extortion threats. Shakeel was angry and wanted to teach Roshan a lesson by killing him.

We found that Shakeel was actively pursuing Shah Rukh Khan to get him to work in his movies. He asked Nazim to get details of Khan's schedule and his whereabouts so that he could be approached for negotiation. Listening to this conversation had us worried, because we had to quickly decide on a course of action as we couldn't let Shakeel get close to Khan or any other individual from the film industry.

In late 1999, the situation was turning dangerous, as the talks were getting more serious. Nazim's movie *Chori Chori Chupke Chupke,* which was being funded by Shakeel, was due to be released soon; however, the release date clashed with one of Ajay Devgn's film. It was being discussed that if the two movies released on the same day, Nazim's production may not get as good a response and would suffer losses. Shakeel started developing a plan to prevent Devgn from releasing his movie on the same day as *Chori Chori Chupke Chupke.*

The extent to which Shakeel was interested in the film industry was demonstrated by the intricate details he was heard discussing with Nazim Rizvi about the publicity and release of their movie – how they would sell the rights to various TV channels and the kind of money they were expected to make once the movie was released. Looking at the way the music industry was booming, Shakeel was also talking of taking possession and control of the Venus Music Company. It was among the top music promoters of the time. They also spoke regularly about Bharat Shah.

Another conversation revealed how they were laundering money through *hawala*. The transactions were happening in Dubai, wherein American dollars were being collected by sharing a code number and then transferring them to Shakeel.

One day, Temkar heard a conversation which alerted him. Shakeel was in a heated discussion with Rizvi over some newspaper articles that mentioned that *Chori Chori Chupke Chupke* was being financed by Shakeel. He wanted to know from Rizvi how the papers knew about it and what was happening in Mumbai.

Sensing trouble, Shakeel immediately warned Rizvi that their phones might by tapped and intercepted. Worried, he asked Rizvi to start taking all possible precautions in case the police or any other investigative agency started looking into this issue. Shakeel gave Rizvi a to-do checklist to be followed in case the police or income tax authorities questioned him.

Temkar immediately informed me about the development. We were now facing a predicament. It was clear that the gangsters would henceforth be very careful when they talked over the phone and would take a lot of precautions when discussing important matters. So, the tapping and surveillance might no longer be useful. Also, most important, there was a possibility that the gangsters would panic and do something dangerous.

Faced with this dilemma I carefully studied all the evidence (documentary and electronic) that I had and decided to go ahead and register a case under the stringent Maharashtra Control of Organised

Crime Act (MCOCA). This was done so that the police could take immediate and preventive action and expose any plans the underworld had to take control of Bollywood. There was also a very pertinent threat to the lives of a lot of prominent people in the film industry.

In the absence of any immediate complaint or complainant, I decided to do something that is rarely done – I asked Temkar to be the complainant and register an FIR.

On 12 December 2000, Police Inspector Sunil Temkar lodged FIR No. 112 of 2000 at the Mumbai Crime Branch. The police made a note that Rizvi was indeed an active member of an organised crime syndicate run by Chota Shakeel, and that Shakeel had financed the movie *Chori Chori Chupke Chupke.*

Following registration of the FIR, the Mumbai Crime Branch arrested Nazim Hasan Shamsu Zoha Rizvi a.k.a. Rajasaab, and Abdul Rahim Allah Baksh Khan a.k.a. Farooq. In the FIR, we recorded that the arrested accused had knowingly got into a criminal conspiracy with Karachi-based fugitive gangster Chhota Shakeel and his close aides, with the intention to aid and abet unlawful activities in Mumbai. And that this entire operation was being run on behalf of an organised crime syndicate headed by wanted terrorist and fugitive gangster Dawood Ibrahim Kaskar.

The FIR further stated that the crime was being conducted to spread a reign of terror through the Hindi film industry so that the accused could make and produce films and distribute them in India and abroad to make huge financial gains. Through their crime syndicate they also planned to target popular and lead film stars with the intention of forcing them to work with their production house, or else threaten to eliminate them. Nazim Rizvi, Abdul Rahim Khan and Bharat Shah had instigated the wanted accused Chhota Shakeel to commit murders of film stars and producers. They had plans to coerce, force and extort film stars like Shah Rukh Khan, Hrithik Roshan and others to work for them.

Rizvi was in constant touch with Shakeel telephonically, and was passing on information regarding the whereabouts of film personalities with the intention that Shakeel would monitor them and eventually threaten and force them to sign films against their wishes for nominal fees or inadequate consideration, and to facilitate the production of his Hindi film *Chori Chori Chupke Chupke* under the banner of 'Emaar Films International'. Investigations revealed that the film was being financed and presented by Bharat Shah for the monetary benefit of the organised crime syndicate.

It further came to light that Nazim Rizvi had asked Shakeel to cause the death of film personalities Shah Rukh Khan, Hrithik Roshan and Rakesh Roshan, and high-profile police officers Pradeep Sawant (Deputy Commissioner of Police), Pradeep Sharma (Police Inspector), and Daya Nayak (Police Sub-inspector), or to cause grievous injury to them.

During their continued investigations, the police stumbled upon evidence that between 1 August 2000 and 2 January 2001, Shah was in telephonic communication with Ahmed Shamsuddin Mohammad Salihu to remit money through *hawala* transactions to Shakeel. Shah was also in touch with Nazim Rizvi.

The questioning of Nazim Rizvi and Abdul Rahim Khan revealed that Shah had spoken to Shakeel along with Rizvi. Immediately, the Mumbai Crime Branch recovered those voice samples and matched them with Shah's. We were aware that Shah was influential in business circles and beyond. We did not want to take any chances hence we had the voice samples matched forensically. Once the forensic scientists confirmed that the voice on the phone that spoke to Shakeel was indeed that of Shah, the Mumbai Crime Branch finally arrested Shah on 8 January 2001.

It was at a time when Shah was considered invincible. He was the richest film financier in Bollywood and one of India's top diamond merchants. Perhaps the most powerful movie mogul of his time, Shah was caught on tape talking to Shakeel about how to extort money from Bollywood stars. Such was the shock of Shah's arrest that people found it hard to believe that such a powerful and well-connected wealthy business tycoon could become involved with the underworld.

Initially, the support for Shah was great – people from the diamond industry felt that he was a victim of the underworld and was being unnecessarily targeted by the police. In fact, diamond traders from Mumbai had even gone on a day-long strike to protest his arrest.

For several years, Shah was among India's biggest diamond exporters, having traded in diamonds worth billions of dollars. He had so much money that he could finance several Hindi films at once. He was also considered to be extremely powerful, with friends in the corridors of power spread across the country, from Mumbai to Delhi. The grand marriage of his children was held in a huge cricket ground and was attended by prominent members of society ranging from top politicians to bureaucrats and film stars.

Following Shah's arrest, we recovered lots of material with regard to *Chori Chori Chupke Chukpe* from his office and residence. Shah's voice samples were also collected to match them with the intercepted telephone conversations he had had with Shakeel and Rizvi.

Investigations also revealed that Shakeel had extorted money from Mansoor Siddiqui and the Morani brothers. Shah had aided and abetted the extortion by collecting jewellery and property documents from Mansoor on behalf of Shakeel. We also found that ₹ 5 crores was demanded from the Morani brothers as extortion money by Shakeel. Shah had intervened and asked Shakeel to reduce the amount, assuring him that he would recover the balance from the Moranis later.

It was revealed that Shah had also accepted jewellery and property documents from Ali Morani on behalf of the crime syndicate. Shah's role was further exposed when investigators stumbled upon the information that he, through his accountant and close confidant Tarun Shah, had transferred ill-gotten money to Salihu through *hawala* in Dubai. Salihu owned Sembi Trade International and Sembi Jewellers located at Gold Suk, Diara, Dubai, UAE. Through this firm Bharat Shah reportedly laundered money to Shakeel in Karachi.

We also found that even though Rizvi was not a big name in the industry, he was able to sign lead actors for his film because of Shakeel and with assistance from Shah. Nazim Rizvi was running a company by the name 'M/s Mega Bollywood Pvt. Ltd.,' and had agreed to become the presenter for *Chori Chori Chupke Chupke* even though he was fully aware that Shakeel was the main financier and had a pecuniary interest in the film.

Shah reportedly told Shakeel to approach Hrithik Roshan and Rakesh Roshan for extortion. Rizvi sought the underworld's help in coercing Hrithik through his father Rakesh to agree to work for the film at a nominal fee.

Shah's arrest caused a nationwide sensation and sent ripples down the spine of Bollywood and, to a great extent, the underworld. The fact that the Mumbai Police had taken the bold step of arresting a top Bollywood producer threw up questions as to whether the police had enough evidence against him.

Talking to the media after Shah's arrest, I said that the police had not taken any action before gathering enough intelligence and evidence. While we were monitoring Rizvi's phone, we stumbled upon conversations between Bharat Shah and Chota Shakeel. After recording calls between Shah and Shakeel, we had Shah's voice forensically tested in a laboratory in Delhi, which certified that the voice was indeed his.

The Mumbai Police was keeping a close watch on all crime and underworld related activities in Mumbai; Shah had never been on their radar. He was arrested for abetting a crime and the fact that he had helped the gangsters with extortion activities. I assured the press that the police had strong evidence against Shah. I would be risking my job if I had acted without that.

A few days after his arrest and some very difficult days in jail, Shah applied for bail in the special TADA court. It was rejected by the court seven times. A dejected Shah then knocked on the doors of the Bombay High Court; there too the court did not consider his plea worthy of bail and rejected it. Shah had to continue being incarcerated in a dingy cell in Arthur Road Jail. Finally, after 14 months of languishing in prison, the Supreme Court granted him bail.

After the investigations were finally complete, more than two chargesheets were filed in the case under various sections of the stringent MCOCA, IPC and Arms Act. And thus began a unique trial in the Sessions Court of Mumbai. Unique because a slew of top Bollywood stars had been lined up as witnesses by the Mumbai Police.

A total of 76 witnesses were examined in the trial, of which 14 were top film personalities. The likes of Shah Rukh Khan, Salman Khan, Preity Zinta, Rakesh Roshan, Sanjay Gupta, Mahesh Manjrekar, Anees Bazmee and producers Harish Sugandh, Ratan Jain and Mohammad Morani were produced as witnesses in the case.

We put them on the stand to prove that these stars were victims of the high-handedness of the underworld, all of them at one point targeted by Shakeel. However, all of them, except for actress Preity Zinta, turned hostile and did not say a word against the underworld. Only Preity, the heroine of Rizvi's film *Chori Chori Chupke Chupke,* stood by the statement she had given to the police. She told the court about the threats and extortion demands she had received from the underworld, thus proving our Mumbai case against Rizvi, Shakeel and Shah.

During the hearing, we told the court that the case demanded strict action, because it showed the larger conspiracy by the underworld. We informed the court that the underworld was planning to take over the film industry and rule it. Films are a powerful medium through which the thought process of a nation and society can be shaped. If such a powerful medium had fallen prey to the underworld, then the gangsters would be able to shape the narrative of our society and country as per their own whims and fancies.

After two years the trial ended, and special judge A.P. Bhangale found Bharat Shah guilty and convicted him. While convicting Shah, the court observed in its order that there was reason to believe that Shah, in the course of financing the film *Chori Chori Chupke Chupke* learned in October 2000 that Nazim Rizvi was a conduit for Shakeel and that they were planning to extort huge sums of money from prominent film personalities known to Shah. Right then Shah ought to have approached the police; instead, he adopted a submissive and docile attitude and did not inform the authorities.

The court, however, found that the one solitary conversation that Shah had with Shakeel was fraught with laxity by the police with regard to collecting evidence and making the *panchanama*. Shah was found guilty under section 118 of the IPC and section 3 (1) (11) of MCOCA for voluntary illegal omission to inform the police and/or competent authority about Rizvi's connection to the underworld. Shah was sentenced to one-year's rigorous imprisonment. Since he had already spent 14 months as an undertrial, he did not have to return to prison to serve his term.

The court further said that the 17 telephonic conversations presented by the police as evidence against Nazim Rizvi and Abdul Rahim Khan were clear proof that both were hand in glove with the crime syndicate. Based on the evidence produced by the police, the court found that Rizvi and Khan had active links with the underworld and were intentionally engaged in the activity of targeting film personalities for extortion.

Nazim Rizvi was found guilty and convicted under MCOCA and sentenced to six years' rigorous imprisonment and a fine of ₹ 5 lakh. Abdul Rahim Khan was found guilty and convicted under MCOCA and sentenced to six years' rigorous imprisonment and a fine of ₹ 5 lakh. And Bharat Shah got a one-year prison term. The conviction stands till date.

With a sure conviction in this case, the Mumbai Police successfully scuttled the underworld's bid of a hostile takeover of the Hindi film industry, popularly known as Bollywood. Had the police not done what it did, the underworld may have taken over the Hindi film industry and run it as their fiefdom.

The successful investigation and conviction is entirely due to the support of my CP, Mr. M.N. Singh, IPS (retd.).

No praise is enough for Ms. Vijaya Tahilramani, our Special Public Prosecutor for the Bharat Shah case. She made a remarkable case and arguments, understood the nuances of MCOCA, which was a new law and was not easy to understand.

Her prosecution of the case and the arguments in the court was the stuff of legal folklore. It was due to her legal acumen that the Mumbai Police managed to get a conviction in the case. In fact, she put up such a strong case that it held good right up to the Supreme Court.

After her stint as the Public Prosecutor, Ms. Vijaya Tahimramani went on to become a judge in the Bombay High Court and later became Chief Justice of the Madras High Court before her retirement.

♦♦♦♦♦♦

Chapter 8

UNDERWORLD MURDERS THAT SHOOK MUMBAI

This chapter highlights some of the most daring, horrific and shocking cases in which the Mumbai underworld showcased its darkest side. Listing and describing all the cases would be extremely difficult, as there are hundreds registered in Mumbai and other parts of the country.

The attempt in this chapter is to give the reader an idea of how dreadful the underworld was in its heyday and the kind of fear Mumbaikars were living in, witnessing horrendous crimes being committed in the streets. Cases mentioned in this chapter are a mere sample of the havoc the underworld had spread across Mumbai. And it is evidence of the quality of crimes and criminals the often under-staffed and poorly-armed Mumbai Police had to deal with.

- **The Murder of Rajan Nair by Chandrashekhar Safalika on 21 September 1983**

In 1986, Sadanand alias Sadhu Shetty was running the Sridevi Bar in Thane. There he met Abdul Majid, a local goon from the Castle Mill area of Thane (West). Majid resided in the hutments near the bar and would collect monthly protection money of ₹ 3,000 from Shetty.

One evening in April 1986 at around 7.30 p.m., when Shetty was managing his bar, Majid walked in with a youngster and sat at one of the corner tables. After a while, Majid called Shetty to the table. They had beer together and chatted. After some time, Majid asked Shetty if he recognised the lad with him. Shetty looked at him but had no clue who he was. Majid asked him to look carefully; Shetty still didn't recognise him.

Majid told him the youngster sitting with him was Chandrashekhar Safalika, the same person who had killed Rajan Nair inside the Esplanade Court on 21 September 1983. Unknown to both Majid and Safalika, the former had unwittingly signed the latter's death warrant.

Both were unaware that Shetty was extremely close to Chhota Rajan; he was among the top three members of the Chhota Rajan gang. Ever since Nair was murdered, Chhota Rajan had been baying for the blood of his killer. Safalika was an absolute newcomer on the underworld circuit, so no one knew about him or his whereabouts. He had gone underground after the murder and was nowhere to be found.

A shocked Shetty couldn't believe his eyes and ears when he heard that the young man sitting right in front of him was the most wanted killer for the Chhota Rajan gang. However, Shetty maintained his composure and sat with the duo, drinking beer.

At around 11.00 p.m. Majid left the bar, leaving instructions with Shetty to ensure that Safalika ate and drank to his fill. He asked Shetty to give him ₹ 200 for conveyance whenever he decided to leave. After Majid left, Shetty prodded Safalika into telling him the entire story of how he planned and killed Rajan Nair. During their conversation Safalika also told Shetty that he was in dire need of money and wanted to know the various ways in which he could commit robberies and dacoities.

At around 1 a.m., Shetty took a completely drunk Safalika to his club near Louis Wadi in Thane. There, Shetty asked the young man to sleep in one of the rooms as he was in no shape to travel. Once

Safalika was fast asleep, Shetty rushed to meet a close associate called Chandrakant Chavan, who lived nearby.

Shetty took Rama Naik and Babu Reshim's number from Chavan. He immediately called Naik but he was not available. He then phoned Reshim, who replied immediately. Shetty narrated the entire episode of that evening and told Reshim that Safalika was sleeping in his club.

Reshim too was stunned and reconfirmed with Shetty if it indeed was Safalika. On his confirmation, Reshim asked Shetty not to alert the police and to ensure that Safalika did not leave the club; he further said he was sending his men to pick up the young man.

Shetty returned to his club and waited, keeping an eye on Safalika. At around 4 a.m., Shree Mama, Sanjay Raggad, Naresh Jukkar, Diwakar Churi and Anil Parab arrived. They had driven there from Dagdi Chawl in Agripada in a Fiat, with Churi at the wheel.

Shetty woke Safalika and informed him that his friends were going to commit a dacoity and that he should accompany them. Safalika instantly agreed. Shetty told him that since he was looking for an opportunity to commit robbery or dacoity, this would be a good experience.

An unsuspecting Safalika got into the car with Shetty, Churi, Raggad and Parab, while the rest hired a taxi. They drove to Byculla and took Safalika to Rama Naik's storeroom in the Lal Vitachi Chawl (a building built using red bricks). There they met Reshim, Ghanshyam (Rama Naik's brother) and Ashok Chowdhary alias Chhota Babu. Reshim asked Safalika a few questions to verify his identity. By this time Safalika was sober and knew that something was amiss.

At around 8 a.m., Anil Parab brought Chhota Rajan to the storeroom. Rajan ordered his men to take Safalika to Noora's (Dawood Ibrahim's younger brother's) godown in Nagpada. News of Safalika being caught was big for both the Rajan and Dawood gangs.

A few minutes later, Dawood Ibrahim, Hanif Kutta, Lambu Shakil, Chota Shakil, Iqbal Kaskar (Dawood's youngest sibling), Satish Raje, Chikna Raju and a few others came to Noora's godown. They started questioning Safalika and asked him to explain how he had gone about planning and murdering Rajan Nair. With almost half the underworld in the storeroom, young Safalika soon realised that his life was in danger. He told the group the entire story of how he had killed Rajan Nair.

He said that he was an autorickshaw driver who lived in the Shell Colony in Chembur. A few days before the murder of Nair, Safalika was badly in need of money for his sister's wedding, so he approached gangster Abdul Kunju, who lived nearby. When, on 6 September 1983, Rajan Nair alias Bada Rajan along with his close associate David Pardesi killed Amirzada in a daring shootout inside the Sessions Court in Mumbai, the Pathan gang started looking for revenge.

Dawood Ibrahim had given *supari* of a huge amount to Bada Rajan to kill Amirzada to avenge the murder of Dawood's elder brother Shabbir. Bada Rajan was arrested by the police as he tried to escape.

Abdul Kunju, a close associate of Samad Khan, was entrusted with the work of planning the revenge. Kunju decided to employ a new face, because most gang members were known to rivals as well as the police, who would never allow any of them anywhere close to Bada Rajan, who was in police custody.

It was then that Kunju remembered Safalika and decided to use him. Kunju called the young man and told him that he was willing to give him money for his sister's wedding, on condition that he would do a job for Kunju and the Pathan gang. Safalika was tasked with killing Rajan Nair. He agreed, since he desperately needed the money.

Kunju took him to Shashi Shetty, owner of Akshay Bar situated near the Alankar Theatre in Girgaon. Kunju introduced Safalika to Shetty, Ravi Shetty, Mangesh More and Yeda Gopal. In the presence of everyone, Shetty again questioned if he was willing to kill Nair, to which Safalika replied in the affirmative.

They then took him to Caesar's Palace Hotel, where they introduced him to Mahesh Dholakia, in his office. Safalika was spellbound when he saw bundles of notes stacked up there. Dholakia told Safalika that there was ₹ 50 lakh in cash in front of him and that the entire sum would be his if he killed Nair. Safalika instantly agreed and took ₹ 1 lakh as an advance that he needed for his sister's wedding.

The next day, Safalika was asked to meet Kunju for training. He was taken to an isolated hillock near Parksite in Vikhroli. There they met Ramesh Pujari, Mangesh More and Kalia Anthony alias Francis. For a fortnight, Safalika was trained in the use of a firearm. They fired several rounds in the isolated area without raising alarm. After 15 days they were satisfied with Safalika's skill, convinced that he could hit a target.

Meanwhile, Kunju was already working on a plan to target Bada Rajan. It was known that Rajan would be brought to the Esplanade (Killa) Court situated next to the BMC Headquarters in South Mumbai, on 21 September 1983, for his hearing. Kunju had decided that this was the best time to target Rajan. A few days before the day of the hearing, Kunju brought Safalika to the court and asked him to study the topography of the place. They did a proper reconnaissance and even a mock drill of the entire operation.

D-Day arrived. Safalika wore a white uniform to disguise himself as a navy officer. He got into a green Ambassador car driven by Mangesh More. They left the Shell Colony and reached Crawford Market. Mangesh More parked the car and Safalika got out and started walking towards the Esplanade Court. He was carrying a revolver in the right-side pocket of his trousers. A thick book covered the pocket, so no betraying bulge was visible. Interestingly, the book had a cavity inside to hide the gun. Safalika waited in the court premises.

After Bada Rajan was done in court, the police brought him out, escorting him to the police van parked outside the building. The moment he appeared, Safalika seized his chance and charged towards Rajan, shooting him several times. Before the police could react, Rajan was dead, lying in a pool of blood. And before Safalika could escape, the police had caught him. He was taken into custody and lodged at the Thane Central Jail. From inside prison Safalika sent several messages to Kunju to remit the remaining ₹ 49 lakh, but got no response.

Meanwhile, Bada Rajan's killing was a massive shock to Chhota Rajan and his gang. Chhota Rajan was angry and upset and was looking for revenge. With Safalika in jail, Rajan targeted Kunju and killed him in a daring shootout. (Read about the murder of Kunju on page no. 158.)

After Kunju's killing, Safalika had no hope of getting the remaining money promised to him by Kunju, Shashi Shetty, Mahesh Dholakia and others. He was in jail for more than one and a half years. One day, he was taken to the Sessions Court from Thane jail for his hearing. Later, the police team escorting Safalika stopped at the Siddhivinayak Hotel at Nehru Nagar in Kurla (East) for refreshments. Safalika grabbed the chance and escaped. He went into hiding.

Safalika was in a terrible state financially and needed money desperately. After being underground for a few days, he went to Caesar's Palace to meet Shetty and Dholakia. When he asked for his money, they flatly refused and asked him to leave and never come back.

A dejected Safalika got in touch with Abdul Majid, whom he had befriended when he was in Thane jail. Majid regularly gave him money for survival.

Safalika told Dawood, Rajan and the others gathered in the storeroom that he had gone to Thane to meet Majid to get some money from him. Majid took him to the Sridevi Bar where they met Sadhu Shetty, who had brought Safalika to that room.

After hearing Safalika's story, Dawood and Rajan decided to keep him in their custody till they decided what to do with him. That day almost every member of the Dawood and Rajan gangs came to see Safalika, still shocked about how he had managed to kill Bada Rajan.

The next day, it was decided that Safalika should be taken to a secluded spot and killed. At around 6 p.m., they took three cars – in one sat Dawood Ibrahim, Chhota Rajan, Chhota Shakeel and Chhota Babu. Safalika was placed between Chhota Rajan and Chhota Shakeel in the back seat, while the others were seated in front. The second car was driven by Satish Raje, with Raju Chikna, Sopan, Sanjay Raggad and Sadhu Shetty as passengers. In the third were Amir Lambu and other members of the Dawood gang.

The entourage left from Noora's storeroom in the Bohri Mohalla area of South Mumbai and went to Milan Subway in Santacruz. It was post 8 p.m. and the subway was secluded. Chhota Shakeel and Chhota Rajan forced Safalika out of the car and took him to the side of the road. The three cars halted. Everyone got out and stood there, waiting.

Without batting an eyelid, Chhota Rajan pulled out his revolver and shot Safalika in the forehead at point blank range. Safalika fell to the ground and Rajan pumped four more bullets into his chest. Safalika lay on the ground, dead. All the men got back into their cars and drove back to Bohri Mohalla.

With Safalika's killing, and Kunju's murder a few months earlier, Chhota Rajan had avenged the death of his mentor Rajan Mahadevan Nair alias Bada Rajan.

• The Sensational Killing of Ashok Joshi on 3 December 1983

After the mid-1980s, the underworld was clearly divided into two gangs: the Dawood gang and the Arun Gawli gang. Both had important people at the helm. While Dawood Ibrahim and Chhota Rajan were a formidable pair, continuously giving them a run for their money were Arun Gawli and Ashok Joshi. Both pairs were equal in might and valour and would often take each other head-on.

But Joshi and Gawli were by far the most feared pair, since they were ruthless in their killing of rival Dawood and Rajan gang members. Both were also on-the-ground operatives and would often be in the middle of the action. Dawood, on the other hand, always got someone else to do the work for him.

By 1986-87, Dawood and Rajan had fled to the Middle East and were operating from Dubai. With both absent from Mumbai, Gawli and Joshi had an almost free run and were creating havoc in the D-Company by targeting its men as well as financiers and well-wishers.

A desperate Dawood and Rajan informed their teams in Mumbai that Gawli and Joshi had to be killed. Men were asked to plan and execute the murders and report to Dubai. Joshi and Gawli knew that the D-Company was targeting them and so they maintained a tight layer of secrecy around themselves and their whereabouts. Dagdi Chawl became a fortress – huge iron gates were installed at the entrance and Gawli's men, armed to the teeth, made sure there was round-the-clock security in and around the tenement.

Gawli rarely stepped out of the compound; most of his meetings were conducted in the confines of the *chawl*. Even inside the *chawl* several measures were taken to ensure that in the event of an attack, a counterattack could be instantly launched. To ensure Gawli was not targeted, hiding places, underground tunnels, cavities in the walls and hidey-holes in the floor were made.

Joshi had ensured that he too was surrounded by a blanket of security and secrecy. He would rarely move out of his area in Kanjurmarg and if he had to, he had two cars with bodyguards armed with sophisticated AK-47 and AK-56 assault rifles.

Dawood gang member Anil Parab, after days of persistence, managed to infiltrate the Joshi gang. Parab made an acquaintance with Shyam Sundar Nair, Joshi's driver.

One evening in November 1988, Parab called Nair to Tilak Nagar in Chembur for a meeting. They sat in the middle of the empty ground, drank beer and ate snacks. The meeting lasted for several hours.

Eventually Parab hailed a taxi for Nair, giving him ₹ 100 for the fare. An elated Parab went to a secluded STD booth in Chembur village and made a long-distance call to Dubai. He gave Chhota Rajan the good news that he had managed to turn Nair into an informer and would now get real-time information about Joshi and his whereabouts. Both Chhota Rajan and Dawood were happy with the development.

After the first meeting, Nair started visiting Parab regularly, meeting at the house of another gangster (Danny) in Tilak Nagar. In the last week of November, Nair came to meet Parab hurriedly in Chembur and informed him that both Joshi and Gawli were holed up in a bungalow in Khopoli. Parab immediately informed his gang members and in no time a team of 40 men, including Parab, Danny, Sanjay Raggad, Diwakar Churi, Naresh Jukkar, Subhash Makadwala, Chandya Talegaonkar, Sunil Sawant, Shree Mama, Dinesh Patel, Shirish Pawar and Mangesh More started for Khopoli in a dozen cars. They were armed like a small military unit with revolvers, pistols, AK-47s and AK-56s, and a lot of ammunition. But when they reached Khopoli they were unable to identify the bungalow – the information and operation turned out to be a hoax. The entire team drove back to Chembur.

On 3 December 1988, sometime around noon, the telephone in Danny's house rang. It was Shyam Sundar Nair wanting to speak to Parab urgently – he said he would call back in a few minutes. Danny immediately fetched Parab.

A few minutes later the phone rang, and Parab answered. It was Nair who said that Joshi and Gawli were back in Mumbai, in Dagdi Chawl. They were scheduled to travel to Pune around midnight the same day in a silver Maruti car, registration number MFF 788. Then the line went dead.

Parab realised that the information that he had just received was huge and it was probably their golden opportunity to target Joshi and Gawli at the same time in a single operation. Parab immediately called Chhota Rajan in Dubai and updated him. They had less than 12 hours to organise and execute the operation. Rajan asked Parab to immediately gather all the gang members and he himself called some of them.

After a few minutes Rajan called back on Danny's number and spoke to Parab, assuring him that the best sharpshooters and top gangsters from the Dawood and Rajan gangs would assemble in Chembur at around 7 p.m. After that, Parab would lead the operation.

As decided, around 7.30 p.m. most of the men had assembled in Chembur, including Ganesh Ram Soradi aka Honey, Ramesh Devisingh Bist aka Danny, Bandya Mama, Sadhu Shetty and Sunil Manya. Gangsters started arriving in cars and SUVs. Shrikant Desai and Dinesh Patel came in Maruti cars with seven or eight of their men. Sunil Sawant, Madhu Nigade, Shrikant Pawar and Mangesh More, along with five or six of their gang members reached Chembur in a car and an SUV.

Fugitive gangster Sharad Shetty sent Suresh alias Suru, who drove there in a Premier Padmini 118NE along with four men. Shetty also sent two brand new Jeeps and two Maruti cars for the operation. Subhash Makadwala, Chandya Talegaonkar, Arun Rajdeo, Naidu and 15 men reached there in five cars. Naresh Jukkar, Sanjay Raggad, Diwakar Churi came from Dadar in their cars with four or five people. Mobin Khan, Vijay Singh Rajput arrived from Kurla.

Sunil Sawant had an AK-47 assault rifle, 15 revolvers and pistols. Anil Parab was carrying one AK-56, 20 revolvers and pistols. Sharad Shetty had sent ten revolvers and pistols with his men. Bhai Thakur had sent the same number of guns all the way from Virar. Seven or eight revolvers were collected from Tilak Nagar by Rajan's men. Chhota Shakeel had sent that many licensed revolvers.

More than 50 men, 25 cars, two assault rifles, over 30 revolvers and pistols, ammunition and more were ready and primed for use. It looked like a war would soon be waged.

The posse left from Chembur at around 8.30 p.m. Bandya Mama was asked to stay back and monitor the telephone in case messages and information needed to be passed on.

As per the information received, Gawli and Joshi were going to leave from Kanjurmarg at midnight in a Maruti van, and head to Pune. The plan was to ambush the car in Panvel – this was decided since it was close to Mumbai, so that after the operation the gang members could rush back to Mumbai and hide in their own areas.

They reached Panvel at about 10 p.m., parked their vehicles around the Panvel ST stand and waited. It would not be before 1.30 a.m. that they would see action. If Gawli and Joshi were going to leave Kanjurmarg at midnight, they would not reach Panvel before 1.30 a.m.

They waited until 4 a.m., but there was no sign of the Maruti van or any other vehicle carrying their targets. A few minutes later, Sadhu

Shetty alerted the team after he saw a car at a distance and vaguely identified Joshi sleeping in the left corner of the rear seat. The alert gangsters started following the vehicle.

The car in which Sadhu Shetty was travelling took the lead for some distance, intercepting it near the Persian Darbar hotel in Panvel (the same place where one of the conspiracies of the 1993 serial bomb blasts in Mumbai was hatched) on the old Mumbai-Pune highway.

Raggad, who was travelling in the same car as Sadhu Shetty, fired the first shot at Joshi and injured him. Immediately after, a hail of bullets rained down on the car.

Shyam Sunder Nair, who was driving the car, immediately stopped in the middle of the road, got out and started running. An injured Joshi saw him and immediately realised something was amiss. Instead of speeding up and taking him to safety, Nair had stopped the car in the middle of the road. Instead of helping Joshi, Nair was running away. In that moment, the injured Joshi realised that it was Nair who had tipped off the Dawood gang about his plans. Even though he was injured, Joshi took out his weapon and fired at Nair, who was hit in the head and chest and died instantly.

As he fired at Nair, the rival men shot him multiple times and he was killed. Parab and Sunil Sawant pulled Joshi's bullet-riddled body from the car and laid him on the ground. They got a large hammer from their car and bashed Joshi's head and testicles repeatedly with it. The lifeless body shook with the impact of the blows.

By battering Ashok Joshi's head and private parts with a hammer, Sawant took his long pending revenge. A few years earlier, when Sawant was in jail, Joshi was there too. Since Sawant was from the Dawood gang, Joshi and his gang members had stripped him naked and pounded his testicles with a hammer.

In a matter of minutes, the operation was over. Ashok Joshi, Shyam Sundar Nair, Karunakar Hegde and Dilip Landge were shot dead by Anil Parab and his gang. Hegde and Landge were close aides of Joshi, travelling in the same car. From the attacking side, Subhash

Makadwala was the only person who sustained bullet injuries. He was immediately rushed to Thane for medical treatment.

Leaving the bullet-ravaged and battered body of Joshi with the dead Nair and others on the ground, the entourage left before the police could reach the spot. The deadly assault rifles and other weapons were stored in the Premier Padmini 118NE, which would be driven to Navi Mumbai and parked in a garage near the LP Company. When the gangsters reached Chembur and informed Bandya Mama about the success of the operation, he immediately called Chhota Rajan and gave him the good news. Bandya Mama also phoned Chhota Shakeel with the news; he informed Shakeel about the Premier Padmini 118NE in Navi Mumbai that needed to be brought back to Mumbai. Shakeel immediately called his men in Nagpada, who dispatched five women to Navi Mumbai to drive back in the Premier Padmini 118NE. Once in Nagpada, the car and the weapons were hidden.

Before the operation, Parab had promised to give Nair ₹ 5 lakh for his information. He had given him an advance of ₹ 2 lakh, and the rest was given to Nair's wife after his death.

Three days after the killing, Vijay Singh Rajput, Madhu Nigade, Arun Rajdeo, Chandya Talegaonkar and Momin Khan surrendered to the Panvel police in the Ashok Joshi murder case. In February 1989, Sadhu Shetty surrendered in the same case.

It was never revealed why Gawli was not travelling with Joshi, as they had heard he would. Whether the information was wrong or Gawli found out about the operation and backed out at the last minute, or perhaps travelled by a different route, was never known.

However, Ashok Joshi's killing had dealt a heavy blow to Arun Gawli, and his gang was never the same again.

• The Murder of Abdul Kunju in 1987

Things changed for the gang in 1984, when Abdul Kunju plotted to kill Bada Rajan. Before 1982, Kunju, a gangster from Shell Colony in Chembur, was a member of the Bada Rajan gang. However, in 1982,

Rajan molested Kunju's fiancé in his absence. Kunju found out and was furious. An angry Kunju left Bada Rajan's gang and swore revenge.

It took him almost two years, but he got payback in the most daring style. Kunju hired a hitman named Chandrashekhar Safalika to kill Bada Rajan. He planned the entire operation – Safalika, dressed as a Navy officer, fired at Bada Rajan in the compound of the Esplanade Court in South Mumbai when the latter was brought there for a hearing on 21 September 1983.

Kunju got his revenge, but he had angered Chhota Rajan, who swore to avenge his mentor's death. At that time Rajan did not know much about Kunju. A few days later Rajan learned that Kunju was a cricket buff and liked to play. In fact, such was his love for the game that he would often arrange matches in large grounds and invite people to watch him play. This was what Rajan was waiting for. He alerted his gang members and asked them to keep a close watch on Kunju, especially when and where he was going to play cricket.

One Sunday afternoon Rajan got a tip-off that Kunju would be playing cricket at a particular ground in front of a large crowd. He decided that it was the day to carry out his operation. Almost immediately he, along with close aides Sanjay Raggad and Sadhu Shetty, left for the venue.

Dressed in T-shirts, jeans and sports shoes, the trio mingled with the crowd and watched Kunju bat while they lay in wait for an opportunity. That presented itself when Kunju hit the ball in their direction … and it crossed the boundary. Rajan quickly seized the opportunity and grabbed the ball. He asked Raggad and Shetty to follow him. On the pretext of returning the ball the trio walked across the ground towards Kunju.

Kunju had no reason to suspect anything when he saw three youngsters coming towards him to return the ball. When they got closer, Rajan handed over the ball to Kunju and, before he could bat an eyelid, all three of them whipped out their weapons and opened fire point blank at him. Kunju was hit several times and collapsed on the ground, dying almost instantly. The crowd was stunned and stood there watching, aghast. Before anyone realised what had happened, the trio walked out of the ground and vanished into thin air.

It was one of the most daring shootouts of its time and, more importantly, it catapulted Rajan to fame in the underworld almost overnight. He was asked to take his mentor's place and was anointed 'Chhota Rajan'.

• The Gut-wrenching Killing of Babu Reshim on 5 March 1987

The wee hours of 5 March 1987, witnessed another gruesome killing in the history of the Mumbai underworld, this time within the premises of a police station.

A team of ten gangsters: Ravindra, a.k.a. Ravi Bansi Gohar, Rajendra, a.k.a. Raju Bhai, Tarachand Sankat, Kishor, a.k.a. Kishya, Amarsingh Maheshkar, Vinod-Bhika Maria, Rajesh Utekar, Mahesh Maskarm, Kishore Kanjari and Ravi Kanjari, hailed two taxis from Bombay Central and asked the drivers to head in the direction of Nana Chowk. From there they went to Chowpatty and then to Teenbatti (Walkeshwar) at Malabar Hill. They stopped the taxis in an isolated lane and started beating up the drivers. Threatening the men with dire consequences, they forced them out of their cabs, carjacked the vehicles and sped away.

They went directly to Saat Rasta or Jacob Circle and parked the taxis in the Sane Guruji Marg, adjacent to the police lock-up. All ten disembarked and started walking towards the lock-up. There was an opening in the compound wall that they entered through and reached the main gate.

They asked the constable who was on night duty to hand over the keys. When the constable refused, they threw a bomb at the entrance gate, following it up with three or four more – the impact of the explosions was such that the iron gates broke open.

There were seven policemen (Nandkumar Takke, Rajendra More, Maruti Mane, Dashrath Narsu Kokitkar, Madhav Karande, Prakash Pachale and Hari Shravan Ahire) on the premises that night. Two were on duty when the attacks started; the others were asleep. They were armed with their .303 service rifles, but were outnumbered, their weapons being no match for the bombs that were hurled at them. It was a battlefield. Constable Hari Shravan Ahire, who was on duty, was seriously injured. Others sustained minor injuries as they rushed to take cover and call for back up.

The police lockup was filled with smoke. The assailants had access to the main door after it was ripped open by the blasts. They entered and headed straight for cell number 1, where Babu Gopal Reshim was lodged along with another criminal. While entering the building, one of the invaders shouted at the policemen, *"Jisko bhaagna hai, bhaag jao!"* (Those who want to run away, run now.)

By now, Reshim knew something was wrong. He was awake and striding around in his cell when Ravi, Raju Bhai, Kishore and Vinod reached there. Reshim saw them and instantly knew that they had come for him. Without hesitating they hurled a bomb into the cell – it exploded with a loud bang and injured both Babu Reshim and his cellmate, Mohan Kudappalli. Reshim was knocked off his feet and sat on the floor with his back against the wall. In a semi-conscious state, he looked at his assailants and said, *"Ye achha nahin hai. Jo kuch hai, bhai hai."* (This is not good. No matter what has happened between us, you are my brother.)

Seeing him helpless, the assailants began a volley of attacks of a ferocity never heard of. They first burst open the cell door with a bomb. More than 35 rounds were fired, and three bombs were hurled, of which one did not explode. If this wasn't enough, they bludgeoned Reshim's head with a sledgehammer.

Once they were sure their target was dead, the assailants left. The entire operation was over in a matter of 10-12 minutes.

On the way out they again hurled bombs into the premises and then walked in the direction of Sane Guruji Marg. They got into the carjacked taxis and fled – the taxis were later found abandoned in the Deonar area of Chembur by the police.

By now the Agripada police and main control room had been

alerted to what had happened. Police Inspectors Madhukar Zende and Bhalerao, along with a police team, rushed to the spot to see the devastation. When they entered cell number 1, they were dumbstruck by the macabre sight.

Babu Reshim's lifeless body lay in the south-west corner of the room, resting against the wall. His tongue was protruding, his body covered in blood. There was a country-made bomb lying near his legs. A sledgehammer was seen near the body. Blood was everywhere. Bullet holes pockmarked the wall. Near the body 17 spent shells were found.

Mohan Kudappalli, who was injured, was immediately rushed to the nearby Nair Hospital. The injured policemen were also taken to the hospital. Reshim's body was sent to the Sir J.J. Hospital for a post-mortem. Police constable Ahire, who was severely injured, succumbed to his injuries a few days later.

After studying the way the operation had taken place, the Mumbai Police decided to set up a team to apprehend the assailants. It took them over two months, but on 28 June 1987, ACP Dhond got information from the Ulhasnagar police station that they had arrested a few people, some probably linked to the Babu Reshim murder case. Following this, a team from the Mumbai Police rushed to Ulhasnagar and found that three of the accused, Ravi, Raju Bhai and Kishore, were involved in the attack on the police lock-up at Jacob Circle.

All three were brought to Mumbai and the case was transferred from the Agripada police station to the Mumbai Crime Branch (DCB CID). In the months of investigations that followed, the police eventually arrested and charge-sheeted more than 12 persons. In its final verdict the Sessions Court acquitted all except four: Ravi, Raju Bhai, Kishore and Vinod. Their roles were confirmed, and they were convicted. The court sentenced them to death, which was ratified by the Bombay High Court in 1997.

- **The Dramatic Shootout at Sir J.J. Hospital on 12 September 1992**

If there is one case that can be singled out to highlight how the underworld functioned in Mumbai during its heyday, it would have to be the J.J. Hospital shootout. It is a showcase of how heinous the underworld was, how it fought an ugly battle on the streets of Mumbai and how it spread panic and fear.

In the late 1980s and early 1990s, the rivalry between the Dawood Ibrahim gang and the Arun Gawli gang was at its peak. It was a battle for supremacy in South and Central Mumbai – an ugly turf war. This battle reached its zenith on 26 July 1992, when Dawood's brother-in-law Ibrahim Parkar was shot dead in his residence in Nagpada, South Mumbai. Parkar was Dawood's most trusted lieutenant in Mumbai and his favourite as well. Dawood liked him so much that he got his sister to marry him.

Parkar's killing not only saddened Dawood but enraged him to the extent that he swore a revenge that would send shockwaves through his rivals. The entire Dawood gang had just one aim: find the killers of Ibrahim Parkar.

The Mumbai Police knew that Parkar's killing would result in an ugly war in the underworld that would spill out onto the streets of Mumbai, making the city unsafe. The police started investigations into Parkar's killing and soon found that it was Gawli's trusted aide Shailesh Haldankar who was involved. Haldankar had helped the killers identify Parkar at his residence.

The Mumbai Police soon started looking for Haldankar. Word reached the Dawood gang, and they too started looking for Haldankar – they wanted to get to him before the police did.

Within a few days, on 30 August 1992, there were gunshots fired in the Kumbharwada area of South Mumbai. An individual by the name of Mansukh Rawat was shot at. Investigations revealed that Shailesh Haldankar, Bipin Shere, Raju Batata and Santosh Patil had fired on Rawat and fled. It was now clear to the police as well as the

D-Company that Haldankar was in Mumbai. They intensified their search for him.

The police caught a lucky break on the morning of 2 September 1992, when they were tipped off that Haldankar, Shere and Batata were seen in Kumbharwada. A team immediately rushed there and instantly identified all three men, asking them to surrender. Caught completely by surprise, the gangsters tried to intimidate the police by brandishing weapons like swords and choppers at them.

However, something happened that neither the police nor the gangsters had foreseen. Seeing the stand-off between armed gangsters and the police, local people and bystanders got into the act and overpowered Haldankar and Shere. They started beating them up; before the police realised what was happening and moved in to stop it, the two gangsters had been assaulted quite severely. The police team rescued both men and apprehended them. However, in the melee, Raju Batata managed to escape.

Considering the severity of their injuries, the police immediately took the duo to the J.J. Hospital for medical treatment. The doctors examined them and decided to admit them, as the nature of their injuries required them to be under medical supervision for more than 24 hours. Following this, they were admitted to Ward no. 18 on the third floor of the hospital.

A team of one head constable and two constables were posted on duty 24x7 to ensure that the injured men did not escape. Unknown to the police or Haldankar, his arrest and hospitalisation had revealed his location to the D-Company. They now knew where he was and the fact that he was not going anywhere.

Dawood, who was still mourning the death of Parkar, decided to seek an audacious revenge. He put together his A-team, with his closest aide Chota Shakeel in charge of the operation. Shakeel called upon the D-gang's most dreaded henchman Subhash Singh Thakur to plan and execute the operation.

In those days Thakur was in Kathmandu, Nepal, along with Sunil Sawant alias Sautya. Thakur had reportedly killed Paul Patrick

Newman, a henchman of Arun Gawli, and fled to his safe haven of Nepal, where he usually escaped from law enforcement agencies in India. His mentor, Khim Bahadur Thapa, was from Kathmandu and was a very influential person in the mountain nation.

However, rival gangster Chhota Rajan had Thapa killed, which enraged Thakur, who decided to seek revenge. Following Thapa's killing, Thakur travelled to Delhi and stayed there with Sawant and Brijesh Singh. As part of his revenge against Chhota Rajan, Thakur managed to kill Sanjay Raggad, Diwakar Churi and Amar Jukkar, all Rajan's men, and thus avenged Thapa's killing. He did it with the help of Brijesh Singh.

Thakur and Sawant were whiling away their time in Delhi when Shakeel called to give them the task of teaching Arun Gawli and Haldankar a lesson that would send a strong message through the underworld: don't mess with Dawood. The men left for Mumbai and began planning what would be the most audacious underworld operation of the time.

After Haldankar and Shere were arrested and admitted to the hospital, for ten days things were quiet. There was a round-the-clock vigil on them, and everything seemed normal. However, what they did not know was that there was constant surveillance, with their every move being tracked, by members of the Dawood gang.

Thakur and Sawant reached Mumbai and started living in a flat in Queens View Apartment near Lido Cinema, Juhu. Sawant was in constant touch with Dawood and was taking instructions from him on the phone.

On 11 September, after one such call, he told Thakur that Dawood had instructed them to kill Haldankar. At around midnight, Sawant asked Singh to go to the hospital and find out what the situation was there. Brijesh Singh came back after an hour with the information that there was only one constable on duty, so it would be the ideal time to conduct their operation.

What was about to happen was something no one could have foreseen or even imagined in their wildest nightmares. It was a day that would change the equation between the Mumbai Police and the underworld forever.

Immediately after getting this information, on 12 September 1992, Thakur and Sawant decided to go ahead with the operation. They armed themselves with some of the most sophisticated weapons available in those days, including AK-47 assault rifles, pistols, revolvers, dynamite and hand-grenades.

Around the same time, in the hospital, Police Sub-inspector (PSI) Krishnavatar Thakur was on duty, on rounds at the J.J. Hospital. He checked on Shere first and then went to Ward no. 18 to check on Shailesh Haldankar. He saw that Haldankar was asleep on his bed, handcuffed to the rails. Police Constable Nagare was sitting on a stool between Haldankar's bed and that of another patient, Siddiq Ahmed. Head Constable Javsen and Constable Bhanavat were sitting on the bed on which Haldankar was sleeping. Thakur proceeded to join them on Haldankar's bed.

Within a few minutes, two Fiat cars and a two-wheeler screeched to a halt near the west entrance gate of the hospital. At least ten armed men got out and walked into the main entrance.

Shankar Ramchandra Jadhav was on duty as a night watchman, sitting near the elevator in the main building. He saw the gangsters walk in, and when he saw the weapons they carried, his initial thought was that they were policemen. When he asked, one of the gangsters caught him and ordered him to be quiet. At the same time, Bachchi Singh slammed Jadhav's face with his revolver with such force that the watchman was knocked out instantly.

They then went to the third floor to Ward no. 18, where Haldankar and Shere were. Storming into where Haldankar was, in a pre-decided move, Brijesh Singh held Ravi Sorte (his accomplice) by the shirt collar, pushed him into the ward and shouted, "*Saale, tumhare baki sathi dikhao!*" (Rascal, identify your accomplices!). It was made to look as if a policeman had caught a gangster and was asking him to identify his gang members.

A policeman who was on duty immediately realised that something was wrong and shut the main door of the ward. The armed gangster tried to push open the door, but couldn't, so he fired at it with the AK-47, bursting it open. The gangsters were taken aback when they faced heavy retaliatory fire by the policemen inside the ward.

A stand-off ensued between the heavily armed criminals and the policemen. The armed conflict was tilted in favour of the attackers, since they were armed to the teeth with sophisticated weapons; the brave policemen had only their service rifles and revolvers with limited ammunition. By this time, a scared Haldankar hid below his bed. He told a constable to release him from his handcuffs as the gangsters had come to kill him.

When they were unable to enter the ward, the criminals blew the door out with a hand grenade. As they rushed in, Subhash Singh Thakur started firing indiscriminately with his AK-47 at Haldankar and the two constables guarding him.

Within minutes, Shailesh Haldankar, Police Head Constable Chintaman Gajanan Javsen and Police Constable Kawal Singh Baddu Bhanavat had been killed in a manner never seen, heard of or imagined before by the Mumbai underworld. A few others, including a couple of policemen, were severely injured.

It was the first time that an AK-47 was used by the underworld. More than 500 bullets and half a dozen hand grenades had been spent in one of the biggest government hospitals in the country, leaving two policemen and a gangster dead.

While they were leaving, the killers realised that one of the gangsters had been hit by a bullet fired by the police, injured severely in the abdomen. They rushed to their parked cars and fled the scene, leaving behind a trail of blood. They reached Najir Jariwala's (one of the assailants') house and saw that Pradhan was badly hurt, with a bullet through his abdomen. He was bleeding profusely, and it was clear that if he didn't get immediate medical attention, he would die.

The gangsters immediately contacted Chota Shakeel in Dubai and updated him. He assured them that Dawood himself would investigate the matter and arrange for a doctor at the earliest. About half an hour later, Dawood called them and told them a doctor would be arriving soon. When the medico saw Pradhan's condition, he immediately gave him an injection and medicines, but told Shakeel that the patient would need surgery urgently, which he was not equipped to do. Shakeel then contacted another of Dawood's trusted aides, Sham Kishore Garikapatti, asking him to arrange for a doctor to treat Pradhan.

Garikapatti, a resident of Ghatkopar, was a well-networked, educated and intelligent member of the D-Company. He was the son of a customs officer and had grown up near the Hyderabad House locality of Nepean Sea Road. Hyderabad House is a colony where some of the highest-ranking central government officers stay while they are on duty in Mumbai. After understanding all that had happened during the night, he realised that Pradhan would have to be transported to a facility and treated in secrecy.

Garikapatti arranged for a doctor in Andheri. However, he was faced with the problem of transporting Pradhan from South Mumbai to Andheri without being detected. He therefore called upon the services of Jaywant Dattatray Suryarao, President of the Bhiwandi Nizampura Municipal Council (BNMC), who had an official government car – a white Contessa with a red beacon. He also had a police bodyguard.

Early the next morning, Garikapatti asked him to come to Ghatkopar urgently. Suryarao was tasked with the job of taking Pradhan in his official car from South Mumbai to Andheri. During the journey, he heard about everything that had happened the previous night. After dropping Pradhan at Andheri, a scared Suryarao went back to Bhiwandi.

Meanwhile, the Mumbai Police had affected a lockdown in the entire city and were hunting the shooters. The entire incident at J.J. Hospital had not only shocked them but was also of great embarrassment to the law enforcers. They had resolved to nab the killers.

The next day, Subhash Singh Thakur and Sunil Sawant met Garikapatti and asked him to arrange for their safe passage from Mumbai, as there was police *nakabandi* across the city and it was almost impossible to escape without being discovered. Garikapatti once again called upon Suryarao and asked him to go to Mumbai with his official car and police bodyguard.

A scared Suryarao tried to refuse, but Garikapatti threatened him with the death of his family and himself if he refused. Reluctantly, Suryarao drove to Mumbai. Garikapatti took him to a hotel in Juhu where they met Subhash Singh Thakur and Sunil Sawant. Together, they left the city in Suryarao's car.

They stopped at a petrol pump in Vasai. Garikapatti asked Suryarao to leave, but kept his official car, driver and police bodyguard, because they were planning to go to Delhi – travelling in an official government car with a police bodyguard would not arouse suspicion. Suryarao managed to persuade Garikapatti to not take his police bodyguard along. He, however, agreed to give his official car and driver, who then took Subhash Singh Thakur and Sunil Sawant towards Gujarat, from where they fled to Delhi.

Garikapatti gave Suryarao another car to travel to Bhiwandi. It was this car which helped the police get the first lead in the case. The same car had been used by the shooters to drive to the J.J. Hospital and escape from there. An eyewitness had recorded the number of the car and given it to the police, who traced the car to Suryarao and arrested him.

After his arrest Suryarao spilled the beans on everything that had happened. Based on his information, the police arrested Garikapatti and through him, almost everyone else, except for Subhash Singh Thakur and Sunil Sawant. Thakur had fled to Delhi, while Sawant had reportedly left the country.

Subhash Singh Thakur was arrested almost a year later in July 1993 by the Delhi Police and eventually handed over to the Mumbai Police.

A total of 41 accused were charge-sheeted, of which only nine stood trial – the others were either discharged, absconding or killed by rival gangsters or in police encounters.

I was appointed as the Joint Commissioner of Police (Mumbai Crime Branch) while the trial was in progress. I immediately took a status report of the case, understood the details from the investigating officer and ensured that we put up a strong case with irrefutable evidence in the court.

The trial ended within a few months and on 7 August 2000, designated special TADA court judge P.K. Chawre finally gave his verdict. Thakur was found guilty under various sections of the TADA Act and under section 302 of the Indian Penal Code. He was sentenced to death.

Garikapatti was found guilty and sentenced to ten years' imprisonment, while Suryarao was sentenced to seven years' imprisonment. Six others were given the benefit of the doubt and acquitted.

After being on the run for several years, gangster Brijesh Singh was arrested in January 2008. He was, however, later discharged from the case for lack of evidence against him. Subhash Singh Thakur's death sentence was later commuted to life imprisonment by the Bombay High Court.

- **The Murder of Tanya Koli on 17 September 1993**

In 1990, Arun Gawli's close aide from Sion, Guru Walawalkar, was lodged in the Nashik jail in a murder case. During this time, Guru met gangster Tanya Koli who was imprisoned under the National Security Act (NSA).

Koli was a local goon from Kumbharwada area of South Mumbai and an arch-rival of Shashi Anna Shetty, owner of the Akshay Bar in that area. Shetty was also close to the D-Company.

Guru and Tanya both realised that they had a common enemy, and they could come together and help each other. They soon became close friends. After their release from jail, Guru took Tanya to Dagdi Chawl to introduce him to Arun Gawli.

Gawli took an instant liking to Koli and made him part of his gang. Soon, Koli became Gawli's confidant and conducted several operations for him, including killing many of his rivals.

In 1993, relations between the Gawli and Amar Naik gangs soured to the point of no return. In fact, their enmity increased to such a level that they started plotting to kill each other. During this time, Koli was back in Arthur Road Jail on another murder charge. He was suspicious about Ashwin Naik's father-in-law, Jethwa, who had a shop in Kumbharwada. Koli feared that Jethwa could tip off the police with information about Koli or his associates.

Koli also had a history with Ashwin Naik; they had quarrelled and confronted each other a few times when in jail in Nashik. So Koli decided to get rid of Jethwa, which would also be his way of getting back at Ashwin Naik. From inside the jail Tanya Koli planned Jethwa's murder. He delegated the task to his key associates Durga Bhaiya, Baban Patil and Raju Bhatatia. Following Koli's instructions, they shot Jethwa dead near his shop in Kumbharwada.

At that time, both Koli and Ashwin Naik were in Arthur Road Jail. However, Naik learned that it was Koli who was the mastermind behind his father-in-law's killing. He planned to avenge that death by having Koli killed.

Amar Naik ran his own criminal enterprise inside Arthur Road jail – he was extorting money from undertrials who were in jail for drug related offences. After Amar Naik was released, Ashwin Naik continued with the extortion business. Tanya Koli got wind of this money-making enterprise and soon started demanding money from the same undertrials.

This led to tremendous friction between the two gangs and one day they came face-to-face. A major riot ensued. Several undertrials, including gang members from both sides, were severely injured.

To ensure that the incident would not be repeated, the jail administration decided to move Tanya Koli and his associates to Amravati jail.

Ashwin Naik, who was looking for an opportunity to avenge his father-in-law's death, heard that Koli was being moved to Amravati. He immediately decided that it was time to seek revenge. Naik messaged Amar Naik and asked him to do the needful.

On 17 September 1993, Tanya Koli had a court date in Mumbai. The jail administration decided to move him to Amravati after the court hearing. As per the plan, after Koli's hearing was over, a police team escorted him to Victoria Terminus Station (VT Station, as it was known before being renamed as Chhatrapati Shivaji Maharaj Terminus). Unknown to them, Amar Naik and his associates followed them from the court to the station and boarded the same train.

The train left VT Station on its way to Amravati. When it made its scheduled halt at Kalyan, Amar Naik and his associates took the opportunity and attacked the unsuspecting police team and Tanya Koli, indiscriminately firing at them. There was no time to even react. Before they knew what was happening, Koli was dead.

With Koli's murder, Arun Gawli was dealt a massive blow. In a short span of time Koli had become Gawli's Man Friday. A shocked and shattered Gawli swore to take revenge and teach the Naik gang a lesson. He instructed Sada Pawle to plan an operation to kill either Amar or Ashwin Naik, or both.

Sada Pawle identified Ravindra Sawant, a new entrant in the Gawli gang, to be part of the operation. Pawle first trained Sawant for a few days on how to operate and fire a weapon. On 18 April 1994, as per plan, Sawant, dressed as an advocate, entered the compound of the Sessions Court in Kala Ghoda, South Mumbai. Under police escort Ashwin Naik would be produced before the court for his hearing in a TADA case. As soon as Naik was brought there, Sawant fired at him and fled. As luck would have it, Ashwin Naik survived the near fatal attack but was left permanently paralysed. Ravindra Sawant was arrested and after a court trial was sentenced to ten years' imprisonment for attempting to kill Ashwin Naik.

Gawli was not happy with the outcome of the operation. To please him, his associate, Bandya Adilkar, shot dead Hamid alias Temba Babu at NM Joshi Marg, near Currey Road. Hamid was a close associate of Amar Naik, instrumental in harbouring his gang members. Even though Hamid's murder was a major blow to Amar Naik and his team, Gawli was not happy. He wanted to kill either Amar Naik or Ashwin

Naik to avenge Tanya Koli's death.

About two months after Hamid's murder, Bandya Adilkar abducted Amar Naik's close associate, Sudhakar Naik. He was brought to the Dagdi Chawl and interrogated, gangster style. Gawli forced him to reveal Amar Naik's whereabouts, but Sudhakar Naik did not give in. Frustrated, Bandya Adilkar took him to a secluded place on NM Joshi Marg near Currey Road and shot him dead.

Unhappy with the way things were going, Gawli continued his pursuit to kill Amar Naik and Ashwin Naik. He decided to go after Amar Naik's finances. Babubhai Shah, owner of Sheetal Departmental Store and a chain of other outlets, was allegedly a top financier of the Naik gang. Shah had also reportedly made a fortune dealing in duplicate foreign liquor. Gawli sent a message to him to stop financing Amar Naik and his gang, but Babubhai Shah did not pay heed to his threats. Following this, Gawli ordered his associate Shekhar Mirashi to take care of Shah.

Mirashi and a few of his men went to the store near Lamington Road. They waited for Babubhai Shah to come out, and the moment he did, they attacked him, stabbing him several times until he was dead.

In retaliation, Amar Naik killed Dhanraj Chowdhary, Arun Gawli's financier.

• The Murder of Pradeep Jain on 7 March 1995

When in 1979 and 1981 the Jain brothers purchased a huge plot of land in the secluded area of Kol-Dongri in Andheri (East), little did they know that the transaction would come to haunt them more than 15 years later in 1994-95.

The four Jain brothers – Ashok, Suresh, Pradeep and Sunil – owned a company called 'Kamla Constructions'. Through this company they had two sets of transactions, one in 1979 and the other in 1981, for two parcels of land in Kol-Dongri, purchased from the Yadav family, the original owners of the property. After conclusion of the sale, the Jain brothers built two multi-storey buildings on one plot of land, while the other was left untouched for future projects.

Everything seemed fine for almost 15 years. In August 1994, things changed. One evening, a man named Shaukat Ali Jamal Mistry, who claimed to be a real estate agent, approached the Jain brothers in their office. He asked them to sell their Kol-Dongri property to another company. What shocked the brothers was that the offer which Mistry gave was ridiculously low. They instantly declined.

Unknown to the Jains, Subedar Singh Ramdas Singh Yadav, a member of the family from whom the brothers had bought the property 1981, had entered into a sale agreement with Labh Constructions, an Ahmedabad-based firm, for a sum of ₹ 10.93 crore to sell the same property. Yadav claimed that he, along with his relative Matbadal Yadav, were joint owners of the property and it was within their rights to sell it. However, there was a problem – while Yadav claimed to have rights to sell the property, it was the Jain brothers who owned it and had rightful possession.

To deal with the standoff, Labh Constructions gave an advance amount of ₹ 3.80 crore; it was decided that the amount would remain with their lawyer, and once Yadav was able to get an agreement signed by Jain brothers to waive their rights over the property, the advance and the remaining amount would be paid.

Yadav and his lawyer, Bharat Chaganlal Raghani, met the Jain brothers to persuade them to sell. Raghani had prepared the property release deed, but it was not agreeable to the Jain brothers. Several meetings were conducted in Raghani's office, during which the lawyer told the Jain brothers that their ownership over the property was untenable and would not stand up to legal scrutiny. Despite tremendous pressure from Raghani and Yadav, the Jain brothers did not yield.

As days went by, Raghani and Yadav became restless and decided to use any means possible to get the Jain brothers to sign the release deed. This was the time they decided to opt for Mistry's services. Even though Mistry was a property broker, he was a member of the dreaded

Dawood Ibrahim gang and a history-sheeter. Soon, Mistry started accompanying Raghani and Yadav for the meetings with the Jains.

During one such meeting, things became ugly; in the heated exchange, Mistry threatened the brothers, saying that they would not leave the office alive if they did not sign the papers. Following this, an argument ensued in Raghani's office. An angry Pradeep Jain said to Raghani, "You are a solicitor of repute, how can you tolerate this *hungama* (altercation) in your office?"

In the same meeting, Mistry threatened the brothers, telling them to accept whatever was being offered to them, cautioning that they stood to lose their lives if they didn't agree.

Mistry had been misbehaving and threatening the Jains ever since he first went to their office in August 1994. During his first visit, Mistry met Ashok Jain and demanded that he hand over the property, as a builder from Ahmedabad had purchased it. When Jain told him that they were the title holders, Mistry retorted that the purchaser had connections with the underworld and the consequences would be severe if they refused to sign the papers.

In October 1994 Ashok, Suresh, Pradeep and Sunil Jain went to Raghani's office and in the presence of Raghani, Rajan Robert Fernandes, Mistry and Yadav showed the papers which clearly mentioned that the Jains were the actual owners of the disputed property. A second meeting was arranged in Raghani's office which was attended by Ashok, Pradeep and Sunil, in the presence of Raghani, Fernandes, Mistry and Yadav. Raghani informed the Jains that their documents did not have substance and lacked credibility.

A third meeting was arranged in Raghani's office in November 1994. Raghani told the brothers that the purchaser had offered to give them money to sign the release deed. The Jains demanded to know the name of the buyer. They were told that he was a big man and did not have the time to meet them.

Reacting to this attitude, Pradeep Jain said that he was not interested in the money and would not sign the release deed. An enraged Mistry said that if he did not take the money, then the same amount would be converted into a *supari* (contract for killing) for the murder of the Jain brothers.

A total of six meetings were conducted in Raghani's office to get the brothers to sign off the property. However, they did not relent and eventually the contract between Yadav and Labh Constructions lapsed and Yadav lost the money.

Fernandes, Mistry and Yadav were in touch with Abu Salem. After the fall out with the Jain brothers, the trio called Salem in Dubai. Salem, who was close to Chhota Shakeel, wanted to impress his boss and make a name for himself in the crime world, so he decided to take on the job of forcing the Jain brothers to hand over the property for money and make a name for himself.

In the second week of February 1995, at around 10 p.m., the landline phone at Pradeep Jain's house rang. His wife Jyoti picked up and the person on the other end identified himself as Abu Salem; he said he wanted to speak to Pradeep Jain. Jyoti handed the phone to Pradeep. She saw his face change colour almost instantly – it was obvious her husband was anxious and worried as he spoke. She heard Pradeep tell Abu Salem that he and his brothers were legal occupants of the property and there was no question of them being removed. Pradeep spoke in a stern but firm voice and asked Salem to mind his own business and not to bother him anymore.

When Pradeep Jain disconnected the phone, Jyoti saw that he was worried and asked about the phone call. Pradeep told her that it was Abu Salem on the phone. He had called from Dubai and told him to sign the documents kept ready in Raghani's office. If he didn't, Pradeep should be ready to face the consequences.

In Dubai, Salem was in a rage – more than being told that the deal would not happen, he was livid about the way Pradeep Jain had dismissed him and spoken to him rudely. An angry Salem decided to teach Pradeep Jain a lesson and immediately called his cronies in Mumbai. His main henchmen in Mumbai were Udai Pawar and Rajesh Igwe. Pawar was a close aide of Salem and Anees Ibrahim. He was being paid a weekly salary of ₹ 500-700 by Salem and would get an additional ₹ 5,000-10,000 after every shooting he undertook on Salem and Ibrahim's orders. Pawar knew how to handle firearms like revolvers, pistols and more after his stint with the army attachment of the National Cadet Corps (NCC).

After he spoke to Abu Salem, Igwe told Pawar that Salem had ordered them to kill Pradeep Jain. Salem instructed Igwe and Nair to stand in front of Mithibai College; at a pre-decided time, someone would approach them and show them Pradeep Jain's house.

Udai Pawar got in touch with a few other gang members – Subhash Bind, Shekhar Kadam, Salim Abdul Salim and Sanjay Kadam. They were told that Pradeep Jain was causing obstructions in a land deal, while two brothers were ready to agree. Also, when 'Bhai' (Abu Salem) had spoken to Jain over the phone, the latter was very rude to him, following which Salem was enraged and decided to kill Jain.

After keeping watch on Pradeep Jain and his movements at his residence and office, Igwe decided to carry out the hit. On 7 March 1995, at around 8-8.15 p.m., Mistry called the office of Kamla Constructions. Sunil Jain answered the phone and Mistry asked who was present in the office. Sunil replied that Pradeep Jain and Anil Kumar Pillai were there. Mistry then asked Sunil if everything was alright. Sunil noted that Mistry was being exceedingly polite that day.

Meanwhile, Subhash Bind, Rajesh Igwe, Sunil Nair, Udai Pawar, Shekhar Kadam and Sanjay Kadam assembled near Nair's house in Andheri (West) around the same time. Sunil Nair had a .38 revolver, Shekhar Kadam had a small 7.65 bore pistol, Udai Pawar a .32 bore small pistol, Subhash Bind brought a 9mm revolver and a .38 bore revolver in a plastic bag. A 9mm pistol was with Igwe and a .38 bore revolver was handled by Nair. All the weapons were loaded with live cartridges. After distributing the weapons, the shooters travelled by BEST bus no. 252 to the house of Pradeep Jain. They stood at a distance from the residence and kept watch.

At about 8 p.m.-8.15 p.m., the watchman of Pradeep Jain's bungalow came out with the children. As he was going back into the bungalow, Igwe and Nair caught him and dragged him inside. While this was happening, Kadam and Pawar closed the bungalow gates. Igwe and Kadam entered the bungalow holding the watchman by the collar, while Bind stood outside the door to keep watch.

Still holding the watchman's collar, Igwe and Kadam entered the office and asked, 'Who is Pradeep?'. Without realising what was happening, Pradeep Jain responded and identified himself. In the next instance, before he could bat an eyelid, Igwe and Kadam fired a hail of bullets at him. They continued to shoot till their firearms were empty. Leaving Pradeep in a pool of blood, the shooters ran out. In the firing, Sunil Jain had been hit and was lying injured on the floor.

Bind, who had been standing guard at the entrance gate, heard firing from inside the office. Within a few minutes he saw Igwe, Nair and Kadam running out. Bind immediately opened the gates and all of them fled, leaving Pradeep dead and Sunil Jain seriously injured.

Others in the office immediately rushed the Jain brothers to nearby Cooper Hospital. However, the doctors on duty realised that Pradeep Jain had succumbed to his injuries long before he was brought in. Sunil was rushed into surgery.

The post-mortem report said that Pradeep Jain had sustained 29 bullet wounds. It was a daring murder and made Salem a name to reckon with almost overnight in the underworld.

The blatant way in which the killing was carried out sent shockwaves through Mumbai. It put immense pressure on the Mumbai Police, which was already stressed because of the increasing underworld menace in the city. The Mumbai Police and its elite Crime Branch immediately got into action and investigation started on a massive scale.

Based on information from Pradeep Jain's family and brothers, the police started questioning Raghani, Yadav, Fernandes and Mistry. Soon it was revealed that Mistry had contacted Abu Salem in Dubai. And it was Salem who had planned the entire operation. Investigations also revealed that Salem, along with Anees Ibrahim, Riyaz Siddiqui, Mehendi Hassan Shaikh and Naeem Khan had planned everything in Dubai.

The police got into action and soon arrested Bind and his associate, who confessed in a statement recorded by a Deputy Commissioner of Police (DCP)-level police officer on 21 August 1995 and 28 August 1995 under the TADA Act.

In his statement, Bind revealed details of how the assassination had taken place and the whole conspiracy.

The police named the following as accused in the case:

- Bharat Chaganlal Raghani
- Rajan Robert Fernandes
- Subedar Singh Ramdas Singh Yadav
- Shaukat Ali Jamal Mistry aka Chauhan
- Subhash Bind
- Shekhar Kadam
- Salim Abdul Salim
- Abu Salem
- Anees Ibrahim
- Rajesh Igwe
- Sunil Nair
- Udai Pawar
- Sanjay Kadam
- Riyaz Siddiqui
- Mehendi Hassan
- Virendra Kumar Jhamb
- Naeem Khan

Raghani, Yadav, and Fernandes were arrested, while the others were absconding and shown as 'wanted'.

While the Mumbai Police continued to search for the accused in the case, their investigations led them to track Mistry, Salim, Igwe, Pawar and Kadam. The police managed to locate them individually. However, all of them resisted arrest and were shot dead in separate police operations in 1995 and 1996.

When the Mumbai Police finally filed its charge sheet, Abu Salem,

Mehendi Hasan, Naeem Khan, Anees Ibrahim, and Riyaz Siddiqui were shown as absconding and wanted.

After having gone through the special TADA court and the Bombay High Court, the case reached the Supreme Court, where the apex court gave its final verdict. In the verdict, the court said that it was satisfied that there was no established connection between Raghani, Fernandes, Mistry, Yadav and the killers and planners, hence they could not be said to have been involved in the conspiracy and murder of Pradeep Jain.

The SC in its judgement further mentioned that the cause of murder as disclosed in the confessional statements, was the refusal of Pradeep Jain to part with the property and talking rudely to Salem. It cannot be said beyond reasonable doubt that the four accused (Raghani, Fernandes, Mistry and Yadav) were party to the crime. Thus, Raghani and Fernandes were acquitted.

The SC, however, found Yadav guilty of extortion and sentenced him to two years' rigorous imprisonment and a fine of ₹ 5,000. Bind and Kadam were found guilty of murder and sentenced to life imprisonment.

Meanwhile, on 18 September 2002, Abu Salem and actress Monica Bedi were arrested in Portugal, extradited and brought to India in 2005. The extradition was granted for Salem in respect of the Pradeep Jain murder case, the Bombay serial bomb blasts case and the Ajit Diwani murder case. Salem was charged along with Mohd Naeem Abdul Rahim Khan, Riyaz Ahmed Siddique, Mohd Hassan Mehendi Hassan and Virendra Kumar Biharilal Jhamb, for conspiring in Dubai to murder Pradeep Jain and that in pursuance of this conspiracy, Pradeep Jain was murdered on 7 March 1995.

The case was tried in the special TADA court and in February 2015, the court found Abu Salem guilty and convicted him. After the conviction Special Public Prosecutor Ujjwal Nikam said that it was probably for the first time that a conspirator (Salem) who hatched a criminal conspiracy outside India for an act committed in India had been found guilty and convicted on the charge of murder.

Special TADA Judge G.A. Sanap in his judgement said that the Mumbai Police had proved beyond reasonable doubt that the conspiracy to kill Pradeep Jain was hatched in Dubai by Salem, Khan, Hassan and Anees Ibrahim to pressure and force the Jain brothers to give away their property at a throwaway price.

Abu Salem is currently in Taloja Jail serving his sentence in the Pradeep Jain murder case; he is also an undertrial in several cases registered against him in Mumbai, Maharashtra and other states of India.

• The Murder of Dr. Datta Samant on 16 January 1997

Perhaps it was coincidence or premonition, but when two days before his murder, high profile union leader Dr. Datta Samant claimed that he was going to die an unsung hero, little did he or anyone know that death was looming just a couple of days away. Exactly two days later, on 16 January 1997, Dr. Samant was brutally murdered outside his house in Powai by four assailants belonging to the Chhota Rajan gang.

Even though he was not connected to the Mumbai underworld, Dr. Datta Samant had an uncanny connection to it. In 1982-83, Dr. Samant led one of the biggest and longest stand-offs between the mill workers' union and the mill owners in the form of a strike, which lasted for several days and months. The strike resulted in thousands of mill workers losing their jobs and eventually leading to suffering for them and for their families.

Several mill workers and their children entered the crime world out of desperation to make ends meet and to earn some money for their families. Otherwise, they were in fear of dying of hunger. Several prominent gangsters such as Arun Gawli, Suresh Manchekar, and Amar Naik took to crime because they had lost their jobs in mills and had no other means of supporting their families.

Dr. Dattatraya Narayan Samant, popularly known as Dr. Datta Samant, a well-known trade union leader, was assassinated on near his house, while he was travelling in his Tata Sumo SUV driven by his driver Bhimrao Sonkamble.

Dr. Samant resided in a bungalow named 'Sundar Narayan Niwas' at Padmavati Road, near IIT Powai, Mumbai. On the fateful day, he came out of his bungalow to go to his office at around 11.10 a.m. and sat in his SUV bearing registration number MH-03-H-2814.

As the SUV travelled a few hundred metres from Dr. Samant's bungalow, an unknown person riding a bicycle ambushed the SUV and threw his bicycle in front of the SUV, forcing the driver to screech to a sudden halt. Within moments four individuals, including the bicycle rider, surrounded the SUV and started indiscriminate firing at the SUV, targeting Dr. Samant in particular. They fired a volley of bullets and fled from the spot.

The driver, Sonkamble was also hit and injured. In the mêlée, when he looked back at Dr. Samant, he saw his body riddled with bullets and lying in a pool of blood in the back seat of the SUV.

A severely injured Sonkamble managed to get out of the car and started running towards Dr. Samant's bungalow, but he was injured so badly that he fell unconscious in the middle of the road.

Hearing the shots and the commotion that followed, Dr. Samant's son, Bhushan, rushed out of the bungalow. Realising what was wrong, he ran towards the SUV, got into the driver's seat and rushed the injured Dr. Samant to the nearby Aniket Nursing Home for medical assistance. The injured Sonkamble was rushed to the Rajawadi Hospital by passers-by.

Dr. Samant was declared dead on arrival at the hospital by the doctors. Dr. Samant had sustained as many as 11 bullet wounds. The daring daylight killing of Dr. Samant sent shockwaves across the city and the Mumbai Police and Crime Branch almost immediately got down to investigating the case. It was going to be a high-profile investigation and the police knew their task was cut out from the start.

Police teams stormed the length and breadth of the country to nab the killers. After almost six days, the police tasted success when they arrested Arun Ananda Londhe and Vijay Ramchandra Thopate from Kolhapur.

The duo was holed up in room no. 312 of Hotel Ayodhya situated on the Kawala Naka in Kolhapur. At the time of the arrest, Londhe was found to be in possession of a 9mm imported pistol while Thopate was in possession of a German-made 7.65mm automatic pistol.

Over the course of investigations, a total of nine accused were arrested and chargesheeted. Chhota Rajan, Guru Satam and Bharat Nepali were shown as wanted accused and absconding.

Investigations revealed that Dr. Samant was targeted on account of union rivalry in Premier Automobiles Limited in Kurla. Bharat Nepali had planned and masterminded the entire conspiracy of killing Dr. Samant and had been given the *supari* by Chhota Rajan and Guru Satam. A total of 16 people were named as accused in the case.

Almost three years after the incident, the Sessions Court in Mumbai gave its judgement in the case on 25 July 2000. The court convicted four shooters, while others were declared absconders.

◆◆◆◆◆◆

Chapter 9

THE JUSTICE AGUIAR COMMISSION REPORT

In the early to mid-1990s, the underworld was at its peak in Mumbai. Especially after the 1993 serial bomb blasts which ripped through the city, the underworld was running amok, causing havoc.

Every day there was a shootout or a bloodied fight on the streets due to inter-gang rivalry. Dawood Ibrahim and Chhota Rajan, who were once a formidable team, split after the blasts and had become staunch enemies. They targeted each other's gangs and those associated with them.

Mumbaikars were weary of living in constant fear of the underworld and looked to the police to do something about it. The Mumbai Police had become aggressive against the underworld after the terror attack masterminded by Dawood in 1993, which killed more than 257 innocent Mumbaikars and injured over 700.

Between 1993 and 1997 the Mumbai Police had killed several underworld gangsters in encounters. After a few such incidences, the underworld realised that if this style of the Mumbai Police continued, it would be difficult for them to operate in the city, since no one would want to be part of the gangs for fear of being killed in an encounter.

Among the most high-profile police operations conducted during those days were the killings of Manya Surve and Maya Dolas, in separate incidents in Wadala and Lokhandwala respectively.

The underworld tried to sway public opinion against the Mumbai Police and their encounters through the media and their cronies in the political world to criticise how encounters were being done. They wanted to show people – especially the judiciary – that the police were behaving like extra-judicial authorities and giving capital punishments to gangsters without a fair trial. Initially, this did not receive much support from the citizens or the judiciary. However, as the number of encounters grew, the way they were conducted started raising a few eyebrows.

The underworld and the anti-police forces got their chance when, on 28 August 1997, the Mumbai Police claimed to have killed a gangster by the name of Javed Abu Talib Shaikh alias Javed Fawda. However, it was alleged that the person killed was not a gangster, but a peanut vendor named Abu Sayama. This operation was conducted by a team of police officers led by Police Inspector (PI) Vasant Dhoble. This was the first time that serious allegations were made against the Mumbai Police that the encounter was fake and that the person who was killed was an innocent person and not a gangster or a criminal.

A month later, on 26 September 1997, another sensational dual encounter took place at Rajawadi junction, Ghatkopar (East), in which high profile gangsters Sada Pawle and Vijay Tandel, both belonging to the Arun Gawli gang, where killed. This operation was conducted by a team of police officers led by then Assistant Police Inspector (API) Vijay Salaskar.

Vijay Salaskar was killed while on duty during the 26/11 terror attacks. He was driving the police vehicle in which then Chief of the Maharashtra Anti-Terrorism Squad (ATS) Hemant Karkare, Additional Commissioner of Police Ashok Kamte and six other policemen were travelling. Their vehicle was attacked

by Mohammad Ajmal Kasab and his partner Abu Ismail in the Rang Bhavan Lane, next to St. Xavier's College. The officers were caught unawares and were hit by a hail of bullets fired by Kasab and Ismail from their AK-47 assault rifles.

Vijay Salaskar, Hemant Karkare, Ashok Kamte and five other policemen were killed in the attack in the Rang Bhavan Lane.

The Javed Fawda encounter had already created quite a stir, so when the double encounter followed, some human rights activists decided to approach the Bombay High Court to act against the Mumbai Police.

Non-governmental organisations (NGOs) like the People's Union for Civil Liberties (PUCL), the Committee for Protection of Democratic Rights (CPDR) led by civil rights lawyer P.A. Sebastian, advocates Lalit Chari and Majeed Memon, and Samajwadi Party (SP) leader Abu Asim Azmi petitioned the Bombay High Court via separate petitions to order an investigation into the encounters and to find out if these were genuine cases of retaliatory shootouts in self-defence as was being claimed, or targeted extra-judicial killings by the police.

Samajwadi Party leader Abu Asim Azmi was arrested for his alleged role in the 1993 serial bomb blasts in Mumbai. It was alleged that he had been part of the plan to send 40 youngsters from India to Pakistan for terror training.

Azmi moved the Supreme Court (SC) against his arrest and allegations. The SC cleared him of all charges and discharged him from his role in the 1993 serial bomb blasts in Mumbai.

Azmi filed only one petition regarding the encounter of Jawed Fawda, claiming that the man killed was not a gangster but a peanut vendor called Abu Sayama. The NGOs filed petitions against all encounters conducted by the Mumbai Police over the previous couple of years.

The Bombay High Court held a joint hearing of all three petitions. Based on the submissions made by the petitioners as well as the

Mumbai Police, the court concluded that the evidence presented by the petitioners' prima facie indicated a disturbing pattern in the encounters and should be investigated.

The High Court handed over the responsibility of inquiry to the then Principal Judge of the Bombay City Civil and Sessions Court, Justice A.S. Aguiar. Justice Aguiar later became a judge in the Bombay High Court.

The inquiry was carried out in February and March 1998. For two months non-stop, Justice Aguiar heard evidence and witnesses put forth by the petitioners, and the defence by the Mumbai Police. After finishing the inquiry, Justice Aguiar submitted his report to the Bombay High Court in July.

The report was made public in September 1998. To the utter shock of the Mumbai Police, Justice Aguiar concluded that as many as 99 encounters were fake. He also stated that the encounter of Javed Fawda may not even have taken place – the reason for this was that the petitioners claimed that it was a case of mistaken identity since there were two individuals with the same name, while the Mumbai Police in its defence stood firm on the ground that it was not a case of mistaken identity and they had indeed killed Fawda.

Findings of the Justice Aguiar Commission:

- **In the Javed Fawda case, Justice Aguiar concluded his findings, stating that the deceased Javed Fawda aka Abu Savama aka Javed Abu Talib Shaikh, was not killed in the encounter as claimed by the police. It is doubtful whether any such encounter took place.**
- **Whereas, in the Sada Pawale and Vijay Tandel case, Justice Aguiar stated in his concluding remarks that the encounter in which Sada Pawale and Vijay Tandel were killed, cannot be said to be a genuine encounter.**

The Justice Aguiar Commission Report shook the rank and file of the Mumbai and Maharashtra police. The Mumbai Police was already fighting a losing battle with the underworld and, as if struck by lightning, all the counterattack operations that had begun to effectively quell crime in the city, came to a standstill.

The Maharashtra government and the Mumbai Police almost immediately decided to challenge Justice Aguiar's report to a higher bench in the Bombay High Court.

The underworld rejoiced – it had got a reprieve and was again free to wreak havoc in the city. A reign of terror like never before was unleashed. In fact, statistics of the year 1998 show that as many as 101 people were killed by the underworld, an average of one gang-related killing of an innocent person every three days in Mumbai.

In the middle of this mayhem, I was posted as Joint Commissioner of Police (Jt. CP) in Mumbai and made Chief of the Mumbai Crime Branch on 29 June 1998. It was much later that I learned that a team comprising the then Additional Chief Secretary (Home) P. Subramaniam, then DGP (Maharashtra) Arvind Inamdar, and Mumbai Police Commissioner R.H. Mendonca had studied my career and track record and selected me to lead the Mumbai Crime Branch in its war against the underworld.

My solid work in my earlier postings in the Special Branch for four years helped me. During that tenure I did exceptionally well. After that I was posted with the Intelligence Bureau (IB), where I spent six years honing my skills in intelligence gathering and carrying out sensitive operations. Thereafter, I was posted as Additional Commissioner of Police in Mumbai for three years. This stint helped me understand the city, its demographics, its culture and its people. Subsequently, I was posted in the Naxalite area of Maharashtra, where I conducted anti-naxal operations.

These sensitive and important postings and the experience gathered through them helped me immensely in my strategies in the fight against the underworld.

I took over the reins of the elite Crime Branch at a time when its morale had hit rock-bottom, and it was battling for survival. The city of Mumbai was on tenterhooks. There was mayhem; businessmen, industrialists and Bollywood luminaries were being targeted almost daily. Mumbai had become like a modern-day war zone.

To make matters worse, on the day I took charge as chief of the Crime Branch, two shoot-outs occurred in the city. Some media published news reports saying that the underworld was welcoming the new chief of the Mumbai Crime Branch!

When in September 1998 the Justice Aguiar Commission Report was made public, the image of the Mumbai Police, especially the Crime Branch took a beating. We were once again pushed back into a black hole. The public perception about us had changed and the confidence of the people was shaken. It was going to be an uphill task to claw ourselves out of the hole. As chief and leader of the team, I realised it would need to start with me; I would have to lead from the front.

I decided to take matters in hand. I held multiple meetings with the entire police force of the Mumbai Crime Branch and assured them that I would personally back each one of them in all their cases, but they should continue the quest of taking the underworld head-on, without any fear or favour.

To boost morale and confidence and to send a message that they had their chief's backing, I told them that they were free to add my name to any FIR. The idea behind this was that my team would know they had my total support and in case something went wrong, my name would be in the FIR, so I too would face the consequences.

It was a confidence-boosting measure. Thus, slowly and surely, I started the work of strengthening the organisation. I also assured them that we would fight and win the court case against encounters which had broken the morale of the police force.

Immediately after the report was made public, the Mumbai Police decided to appeal to the higher bench of the Bombay High Court against the report.

A division bench of Justice Ranjana Desai and Justice Arumugam was constituted for our appeal. The Mumbai Police engaged the services of senior advocate V.R. Manohar to defend them. I stuck my neck out and promised my team that I would win this case for them.

Such was the seriousness of the case that Police Commissioner Mendonca and Director General of Police (DGP) Arvind Inamdar were personally monitoring the developments of the case on a day-to-day basis. V.R. Manohar, a towering legal luminary, had agreed to defend Mumbai Police pro bono (free of cost). His presence gave the police much needed confidence.

During the hearing, Advocate Manohar's legal acumen was on display. It was due to his sheer brilliance that the Mumbai Police was exonerated, and the Justice Aguiar Commission report was set aside by the Bombay High Court. While giving the judgement, Justice Ranjana Desai gave a set of guidelines to the police to follow in the event that an encounter took place.

Following are the guidelines set by Justice Ranjana Desai:

1. **Whenever the police receive intelligence or a tip off about the criminal movements and activities pertaining to the commission of grave crime, it shall be entered into a case diary and then be pursued further in accordance with the procedural law.**
2. **After any encounter operation is over and persons are killed or injured and the same is reported either orally or in writing to the police in furtherance of section 154 of the Criminal Procedure Code (CrPC), it shall be registered in the Crime Register of that particular police station and that further the said First Information Report (FIR) along with copies to the higher officials and the Court in original shall be sent immediately without any delay whatsoever through proper channel so as to reach the Court without any delay at all. A report, as enjoined under section 157(1) of the CrPC, shall also be followed necessarily by the concerned police station.**
3. **After setting the law in motion by registering the FIR in the Crime Register by the concerned police officer of the particular police station, the investigating staff of the police shall take such steps by deputing the man or men**

to get the scene of crime guarded so as to avoid obliterating or disfiguring the existing physical features of the scene of occurrence or the operation encounter. This guarding of the scene of occurrence shall continue till the inspection of occurrence takes place by the investigation staff of the police and preparation of spot Panchanama and the recovery Panchanama.

4. **The police officer who takes part in the operation encounter or the investigating officer of the concerned police station, shall take all necessary efforts and make arrangements to preserve fingerprints of the criminals or the dreaded gangsters, of the weapons, of who handled immediately after the said criminal was brought down to the ground and incapacitated, and that the said fingerprints, if properly taken and preserved, must be sent to the Chemical Analyser for comparison of the fingerprints of the dead body to be taken.**
5. **The materials which are found on the scene of occurrence or the operation encounter and such of the materials including the blood-stained earth and blood-stained materials and the sample earth and other moveable physical features, shall also be recovered by the investigating staff under the cover of recovery Panchanama attested by independent witnesses.**
6. **To fix the exact date and actual place of occurrence in which operation encounter has taken place, a rough sketch regarding the topography of the existing physical features of the said place shall be drawn by the police or the investigating staff of the police either by themselves or with the help of the staff of the Survey Department even while the spot Panchanama is prepared.**
7. **The inquest examination shall be conducted by the investigating staff of the police on the spot itself without any delay, and statements of the inquest witness are to be**

recorded under section 161 of the Code of Criminal Procedure. The inquest Panchanama shall also be sent along with the above case record prepared along with the FIR without any delay whatsoever to the Court.

8. **If the criminals injured during the operation encounter are found alive, not only should they be provided medical aid immediately but also arrangements and attempts shall be made by the police to record their statements under section 164 of the Criminal Procedure Code either by a Magistrate, if possible, and if not, by the Medical Officer concerned, duly attested by the hospital staff mentioning the time and factum that while recording such statements the injured were in a state or position that they were able to give statements, and the connected certificates by the doctors appended thereto.**
9. **After the examination of further witnesses and completing the investigation inclusive of securing the accused or accused persons, the concerned police is directed to send final report to the Court of competent jurisdiction as required under section 173 of the Criminal Procedure Code for further proceedings.**
10. **Either in sending the First Information Report or sending with the general diary entry referred in the guideline nos. 1 and 2, the concerned police shall avoid any iota of delay under any circumstances whatsoever so also rough sketch showing the topography of the scene and the recovery of the materials and the blood stained materials with the sample earth and the blood stained earth with the other documents viz, the spot Panchanama, recovery Panchanama – all seems very vital documents – the respondents-police are also directed to send them to the Court of concerned jurisdiction without any delay.**

It was a huge win and a morale booster for the Mumbai Police. In later years the case went in appeal to the Supreme Court, with the Maharashtra government engaging the services of senior counsel and another legal luminary, Harish Salve, to represent it. Salve also agreed to defend the Mumbai Police in the Supreme Court pro bono.

In 2014, more than 16 years later, we won the case in the Supreme Court when Honourable Supreme Court Judges R.M. Lodha and R.F. Nariman, J.J., in their judgement (2014, AIR SCW 5940 dated 23 September 2014) upheld the Bombay High Court's order.

◆◆◆◆◆◆

Chapter 10

THE MULTI-PRONGED ATTACK BY THE MUMBAI POLICE

In its fight against the Mumbai underworld, the Mumbai Police had faced many setbacks. From bootleggers and *matka* operators in the 1950s and 1960s to smugglers in 1970s and the dreaded underworld in the 1980s and 1990s, the most serious setback of all had to be the Justice Aguiar Commission Report.

Made public in September 1998, the Aguiar Commission Report had tarnished the reputation of the Mumbai Police. The efforts of the Mumbai Police had quite clearly not been effective in restraining the monster called the Mumbai underworld, which had now become a bane for the authorities.

Even ordinary citizens were getting weary and increasingly frustrated with the police's inability to control the underworld. The credibility of the police force had taken a massive beating, and I had to think quickly and come up with multiple strategies, including the *Brahmastra*, to tackle the underworld.

Happiest with this development was the underworld. Encounters stopped, the gangsters once again had a free run to target innocent citizens for money and commit various other violent crimes. After the controversy of fake or staged encounters erupted in August and September 1997, such action had stopped. A year and a half later, by end of 1998, the number of shootouts by gangsters had created a record, with more than 100 people killed in various acts of gun violence by the underworld. It was clear that the villains were running amok, and the Mumbai Police was perceived as helpless.

The situation in the city reached a nadir when, in a span of just 15 days, three businessmen were killed in separate incidents. The underworld had targeted them for refusing to pay extortion money.

<table>
<tr><th colspan="6">EXTORTION CASES</th></tr>
<tr><th>Year</th><th>Total cases</th><th>Detentions</th><th>YEAR</th><th>TOTAL CASES</th><th>DETENTIONS</th></tr>
<tr><td rowspan="3">1998</td><td rowspan="3">341</td><td rowspan="3">365</td><td>2002</td><td>175</td><td>281</td></tr>
<tr><td>2003</td><td>142</td><td>165</td></tr>
<tr><td>2004</td><td>190</td><td>137</td></tr>
<tr><td rowspan="3">1999</td><td rowspan="3">297</td><td rowspan="3">638</td><td>2005</td><td>210</td><td>169</td></tr>
<tr><td>2006</td><td>197</td><td>186</td></tr>
<tr><td>2007</td><td>128</td><td>151</td></tr>
<tr><td rowspan="3">2000</td><td rowspan="3">309</td><td rowspan="3">242</td><td>2008</td><td>162</td><td>80</td></tr>
<tr><td>2009</td><td>176</td><td>57</td></tr>
<tr><td>2012</td><td>81</td><td>270</td></tr>
<tr><td rowspan="2">2001</td><td rowspan="2">282</td><td rowspan="2">406</td><td>2013</td><td>86</td><td>343</td></tr>
<tr><td>2014 (JAN)</td><td>74</td><td>39</td></tr>
</table>

Such was the state of fear and anxiety in the city that the business community had called for a 'Black Diwali' that year (1998) and threatened to not celebrate the festival if the police and the government did not do anything to stop the menace. At a meeting organised at the Birla Krida Kendra near Girgaon Chowpatty, more than 800 angry and upset businessmen and traders of Mumbai had gathered.

They expressed their anger and resentment to the then Chief Minister Manohar Joshi, then Deputy Chief Minister Gopinath Munde, Police Commissioner R.H. Mendonca and me (representing the Mumbai Crime Branch). Even though I had worked in Mumbai during an earlier stint as Additional Police Commissioner from 1993-1995, I was only recently posted back in Mumbai as chief of the Crime Branch and was still finding my feet. I found myself sitting on the stage with the CM, Dy CM and Mumbai CP, facing the wrath of angry Mumbaikars.

During the meeting, the Chief Minister and Deputy Chief Minister assured the community that concrete steps would be taken to rein in the underworld. After the meeting, the Chief Minister spoke to the Police Commissioner and directed him to do whatever was needed to tackle the issue.

The situation in Mumbai had touched such a low point that it couldn't go any lower. Under these circumstances, the responsibility of tackling the underworld and bringing the city back to normalcy was entrusted to me by my superiors and the state government. I knew time was crucial.

The Mumbai Police tasted success when on 14 August 1998, two gangsters – Dindayal Singh and Vijay Mishra – belonging to the Dawood gang were shot dead in a police operation in Borivali. Dindayal was a dreaded criminal from Uttar Pradesh and was wanted in several cases there. In fact, the Lucknow Police had even posted a reward of ₹ 10,000 on him. This operation was the much-needed booster shot the Mumbai Crime Branch needed, and it came at the right time.

Then, in September 1998, the Crime Branch arrested another member of the Dawood gang – his name was Rahul Talukdar, alias Bablu. A resident of Malvani, he was arrested with an AK47 assault rifle and more than 230 bullets; two imported Star pistols were also seized from him. He was given the *supari* to kill a prominent businessman in Chembur during the Ganapati festival that year. His arrest was another major victory for us.

But soon thereafter, there occurred two incidents which stirred me up. One was the daylight murder and shootout of the Kurup Brothers in a hotel in Bhandup (West) on the afternoon of 13 October 1998. The other was when a woman who was interviewed by a news channel said that she woke up every day at 4 a.m. to make lunch for her husband, but was always scared and anxious because she was not sure if he would come back home that day. She spoke in reference to the underworld menace in the city and the fear that had engulfed citizens. That was the tipping point for me, and I decided it was time to respond and retaliate.

I formed a crack team of police officers from the Crime Branch. Among the first things I ideated was to craft a strategy and a concrete plan on how to deal with this seemingly insurmountable task. After several brainstorming sessions with my officers, we decided on a path.

The first step was to devise a multi-pronged attack on the underworld. The strategy was that of a *chakravyuh*, attacking the gangs on all fronts, and from all sides at the same time, trapping them without respite, and snuffing out their existence.

I formed a crack team of police officers from the Crime Branch. Among the first things I ideated was to craft a strategy and a concrete plan on how to deal with this seemingly insurmountable task. After several brainstorming sessions with my officers, we decided on a path.

The first step was to devise a multi-pronged attack on the underworld. The strategy was that of a *chakravyuh*, attacking the gangs on all fronts, and from all sides at the same time, trapping them without respite, and snuffing out their existence.

- **The Multi-pronged Attack Strategy**

Worst Year - 1998				
Incidents of Murders with Firearms				
Year	Total Incidents	Victims Killed	Total Victims killed by gang	Killed by Other Accused
1998	93	101	80	21
Extortions - Gang/Petty Criminals related				
Year	Total Incidents	Total Accused Arrested	Gang Related	Petty Criminals
1998	367	604	314	326
Highlights: 32 Film stars had received extortion threats				

1. Boosting morale

A major aspect that had impacted the smooth functioning of the police force was that the morale of its personnel was at its lowest point. Police officers were demoralised because of the constant threat of legal cases against them.

The Justice Aguiar Commission Report had dealt a massive blow to the drive and zeal of the force and had changed the way they now felt about their work. Hardworking and dedicated police officers were depressed and were refusing to work due to fear that they would be targeted, with cases filed against them. We quickly identified this problem and started taking steps to overcome it.

Shootouts By Criminals

Year	Total Incidents	No of Citizens Killed by Gangs	No of Citizens Killed by Others	Total	No of Citizens Injured
1998	93	74	27	101	15
1999	41	10	38	48	28
2000	24	3	22	25	3
2001	18	11	7	18	0

The direct fallout of the Justice Aguiar Commission report was a huge increase in underworld-led shootouts in the city. Statistics show that 1998 and 1999 were two of the worst years Mumbai had witnessed, with hundreds of people in Mumbai targeted by the underworld for extortion and 149 killed in gang-related shootouts.

It was important to boost the morale of the police force and to instil the fear of law enforcement agencies in the minds of the gangsters.

2. Reviving MPDA

An ingenious strategy I adopted was to revive an already existing law that had been gathering dust. We polished it and honed it into an effective weapon.

The Maharashtra Prevention of Disruptive Activities (MPDA) Act, 1981, was resurrected. Even though the MPDA had been in existence since 1981, it had hardly ever been used effectively, even though it had enough teeth in it to be an effective tool against gangsters and criminals.

What is MPDA? Preventive detention is power given to the Police Commissioner under the law to detain a criminal (with certain criteria, well established in law) for a period of one year. The detained person has a remedy under the law – he can file an appeal to the Home Department against his detention and if that is not heard or resolved, then after another 12 days the person can petition the High Court.

Armed with the MPDA, the Mumbai Police started identifying criminals, gangsters, history-sheeters and anti-social elements, and acting against them. Any gangster who was creating a nuisance was detained under MPDA for a period of one year.

P.C.B. CRIME BRANCH, MUMBAI Year-wise information from 1990 to 2025 (Till 06/05/2025) Total number of persons detained under MPDA ACT 1981		
Sr. No.	**Year**	**Detained Persons**
1	1990	18
2	1991	13
3	1992	23
4	1993	11
5	1994	14
6	1995	08
7	1996	19
8	1997	117
9	1998	358
10	1999	638
11	2000	242
12	2001	408
13	2002	281
14	2003	165

15	2004	137
16	2005	190
17	2006	200
18	2007	150
19	2008	83
20	2009	62
21	2010	34
22	2011	13
23	2012	07
24	2013	11
25	2014	06
26	2015	06
27	2016	07
28	2017	08
29	2018	06
30	2019	30
31	2020	07
32	2021	27
33	2022	05
34	2023	15
35	2024	13
36	2025 (Till 06/05/2025)	01

The effect of this action was directly visible on the ground, as these people were unable to operate in their usual areas. They were in jail and 1,600 man-years were spent behind bars. During the time they were externed, they lost significant clout and respect.

In the first six months (from June 1998 to December 1998) of my tenure as Chief of Mumbai Crime Branch, every day two detentions were carried out. In the six months as many as 365 detentions were carried out only in six months of the second half of 1998. In 1999, the Mumbai Police carried out detention action against as many as 642 criminals. In 2000, there were 446 detentions.

A major hurdle which came in the way of acting under MPDA was that there was voluminous paperwork to be done in respect of each detention. As per the law, documents were to be prepared in the mother tongue of the criminal; this took a lot of time because criminals belonged to various linguistic backgrounds. In a majority of cases the police had to translate hundreds of documents in other languages as required by the law. Under the law it was mandatory for the police to provide the detainee with a copy of all paperwork in his native language.

This Herculean task was given to Police Inspector Arun Chavan, who did yeoman work in getting all the documents done within the framework of the law and ensuring that criminals did not get away due to improper or irregular paperwork. Huge credit goes to Arun Chavan for doggedly getting behind each case and ensuring that the detention was carried out thoroughly.

To encourage police officers to work efficiently, I arranged for all the MPDA officers from all police stations of Mumbai to come to the Mumbai Police Headquarters once in three months and rewarded them for their work. For each successful MPDA case, ₹ 3,000 per case was earmarked and, in some cases, actual expenses incurred per case were reimbursed.

A mammoth body of work was undertaken by the Mumbai Police around the detention of extortionists. This had never been done. This resulted in an immediate decrease in the number of cases. As many as 1,600 criminals were put behind bars; this had a direct result on the ground as the number of crime cases in Mumbai reduced drastically.

3. Need for a new law

An in-depth study revealed that laws like the Prevention of Terrorists and Disruptive Activities (POTA) Act and Terrorists and Disruptive Activities (TADA) Act, which were enacted specifically to keep terrorists and terror activities in check, were not effective.

From 1990-1999, these two laws were often misused across the country and were repealed in due course. However, the Mumbai underworld was largely unaffected by these laws because they were primarily designed to tackle the terrorist menace.

It was clear to us that there was an urgent need for another law to deal specifically with the underworld. Thus, the Maharashtra Control of Organised Crime Act (MCOCA) was enacted in record time and implemented. How this Act became the main weapon of the Mumbai Police's fight against the underworld is explained in detail in the next chapter.

Analysis of MCOCA Cases							
Year	Cases Registered	Gangsters Arrested					
		Dawood gang	Gawli gang	Ashwin Naik gang	Rajan gang	Others	Total
1999	19	33	6	0	13	12	64
2000	14	54	0	0	4	7	65
2001	20	51	0	5	38	11	85

4. Upskilling and training of police officers and team building

I realised that we needed trained and efficient manpower, for which police officers would have to be empowered with specific, new-age skills. Such training was immediately arranged, and officers were given the knowledge and skills they needed to take on the underworld.

Several training modules were designed and implemented on a war footing and several officers were given the requisite training.

A stringent training programme was organised by the Mumbai Police for its officials, in the art of surveillance, shadowing and intelligence gathering. We asked the Intelligence Bureau (IB) in Delhi to organise this and to train our officers. It helped tremendously, because it empowered the officers in gathering intelligence without raising suspicion.

Emphasis was put on team-building, wherein officers with specific skills were given specific tasks and they would help each other in every case. For example, if there was an officer who was good at speaking and writing in English, he would be made the face of the department and he would liaise with other departments, states, etc. on behalf of the entire force.

Multi-Pronged Attack on Mafia Gangs				
Year	1998	1999	2000	2001
Detentions (MPDA)	365	683	242	408
Firearms Seized	535	540	443	471
MCOCA Cases	-	19	14	20

The rank and file of Mumbai Police came together and worked as one unit. Almost every policeman from Mumbai responded to the clarion call of annihilating the cancer called Mumbai underworld. I do wish to name all of them, from the constabulary to the most senior IPS officers. It will however be difficult to name all of them, but it will be remiss on my part if I do not name some of them who did yeomen service for the force, the city and the state.

Deputy Commissioner of Police (DCP) Pradeep Sawant, Assistant Commissioner of Police (ACP) Dashrath Avhad, Police Inspectors Ambadas Pote, D.Y. Patil, Jayant Hargude, Kedar Pawar, Fateh Singh Gaikwad, Prafulla Joshi, Vinod Bhatt, Vilas Tupe, Subhash Salvi, Subhash Jadhav, Arun Chavan, Brendan Bracko, among many others. These officers and several others worked selflessly and tirelessly only with one aim – to annihilate the Mumbai underworld.

5. Get police of other states involved

I realised that it was important to get all the concerned parties and stake holders on the same wavelength for the mission to be successful. Based on our suggestions and requests, Mumbai Crime Branch organised an inter-state Police Commissioners conference. This was done with a view to bring the police of all states on the same platform to exchange information.

Police Commissioners from other states were informed about the importance of their help in tackling the underworld menace. Most of the gangsters involved in shootouts in the city were either from other states or went to hide in other states after committing a crime in Mumbai.

Police officers were sensitised about this, and their help was sought in identifying these gangsters and apprehending them.

An inter-district conference of the senior police officers of Maharashtra was organised in Mumbai by the Police Commissioner. This was done with the intention that the crack team of the Mumbai Crime Branch would personally meet senior officers from various districts of the state. They could interact on a personal basis and build a rapport with each other. This would help them when the team had to travel to various parts of the state in search of gangsters.

The conference also provided an opportunity for senior officers of the Mumbai Police to instil a sense of collective mission and pride among their colleagues in the fight against the underworld. Officers who were not from Mumbai would often not understand the seriousness and sensitivity of a particular operation of the Mumbai Police. This lack of awareness would often cost the police a case or a gangster.

Meeting at a conference also ensured that everyone was on the same page, ensuring that the operation went smoothly.

Underworld gangs and their operations had spread out of Mumbai to other parts of Maharashtra and to states such as Gujarat, Karnataka, Madhya Pradesh, Delhi, Uttar Pradesh, Bihar, West Bengal, Kerala and elsewhere, so there was an urgent need for law enforcement agencies all over the country to come together and fight them.

The then Bangalore Police Commissioner, Mr. Revanasiddaiah, 1965-batch IPS officer, had attended the conference. Mr. P. Kalimatthu, 1972-batch IPS officer from Chennai had also come, among many other senior IPS officers from across the country. This one-to-one interaction and meeting everyone face-to-face was a game-changer in establishing an inter-state camaraderie between police departments of various states. This ensured that whenever there was exchange of any information it was swift, and officials understood the importance of such information and intelligence.

A coordinated approach by the Police, Income-tax, Customs and Central Excise Departments, DRI, the Enforcement Directorate and the Narcotics Control Bureau, under the watchful eyes of a central nodal agency, was the need of the hour.

The inter-agency coordination yielded almost immediate results. On 13 October 1999, I received a tip-off from the then Additional Director General (ADG) of Directorate of Revenue Intelligence (DRI) that there were suspicious persons seen in Khar area who were reportedly dealing in firearms and explosives.

On receiving the information, I promptly launched an operation, and a police team laid a trap at the said location – in the premises of Parmeshwari Bhuvan situated on 14th Road, Khar (West).

At around 18.30 hours an individual walked out of the building in a suspicious manner and went back in again, doing this several times. Police Inspector Fateh Singh Gaikwad, who was there, recognised him as Hanif, a known history-sheeter and arms dealer.

When Hanif came out of the building again, Gaikwad and his team stopped him and questioned him. He gave evasive answers at first, but later confessed that he had illegal firearms in his possession and was waiting for a potential buyer.

When the police team searched him and the premises, they found an imported weapon with live cartridges. When they further questioned Hanif, he said the weapon and ammunition were delivered to him a few days ago concealed in the tyre of a truck. He had hidden the tyre on the terrace of the building he was hiding in.

The police team immediately searched the terrace and raided a small room there. To their utter shock they found two AK-56 assault rifles loaded with 20 live cartridges each. Also, 133 live bullets hidden in another bag, along with seven pistols, each loaded with five live bullets were recovered from another bag.

This was a large arms seizure and considering the fact that the weapons were delivered in Mumbai, we had managed to avert a major incident, arrest the perpetrators and seize the cache of firearms and ammunition.

6. Providing adequate resources and legal protection to police officers

As mentioned earlier, the Justice Aguiar Commission report dealt a heavy blow to the morale of Mumbai Police and its officers. The scathing remarks in the report against police officers and their action during encounters scared the officers. Most of them refused to be part of any police operations against the underworld, out of fear that they may have to face legal action.

A key strategy that I employed on priority was to boost the forces' morale by providing them with resources which would enhance their investigative and intelligence gathering skills. Another aspect I concentrated on was to make the force aware of the laws which were in existence, and to follow them.

Based on past cases, one thing was clear – that police officers were always on the underworld's target list. On 12 September 1992, during the Sir J.J. Hospital shootout incident in which gangster Shailesh Haldankar was targeted and killed by Subhash Singh Thakur, two police constables – Chintaman Gajanan Jaiswal and Kewalsingh Bhanawat – were shot dead.

Similarly, on 6 May 1998, less than two months before I became Chief of the Mumbai Crime Branch, Police Head Constable Bhalchandra Dattatray Kardile was shot dead inside the Sir J.J. Hospital by members of the Dawood Ibrahim gang when they attacked the ward to free gangster Feroz Kokani.

These incidents clearly indicated that policemen were being specifically targeted; this also affected the morale of the force.

The police officers were then educated about section 100 of the Indian Penal Code (IPC) and told that in the event that they were targeted/shot at by underworld gangsters, they should retaliate in self-defence.

What is Section 100 of IPC?

Section 100 of The Indian Penal Code, 1860:

7. **When the right of private defence of the body extends to causing death:**

   The right of private defence of the body extends, under the restrictions mentioned in the last preceding section, to the voluntary causing of death or of any other harm to the assailant, if the offence which occasions the exercise of the right be of any of the descriptions hereinafter enumerated, namely:—

   - **First – Such an assault as may reasonably cause the apprehension that death will otherwise be the consequence of such assault;**
   - **Second – Such an assault as may reasonably cause the apprehension that grievous hurt will otherwise be the consequence of such assault;**
   - **Third – An assault with the intention of committing rape;**
   - **Fourth – An assault with the intention of gratifying unnatural lust;**
   - **Fifth – An assault with the intention of kidnapping or abducting;**
   - **Sixth – An assault with the intention of wrongfully confining a person, under circumstances which may reasonably cause him to apprehend that he will be unable to have recourse to the public authorities for his release;**
   - **Seventh – An act of throwing or administering acid or an attempt to throw or administer acid which may reasonably cause the apprehension that grievous hurt will otherwise be the consequence of such act.**

The officers were also made aware that in the event of a police officer retaliating in self-defence resulting in the death of an assailant, the guidelines set by the Bombay High Court should be followed meticulously to ensure a thorough investigation of the event. (The guidelines set by the Bombay High Court have been mentioned in detail in Chapter 9 on page no. 195.)

This move really helped in boosting the morale of the officers. Slowly and steadily their confidence rose, and they felt ready to fight the underworld.

Police Shootout with Gangsters/Criminals

Year	No of Incidents	Notorious Criminals Killed	Notorious Criminals Injured	Policemen Killed	Policemen Injured
1998	39	48	3	3	10
1999	65	83	1	0	15
2000	59	73	0	0	4
2001	70	94	0	0	1

7. Technical breakthrough – telephone tapping

Personally, I have always believed that the technological breakthrough that we achieved by telephone tapping was a masterstroke.

One day, I walked into the Videsh Sanchar Nigam Limited (VSNL) office situated in Fort area of South Mumbai and met the General Manager (GM). I spoke to the officials there and asked them to put a couple of telephone numbers on surveillance and to tap and record all the conversations that happen on those phone numbers.

During this meeting, while I was understanding how the telephone tapping and surveillance system worked, an idea crossed my mind and asked the VSNL officials, if they have the technology to tap into a mobile number which was registered and functioning out of India.

I realised that VSNL, being a department responsible for *Videsh Sanchar,* would have the technical expertise to do that. Unlike MTNL or BSNL, it would have the technical expertise to put surveillance on phones functioning within the country.

To my utter shock and surprise, they said they could do that. I instantly jumped at the opportunity and gave them Chota Shakeel's numbers to be put on surveillance. Almost like magic, VSNL officials did that effortlessly and within no time, Mumbai Police was listening to all phone calls coming in and going out of Shakeel's phones. And the best part was that Shakeel had no clue we were listening to all his calls.

This was a gold mine for us; an oblivious Shakeel was talking on the phone to all his contacts all over the world. He was doing that in a carefree manner without an iota of suspicion that we were listening to his phone calls.

This went on for a long time. Very soon, with the help of VSNL we got a listening unit installed in the Crime Branch premises and the calls were being monitored round-the-clock. This was exactly how Alan Turing had broken into Adolf Hitler's Enigma Machine codes during the Second World War, without Hitler or any of his team members having the slightest clue about it. It was the pivotal moment in the Second World War which tilted the war in favour of UK and its allies. Hitler and Germany were eventually defeated and the Second World War ended.

Similarly, in this situation, underworld gangs had no idea that their calls were being monitored, and that we were listening to each phone call. Within no time, the Mumbai Crime Branch had managed to tap not just Shakeel's phone, but international phone numbers of almost all gangsters, including Chhota Rajan, Chhota Shakeel, Abu Salem, etc. What the gangsters did not realise was that the extortion victims would provide these numbers to the Crime Branch, and we would summarily put them under surveillance.

This surveillance gave us valuable information and intelligence about all the operations that fugitive gangsters were planning to conduct in Mumbai and other parts of the country. We were able to pre-empt all their moves and take preventive action. It resulted in avoidance of many crimes in the city.

8. Seizure of illegal arms

Another strategy we implemented was to seize as many weapons as possible. The idea was – one weapon less on the ground was one crime less in the city. Such was our aggressive approach to seizure of illegal weapons that in a span of a few months the Mumbai Police had seized more than 2500 illegal weapons from Mumbai City.

This strategy dealt a body blow to all the criminals.

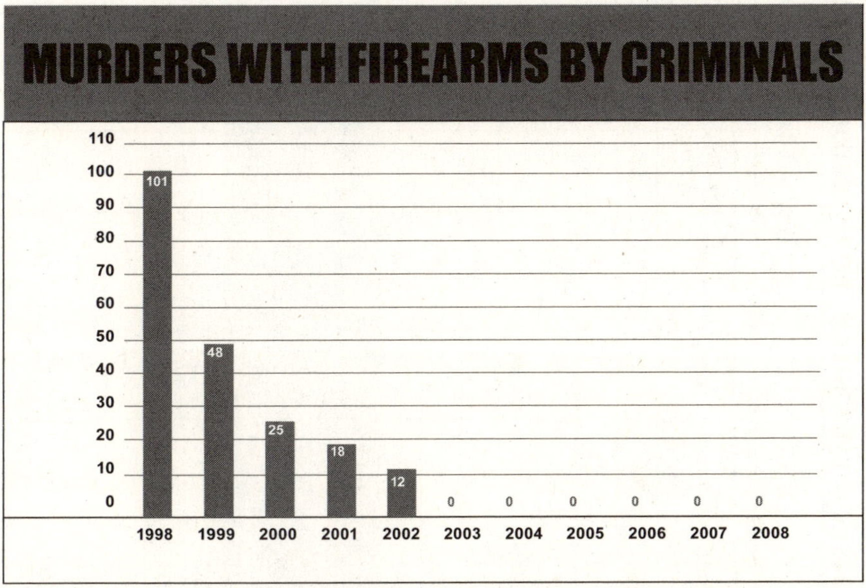

Another aspect I added to the policy was that officers who seized and recovered an illegal weapon were given rewards and certificates; this was major encouragement for the officers, who worked doubly hard to seize as many illegal arms as possible.

Because of all the above-mentioned strategies the murders of businessmen by the mafia gangs came down drastically within three years and from 2002-2025 remained zero. This is the tremendous success achieved by the Mumbai Police. The fear of getting an extortion call or getting a bullet fired vanished for a quarter of a century.

MUMBAI CITY TOTAL FIREARMS RECOVERED 1991-2023													
Sr. No.	Year	Cases Regd.	Persons Arrested	Total Weapons	Weapons Seized 3,25								
					Country made Revolvers	Country made Pistols	Foreing made Revolvers	Foreign made Pistols	Guns/ Rifles	Automatic Weapons (AKR)	Hand Grenades	Rocket Launcher	Cartridges
1	1991	268	268	320	186	40	46	26	10	12	0	0	3708
2	1992	293	293	325	180	55	41	33	10	6	0	0	1655
3	1993	272	380	386	167	51	60	35	14	59	0	0	19587
4	1994	247	308	286	148	44	44	33	10	7	0	0	2543
5	1995	198	251	248	122	31	22	59	12	2	0	0	3586
6	1996	203	256	226	104	47	29	37	4	4	1	0	1679
7	1997	230	328	269	149	27	31	43	9	4	6	0	1165
8	1998	374	531	535	253	35	57	59	8	13	110	0	4994
9	1999	435	653	540	338	44	60	73	5	8	8	4	2506
10	2000	399	585	443	317	15	51	33	15	3	9	0	1468
11	2001	396	541	471	347	20	49	44	11	0	0	0	2290
12	2002	303	391	343	267	13	20	25	14	1	3	0	1247
13	2003	281	340	562	234	21	24	21	6	5	251	0	1340
14	2004	428	577	466	371	30	19	29	17	0	0	0	1970
15	2005	370	530	506	285	32	54	37	98	0	0	0	3302
16	2006	292	413	355	236	39	15	24	27	2	12	0	2170
17	2007	259	375	399	247	80	12	27	26		7	0	1272

MUMBAI CITY TOTAL FIREARMS RECOVERED 1991-2023 (contd. from page 212)

18	2008	205	295	311	198	46	5	22	13	11	6	10	1316
19	2009	273	378	314	220	36	5	12	37	0	4	0	2454
20	2010	214	280	284	179	50	2	11	39	3	0	0	1013
21	2011	208	373	299	161	64	8	9	55	0	0	2	1636
22	2012	144	211	181	116	29	4	5	26	1	0	0	1305
23	2013	150	229	166	75	53	1	9	27	1	0	0	739
24	2014	232	322	271	154	81	3	7	25	1	0	0	739
25	2015	144	250	177	76	78	3	7	13	0	0	0	554
26	2016	120	168	141	64	62	1	12	1	1	0	0	550
2	2017	87	120	93	47	42	0	3	1	0	0	0	347
28	2018	75	140	113	50	52	1	6	4	0	0	0	352
29	2019	178	217	189	117	63	4	4	1	0	0	0	368
30	2020	105	87	87	33	47	2	4	1	0	0	0	255
31	2021	79	125	109	36	71	1	0	1	0	0	0	331
32	2022	61	96	86	13	68	0	4	1	0	0	0	286
33	2023	67	109	75	20	53	0	1	1	0	0	0	138
34	2024	171	278	204	57	132	10	3	2	0	0	0	1597
35	upto April 2025	16	23	29	3	26	0	0	0	0	0	0	86

The Iron Lady

While we were busy strategising and working on the ground taking the underworld head-on, there was one tough soldier who was leading our battle from the front, in court. A special mention needs to be made of Public Prosecutor Rohini Salian.

She fought bravely in court for the Mumbai Crime Branch and won most of the cases for us. She had the challenge of dealing with a brand-new law – MCOCA – which did not have any precedent or case laws to fall back on. She overcame this challenge with aplomb and fought all our cases in an astute manner.

She read and studied the MCOCA law quickly and understood its nuances and legal points. She put all her legal acumen to use and ensured that the majority of our cases resulted in convictions.

◆◆◆◆◆◆

Chapter 11

THE BRAHMASTRA: UNLEASHED

Around 2,400 years ago the cruelty of King Nanda and his family was at its peak. There was great unrest amongst the subjects of the kingdom. Observing all the malicious activities of the king, the great thinker Chanakya (aka Kautilya) took action to dethrone the merciless Nanda dynasty and replace it with a new king: Chandragupta Maurya.

Since it was vital to run the kingdom in the best possible manner, he wrote the *Arthashastra*, which would be helpful to 'acquire' and 'protect' this world and the next. It was a book which educated readers about how to not just create a great kingdom, but to make sure it was a happy one as well.

History repeated itself 2,400 years later. My crack team of Mumbai Police and I sought guidance and inspiration from Kautilya's *Arthashastra* for ways to deal with the underworld. We had realised that in a short span of time, the underworld had become a very serious threat to society. It was ruthless and did not function within any legal or societal boundaries. It was dealing in all kinds of illegalities including narcotics, arms, ammunitions, explosives, etc.

It did not respect national or international boundaries (some of the most dreadful underworld shootouts and operations were conducted outside India. Gangster Sharad Shetty was killed in Dubai, while MP Dilshad Beg was killed in Nepal, and Pillu Khan was killed in Bangkok).

This monster called the Mumbai underworld was fuelled by wealth illegally acquired from innocent people, and procured through various criminal and violent acts like contract killing, extortion, smuggling gold, narcotics, arms and ammunition, kidnapping for ransom, money laundering, match-fixing, land grabbing, etc.

It was estimated that the illegal wealth or black money generated by organised crime syndicates in India was huge. The organised crime mafia was running a parallel economy in our country due to the large amount of illegal money it had acquired.

The underworld had spread its tentacles so far, wide and deep that it was also in cahoots with terrorist organisations and syndicates involved in narco-terrorism, international illegal arms trade, human trafficking, etc. Gangs that had indulged in street fights and petty crimes had become international syndicates operating across several countries and dealing in billions of dollars of illegal wealth, daily.

When all this was assessed and analysed by my team and myself, we realised that this monster would have to be dealt with on a much larger scale. Encounters were not going to scare it anymore, and the existing laws were not loophole-safe to rein it in. Also, whenever a gangster was killed in an encounter, the gangs would simply hire services of a fresh recruit from far-flung and remote villages of Uttar Pradesh, Bihar, West Bengal, etc.

It was clear that law enforcement agencies like the Mumbai Police would require the full backing of the law and need be legally armed to the teeth if this mighty Goliath had to be brought to its knees.

After mammoth sessions of discussion, debate and brainstorming with my team, I prepared a report that was handed over to the authorities. I mentioned that there was an urgent need for a new law that would have to be enacted as soon as possible and enforced against the underworld and organised crime syndicates.

The Government of Maharashtra immediately formed a high-level committee led by then Additional Chief Secretary Karun Shrivastava, Law Secretary from the Law and Judiciary Department Ms. Pratima Umarji, then Additional Director General of Police S.S. Puri, and then Mumbai Police Commissioner R.H. Mendonca.

The committee studied several existing national and international laws. The American and Canadian legal systems had interesting specifications that were similar to our needs and demands. Loopholes and weaknesses of existing and previous laws like TADA and POTA were also studied by the committee.

The team got to work almost immediately and within a year, by the end of 1999, a draft of the new law was ready. It excited the police and its legal department. It was designed to be among the most stringent laws in the country, with tough measures proposed against the underworld and organised crime syndicates. It also had several measures to check and balance the actions of police as well, so that there was no scope for misuse like other laws. It was presented to the Government of Maharashtra.

Full credit goes to the Maharashtra state government – the draft bill of the Act was cleared expeditiously. The central government also cleared the act in a record time of two or three months and, at the start of the new millennium, in the year 2000, a brand-new law was enacted.

It was called the 'Maharashtra Control of Organised Crime Act (MCOCA)'. The Mumbai and Maharashtra police had their newest weapon, one so powerful – like a *Brahmastra* – that the underworld would not know what hit it and would have no counterattack ready.

The basic essence of the law was that it would be very difficult for the police to book a person under MCOCA, but once booked, it would be extremely difficult for the person to come out of it.

Seeing its effect and results, in later years the governments of Delhi and Karnataka adopted MCOCA as it was, verbatim. They even kept the name: MCOCA!

Some of the Act's salient features, which gave a lot of power to the police to act against the underworld, are:

- An individual could now be booked under MCOCA if he/she has been involved in at least three other crimes in the last ten years. The crime should be punishable with imprisonment upto three years. The case should have been charge-sheeted, and the court should have taken cognisance of the charge-sheet.

- If the Investigating Officer (IO) wished to apply MCOCA on a particular case, then the IO must apply to an officer of the rank of Deputy Inspector General (DIG) of Police. The DIG must recommend it, and the Inspector General of Police (IGP) or Joint Commissioner of Police (Jt.CP) must approve it. It has then to be ratified by an officer of the rank of Additional Director General (ADG), with application of his original mind. All these officers are grilled in the court of law during the trial of the MCOCA case. So, they must be extremely careful while suggesting implementation of MCOCA to a case. This would help to keep a check-and-balance and ensure that the law is not misused.

- MCOCA made it very difficult for an accused to get bail. This became the biggest deterrent for the underworld. It scared the gangsters, because before this they had never feared the law since they could get bail easily. MCOCA ensured that they didn't get bail.

- Confession by a criminal before a police officer (not below the rank of a DCP) was admitted as evidence. No other police law allows this. That is why this is a unique law.

- Under MCOCA, the IO was to be a police officer not below the rank of an Assistant Commissioner of Police (ACP) or Deputy Superintendent of Police (Dy SP).

- The law gave special powers to the police to take more time to file a charge-sheet. Under existing laws, the mandate was to file a charge-sheet within 90 days of the day of offence or registration of the First Information Report (FIR). The new law proposed to give the police 180 days to file the charge-sheet.

- Under the new law, a co-accused's statement or confession could be used as evidence against an accused.

- Evidence like fingerprints, saliva or handprints on firearms was made admissible as evidence under MCOCA. The police now had powers to make various presumptions based on this evidence and take necessary action.

The Preamble of the Act States:

"To make special provisions for prevention and control of, and for coping with, criminal activity by organized crime syndicate or gang, and for matters connected therewith or incidental thereto.

WHEREAS it was expedient to make special provisions for prevention and control of, and for coping with, criminal activity by organized crime syndicate or gang and for matters connected therewith or incidental thereto.

AND WHEREAS, the Governor of Maharashtra was satisfied that circumstances existed which rendered it necessary for him to take immediate action to make law, for the purposes aforesaid."

Once the MCOCA was effective, all necessary steps and measures were taken to implement it in the state of Maharashtra, keeping Mumbai in mind.

◆◆◆◆◆◆

Chapter 12

MCOCA'S FIRST SALVO SENDS THE UNDERWORLD REELING

The first crime registered under the MCOCA was the attempt to murder Milind Vaidya, the ex-Mayor of Mumbai city. Three others were killed in the attempt. The trial was successfully completed within a year. Three criminals were sentenced to death; seven others got life imprisonment and a collective fine of ₹ 1,01,00,000 was collected. This quick trial and enhanced punishment sent shivers down the spine of the organised crime sector.

- **The Milind Vaidya Firing Case**

In the annals of the history of Mumbai Police and its fight against the Mumbai underworld, 4 March 1999, is a landmark day and date. It proved to be a tipping point for the infamous Mumbai criminal gangs and their nefarious activities. By the time that day had ended, a countdown to its eventual elimination from the streets of Mumbai had begun.

The events that unfolded with the demolition of the Babri Masjid in December 1992, followed by the communal riots in Mumbai at the end of 1992 and beginning of 1993, assumed demonic proportions with the serial bomb blasts in the city.

It also changed the approach of the Mumbai Police in the fight against the underworld. Investigations revealed that Pakistan-based fugitive Dawood Ibrahim Kaskar, along with gangster and smuggler Tiger Memon and the ISI, had planned and executed the blasts as revenge for the communal riots in Mumbai.

The Mumbai Police adopted an aggressive approach against the underworld by resorting to special operations and encounters. While the police were attempting to reclaim their power over the underworld, the syndicates were getting more courageous. The number of shootouts, firings, kidnappings, extortions and territorial rivalry was increasing.

After the serial bomb blasts, Dawood and Rajan split. Soon began a rivalry in the Mumbai gang world that had never been seen or heard of until then. Inter-gang rivalry was not new to the city, but the list of persons targeted by the two gangs was novel and hitherto unknown. Rajan's hit list comprised all Dawood and Shakeel gang members who were on the accused and wanted roster of the *1993 Serial Bomb Blasts* case, while Shakeel's comprised all those who were either indicted or named in the Justice B.N. Srikrishna Commission of Inquiry Report. Incidentally, most of them were leaders and activists of the Shiv Sena, including Balasaheb Thackeray, Manohar Joshi, Madhukar Sarpotdar and Milind Vaidya.

So, while Rajan began to target and kill those accused who were out on bail, Shakeel, on behalf of Dawood, began targeting Shiv Sena activists and leaders in Mumbai, especially those who had played a significant role in the 1992-93 communal riots.

The Mumbai Police was at a loss on how to tackle this latest menace, while the underworld was involved in a bloodbath on the streets. Several people were killed in this unique rivalry.

One person on top of Shakeel's hit list was Shiv Sena politician and former Mayor of Mumbai, Milind Vaidya. He was charged by the Srikrishna Commission for having played a key role in the 1992-93 riots.

On 17 December 1998, Shakeel tried to eliminate Vaidya. He sent two of his shooters to track him. Vaidya, a resident of Mahim, was travelling in his Tata Safari at around 9.30 a.m. near the Mahim-Bandra flyover, when two assailants in an autorickshaw fired one round at him. The bullet grazed Vaidya's jaw. He was rushed to the nearby Hinduja hospital. He was not seriously injured and was discharged after a few days of medical treatment.

The incident was a clear indication that Vaidya was on Shakeel's hit list. He was instantly provided police protection. He started taking his own security measures and precautions and always had a group of security men around him.

The failed killing did not deter Shakeel, and he immediately started plotting another attempt on Vaidya's life. However, he wanted to make sure it wouldn't fail the second time. This time he was making sure there would be no mistake.

Incidentally, around the time that we were giving final touches to the MCOCA before it became an act, Shakeel had put in action his plan to attack Milind Vaidya.

Such was Shakeel's desperation to eliminate Vaidya that he entrusted the work to his most trusted lieutenant, Azizuddin Zahiruddin Shaikh. The 29-year-old Azizuddin was a hardened underworld criminal, trained as a military commando by the ISI, Pakistan's premier intelligence agency.

Who is Azizuddin?

Son of a sales manager at a bidi factory, Azizuddin was born and brought up in Pune. His parents hailed from Jhansi in Madhya Pradesh, and later moved to Pune in search of employment. Azizuddin's journey into the crime world began when he was a teenager working in a garage in Pune to make ends meet. He,

along with four teenaged friends, looted a wine shop owner at knifepoint and stole ₹ 1,800 from him. Azizuddin got ₹ 300 from the take.

He managed to avoid being arrested and fled to Gujarat with his family. However, he had already stepped into the crime world. In February 1993, he, along with two others, murdered a man in the Amberpeth area of Hyderabad with two swords and a knife. Azizuddin had taken a *supari* of ₹ 25,000 for the murder. Even though he was arrested, he somehow managed to evade justice and decided to flee the country.

In September 1993, Azizuddin fled to Riyadh and stayed there for three years. In February 1997, he met Azam Ghouri, a resident of Hyderabad, who was in Riyadh along with Abdul Bari. Both men were preparing to go to Pakistan for advanced training with the Lashkar-e-Toiba (LeT). They influenced Azizuddin to travel with them and partake in the training by LeT in weapons and explosives handling to protect their religion.

In October 1997, Azizuddin, Abdul and Azam travelled to Pakistan and landed in Rawalpindi on a Pakistan Airlines flight from Jeddah. They were received by a retired major of the Pakistan Army who was also working for ISI – his name was Usman.

The Major took them from Rawalpindi to Lahore by car and to a training hideout. There, Azizuddin was given a new name – 'Abu Umar'. Soon, their training began. For 32 days they were given practice in assembling, handling and shooting an AK-47, AK-56, Sniper (a long-range gun), TT (automatic) pistol, RPG-7 (rocket launcher) and hand grenades. They were also trained in first aid and guerrilla warfare.

After completing his training, Azizuddin left Pakistan for Kathmandu, Nepal, and from there entered India by road through Gorakhpur, Uttar Pradesh. He settled in Pune and would often visit Mumbai for odd jobs.

After a failed attempt on Milind Vaidya's life in December 1998, Shakeel called Azizuddin in desperation and said, *"Milind ke upar apne chokre ne misfire kiya. Tu ye kaam karega, kya?"* (My boys have misfired on Milind; will you finish the job?). Azizuddin took the assignment and immediately started planning the hit.

Shakeel arranged to send ₹ 25,000 to him and asked Azizuddin to keep his mobile phone always switched on. *"Mai kabhi bhi kuch bhi kaam bol sakta hoon, kiska bhi kaam ho sakta hai, koi bhi target ho sakta hai."* (I can ask you to do any work any time. Anybody can be a target.)

In the first week of February, Faheem Machmach got in touch with Mansoor Hasan Haji Iqbal Pankar aka Motu, a close associate of Shakeel. As per his instructions, Mansoor picked up a white Maruti 800 from Pila House in Kamathipura and gave it for repairs at the Chhagan Mitha Petrol Pump near Metro Cinema. After the car was ready, Mansoor brought in Azizuddin, and both started using the vehicle for reconnaissance.

Around the same time, Faheem also got in touch with Mohammad Farooq Abdul Gafoor Chipa Rangari, a member of the Shakeel gang, and asked him to arrange for three mobile phones and a huge amount of money. Rangari was asked to hand over the phones and money to Azizuddin.

On 3 March 1999, at around 8 p.m., Shakeel called Azizuddin and asked him to be on stand-by with his mobile phone on. At around 9.30 p.m. Shakeel again called Azizuddin and told him, *"Bismillah Hotel ke saamne jo petrol pump hai, wahan kal subah jaldi aana aur Badi Amma ko utha lena."* (Please go to the petrol pump near Bismillah Hotel early tomorrow morning and pick up Big Mother). The Big Mother or *Badi Amma* that Shakeel was referring to was an AK-47 rifle.

Azizuddin and Mansoor could not sleep all night and wandered the streets of Mumbai in the white Maruti 800, bearing registration number MH-03-H-1749.

As the day of the attack approached, Shakeel and Faheem put into action the next critical phase of their plan. In the characteristic underworld style, a woman was used as a weapons delivery mule, so that it didn't raise suspicion.

Faheem instructed Aslam Mohammad Kutty and Abdul Kadar Abdul Gafoor Razvi, both affiliated to the Chhota Shakeel faction of the Dawood Ibrahim gang, to collect weapons from a woman in Mazgaon on the day of the crime. After collecting the guns, they were instructed to hand them to Mansoor and Azizuddin at Imamwada in the Dongri area of Mumbai.

In the wee hours of 4 March, Mansoor and Azizuddin reached the decided spot. Kutty and Razvi, travelling on a Yamaha motorcycle, came there with a brown leather bag. They handed the bag to Azizuddin and left.

Mansoor and Azizuddin went to Mansoor's house. On reaching there, Mansoor kept the bag, while Azizuddin went home to sleep. He woke at 3 p.m. in the afternoon and went to Mansoor's residence. Azizuddin opened the leather bag and removed the AK-47. He thoroughly checked it and found it was in good condition. He also found two magazines loaded with 28 rounds and 25 rounds respectively.

At around 6.30 p.m. Shakeel called Azizuddin and asked him to rush towards Mahim with the AK-47. Azizuddin and Mansoor did so. Azizuddin stopped briefly at his residence and picked up his pistol loaded with six bullets. They reached Mahim at around 8.45 p.m. Shakeel was constantly monitoring the situation over the phone from Karachi.

When they reached the Mahim signal, Shakeel asked them to go near the Khilnani High School, where three others – Zuber Kasam Shaikh, Fazal Mohammad Shaikh and Abdul Hasan Bande Hasan Mistry – were waiting for them.

At around 9.45 p.m., on the instructions of Shakeel, Fazal Shaikh was asked to walk towards the shed where Milind Vaidya was expected to be at that time. Fazal found Vaidya was indeed in the shed holding a *darbar*, speaking with people. He had his bodyguards with him. Fazal came back and informed the others about the situation.

They decided it was time for action. All of them handed their mobile phones to Mansoor and asked him to go home and wait for them. After Mansoor left, Hasan got into the driver's seat and Azizuddin sat next to him in front. Zuber and Fazal sat behind. All of them checked their weapons – Azizuddin took the AK-47 and his pistol, while Zuber and Fazal held on to the other loaded pistols.

Hasan drove towards Mahim railway station and, in a secluded alley, changed the number plates of the car, installing fake ones (the fake registration number was MH-01-N-7514). After this, they started towards the shed where Vaidya was.

En route, Azizuddin decided that no one would get out of the car and they would shoot at Vaidya from inside the vehicle. When they reached the shed, both Fazal and Zuber identified Vaidya. They now had their target in sight. Azizuddin asked Hasan to drive slowly when the car neared the shed.

An oblivious Vaidya was sitting on a chair under the shed awning and talking to people who had come to meet him. When the white Maruti 800 approached, a loud 'clack' of sound broke the late evening calm of the lane. What followed was a massive volley of bullets tearing through the air in Milind Vaidya's direction. Before anyone knew what had happened or Vaidya's bodyguards could react, gunfire rained down on the shed.

A volley of bullets hit Vaidya and others before the carbine-wielding policemen could retaliate. The two policemen started chasing the vehicle but stopped when Azizuddin fired in their direction from his AK-47.

Azizuddin fired six or seven rounds in the air to disperse the crowd. The shooters then fled from the scene; their car stopped near the Matunga railway station. Azizuddin, Fazal and Zuber got out and went their separate ways, while Hasan was left in the car with the AK-47 and other weapons.

Four people including Vaidya were severely injured and rushed to the nearby Hinduja hospital. Vaidya had miraculously survived the second attempt by Shakeel on his life, but three of his associates –

Vilas Gopinath Aakre, Deepak Sitaram Aakre and Milind Gunaji Chaudhary – died in the gunfire.

Those injured were identified as Babu Kashinath Mangela, Vinay Narain Aakre, Nichal Krishna and Deepak Aakre.

At a time when the Shiv Sena (SS)–Bhartiya Janta Party (BJP) combine was ruling the state of Maharashtra, a near fatal attack on a Shiv Sena leader and a former Mayor of Mumbai was a matter of great concern not only for the state government, but for the Mumbai Police as well. It was a second attempt on Vaidya's life and a far more serious one than the first one.

The news of the attack on Vaidya with an AK-47 spread like wildfire across Mumbai. The entire police machinery swung into action to find out who the shooters were and bring them to justice at the earliest.

Even though the case was registered with the Mahim police, considering its seriousness, it was soon transferred to the Mumbai Crime Branch and Unit IV was given the charge of investigating.

However, it was clear that it was a case fit to be registered under the newly formed MCOCA. Soon, the act was applied on the case and the then Assistant Commissioner of Police (ACP) Pradeep Sawant, a young and dynamic officer, was made investigating officer, with a team of police officers from the Mumbai Crime Branch assisting him.

Meanwhile, within 24 hours of the incident, a desperate Shakeel called Azizuddin, livid that Vaidya had not died. *"Milind kaise bach gaya, target leke nahin mare kya?"* (How did Milind escape, did you not target him properly?) Shakeel asked Azizuddin over the phone from Karachi. By this time, Azizuddin had no idea whether Vaidya had died and asked Shakeel for an update. Shakeel replied, *"Woh admit toh hai, dua karo Allah utha leve."* (He is admitted in the hospital, pray that Allah ensures that he dies).

"Main goli toh barabar mara, teen char lagi hongi," (I shot at Vaidya properly, three or four bullets should have hit him) Azizuddin informed Shakeel.

"Arre yaar, yeh kaise bach gaya?" (How did he escape?) a desperate Shakeel asked. You must have used less bullets, Shakeel insisted.

Shakeel's frustration knew no bounds as he had failed for the second time in his attempt to assassinate Vaidya. He was looking for answers. He kept asking if there was any mistake or default on the part of the driver or anyone else. Azizuddin assured Shakeel that there was no fault or mistake by anyone, and that he had tried his best to eliminate Vaidya.

An exasperated Shakeel, resignedly said, *"Chalo chodo, jo bhi hota hai, Allah ki marzi,"* (Anyway, leave it. Whatever happens is God's will), before disconnecting the call.

Shakeel asked Azizuddin to not communicate with anyone and to flee the city. Azizuddin soon left Mumbai and went to Pune.

The Mumbai Crime Branch, meanwhile, had begun a full-scale investigation into the attack on Vaidya and the death of three others. The incident was significant, as it was among the rare times that an AK-47 was used in a shootout.

Even though it was clear to us that Shakeel was the mastermind, we were having a tough time piecing together the jigsaw puzzle of this massive investigation. However, our tenacity gave us a result as early as the ninth day after the shooting. Based on ground-level human intelligence and thorough investigation, we arrested Mohammad Farooq Rangari on 13 March.

After the arrest of Rangari, we had no success for almost three months. We tried every possible angle to unearth the actual perpetrators of the crime, to no avail. Rangari's interrogation and questioning revealed very little.

In a telephonic interview given to a magazine in the last week of March 1999, Shakeel reportedly confessed to having masterminded the firing on Vaidya. Shakeel claimed that it was a war that was started by Chhota Rajan who had left no other option for Shakeel but to retaliate.

A big breakthrough came when we arrested Aslam Kutty, Abdul Kadar Razvi and Mansoor Iqbal Pankar on 21 June. Within a week, Zuber Shaikh and Fazal Mohammad were arrested, on 26 June. However, the main shooter – Azizuddin – was still elusive.

Azizuddin, meanwhile, was on the run after the shooting. He hid in the Versova area for a few days, then moved to Pune for a couple of months. Sometime in May he got a call from Shakeel, who asked him to go to Lucknow in Uttar Pradesh and purchase AK-47 rifles. In the last week of May, Azizuddin travelled to Lucknow, where he stayed in a guest house.

On 30 May, two individuals – Santosh and Akhil – visited him at the guest house and handed him a brand-new AK-47, three empty magazines, 150 rifle rounds and 93 bullets for a TD pistol.

Interestingly, Azizuddin was given the bag at 7.30 p.m. and at 7.50 p.m., Lucknow police raided the guest house and apprehended him. As part of their investigations into the case of possession of illegal arms, Azizuddin was brought to Mumbai.

Soon after the UP police's investigations were over, the Mumbai Crime Branch finally arrested Azizuddin in the Milind Vaidya firing case on 7 July.

Investigation, interrogation and questioning of Azizuddin revealed that Chota Shakeel had given a kill-list to him in February 1999. Azizuddin, along with Mansoor, had been tasked to identify and locate the people on the list and to eliminate them.

The kill-list included:

1. Former Mumbai Police Commissioner S.K. Bapat
2. Shiv Sena Chief Balasaheb Thackeray
3. Satyavan Jawkar, former Shiv Sena corporator from Dongri
4. Gangster Bachchi Pandey and his group-members at the Sessions Court in Mumbai
5. Golden Akbar, gangster from the Arun Gawli gang, in Pune
6. Chhota Rajan gang-member Datta Khade, a.k.a. DK in Pune
7. Babloo Shrivastava, ace kidnapper, in Delhi
8. Arun Gawli

During interrogation, Azizuddin told the police that neither he nor Mansoor had been able to locate these people.

After the arrest of Azizuddin, the Mumbai Police arrested Abdul Hasan Bande and one more associate. With these arrests, the Mumbai Police had solved a very difficult case.

Armed with their most lethal weapon - MCOCA - the Mumbai Police soon filed a charge-sheet in the special court and the trial began.

The case had already created quite a stir in Mumbai for being the first ever to be tried under the stringent MCOCA. It soon got another distinction as the fastest murder trial ever conducted. Within just 18 months, the special court gave its verdict in September 2000.

The court pronounced Azizuddin, Zuber and Fazal guilty of murder and sentenced them to death. Hasan was sentenced to life imprisonment, while Mansoor was sentenced to ten years' imprisonment and a fine of ₹ 5 lakh. Aslam Kutty and Abdul Kadar Razvi were acquitted. A total compensation amounting to Rs 1.01 crore was imposed upon the accused by the court.

While delivering judgement, Special Judge A.P. Bhangale of the MCOCA court made a special mention of the Mumbai Police and its investigation of the case.

The court opined that in our criminal justice system the police perform a vital role in collecting all the evidence available. If the police team is well-led, well-trained and well-disciplined, the uphill task of investigation becomes easy, and is done fairly.

A just and complete investigation is essential, as it can help the accused have access to a full and fair trial. It can also help the court to do its duty and find the real and untarnished truth for a just decision in the case.

In the Milind Vaidya case, the investigation by the Mumbai Crime Branch deserves congratulations for placing before the court adequate material and evidence which enabled the court to find out the truth and punish the real culprit.

The conviction was a major victory for the Mumbai Police in its fight against the underworld and gave them a new strategic weapon to bring down the gangs and stop their activities by implementing MCOCA.

However, in December 2003, the Bombay High Court, which was hearing the case in appeal, pronounced a judgement acquitting Zuber and Fazal of all charges and reversing the MCOCA court's judgment. The order was given by the division bench of Bombay HC comprising Justice J.A. Patil and Justice A.S. Aguiar.

The court, however, upheld Azizuddin's conviction, but commuted his death sentence into life imprisonment. The HC upheld the conviction and sentences of others in the case.

The decision by the HC left the police and prosecution dejected. They soon approached the Supreme Court and filed an appeal against the HC's order.

Finally, on 18 August 2009, the SC reversed HC's order and sentenced both Zuber and Fazal to life imprisonment. In its decision, the SC observed that the HC had erred in rejecting the prosecution's evidence and acquitting the duo, while the special MCOCA court had rightly convicted them.

The Milind Vaidya firing case gave a boost to the Mumbai Police's fight against the underworld, which had become a menace in Mumbai. In MCOCA, we (the Mumbai Police) had finally found a powerful weapon to take on the might of the underworld and break its back.

The fact that there were negligible shootouts from 2003 till date reveals a clear picture of how the Mumbai Police's MCOCA – its *Brahmastra* – wiped out the entire underworld in one clean sweep. The city of Mumbai till the late 1990s was a perpetual crime scene. From such a dreadful situation to the streets finally being made crime-free in a matter of two to three years is a huge success. The importance and significance of this *Brahmastra* cannot be emphasised enough.

The security blanket thrown over Mumbai by MCOCA continues to remain intact to this day.

◆◆◆◆◆◆

Chapter 13

THE FUTURE – THE WAR IS WON, BUT BATTLES CONTINUE...

The contents of this book on how the organised crime syndicate functions, in what kind of environment it thrives, has never been more relevant than in these post-COVID times and in a world infested with cybercrime and economic offences.

The current scenario of rising unemployment, financial crisis and increasing frustration of citizens is a classic breeding ground for criminals and gangs to flourish.

Even though there is a likelihood that street crimes or organised crimes like those of the Mumbai underworld may not be conducive to today's day and age, the internet could well become a new breeding ground for crimes and criminals as our society progresses.

The circumstances are all present for criminals to thrive in the post-COVID world. The internet is easily accessible. India is a global leader in online payment (UPI) services. In fact, other countries are approaching India to share the UPI concept, software and technology with them.

Cybercrimes, online frauds and scams are on the rise. It is just a matter of time before someone makes it into organised crime and causes online mayhem. Even though governments and law enforcement agencies are aware of this threat and have taken steps to counter technology-driven crimes, they still have a long way to go before everyone feels safe and secure.

I started the first ever cyber cell of the Mumbai Police in 1998. This was more than 27 years ago and the online world has since changed manifold. We are even now catching up with the ever-changing and ever-evolving online medium.

Back in the late 1970s and early 1980s, when the mills of Mumbai were experiencing lockdowns, and the massive strike organised by then union leader Datta Samant dealt a body blow to the mills of Mumbai, thousands of people lost their jobs. The middle class suddenly saw itself staring at a bleak future. Coincidentally, most of the gangsters that you read about in this book came from families that were severely affected by the strike. Those include Arun Gawli, Suresh Manchekar and Amar Naik among others.

The situation was an ideal incubator for youngsters who found themselves unemployed. Gangs grabbed the opportunity and showed them a mirage of quick and easy money, and lavish and luxurious lifestyles. Hundreds of young people seized the opportunity and became gangsters almost overnight.

The government and law enforcement agencies were not able to foresee this and were caught unawares by the sudden explosion of crime and criminals in the city.

The current years are similar, given the fact that crores of people lost their jobs during the pandemic, and crores are facing the same fate as industry and markets are on a downward spiral. There may soon be a scenario where unemployed youth will be vulnerable to manipulation by criminal gangs into becoming criminals themselves. And in no time the city of Mumbai and state of Maharashtra and our country could see a massive surge in crime.

The nature of crimes may change – we may not see many street crimes, but we may be exposed to more dangerous and invisible types of activity like cybercrimes, terrorism, narco-terrorism, economic offences and cyberwarfare. Even petty crimes like pickpocketing, chain-snatching, looting, burglary, dacoity are likely to fade. Cyberworld is where the action has moved.

A time may soon come when our pockets will be picked even though we haven't stepped out of our homes. An invisible and unknown person or computer may empty our coffers to the tune of millions of rupees without us even knowing. Some of it is already happening and it will just keep getting worse as more technological innovations are developed. Digital deep fakes, artificial intelligence-generated human voices, images, photos, digital arrests, etc., are already creating vulnerability.

The authorities and law enforcement agencies should be wary of this and keep a close watch on crimes and criminals.

Just as the nature of crimes and criminals has evolved in the past 75 years after Independence, the future will also see changes.

The millennials – or Gen Alpha,as the current generation is called – will never be able to fathom the shadow of fear and insecurity under which Mumbaikars lived in the 1980s and 1990s. There was an atmosphere of dread; people couldn't walk on the streets without either witnessing a crime or becoming victims of it. Having wealth or showcasing it attracted a visit from gangsters who would then demand money. People were afraid to arrange lavish weddings for their children because, invariably, they would be forced to pay the underworld.

Businessmen, industrialists, merchants, jewellers, real estate developers, hoteliers, film personalities and anyone of prominence would be under constant threat of extortion, kidnapping or death.

Inter-gang rivalries would result in shootouts, daylight murders, kidnappings, etc., on the streets of Mumbai.

This book is an attempt to give an idea of how the situation was back then and how the Mumbai Police managed to do the near-impossible job of wiping the underworld off the streets of Mumbai.

The Mumbai that we all love today has been made peaceful, cheerful and vibrant because of the effort, hard work, dedication, sacrifice, sweat and blood of the brave officers of the Mumbai Police.

This book is dedicated to those Bravehearts of Mumbai Police who went beyond the call of duty to ensure that we, the people of Mumbai, live in peace, safety, security and harmony.

Jai Hind!

◆◆◆◆◆◆

Chapter 14

MY PERSONAL ROLLER COASTER RIDE

In June 1998, when I was posted as the Deputy Inspector General (DIG) of Police, Nagpur Range, the then Chief Minister of Maharashtra, Manohar Joshi, had come on a visit to Chandrapur. As part of protocol, I had gone there as part of the police team to receive him and be prresent for his visit. During that visit, when I met him, Manohar Joshi advised me to be prepared for a 'very special task' that the state government was about to entrust me with.

His words intrigued me, and I kept wondering what that 'very special task' would be. I did not have to wait long, as within a few days I was promoted to the rank of Inspector General of Police (IGP) and got my posting as Joint Commissioner of Police (Jt.CP) in Mumbai Police and was thereby tasked with heading the Mumbai Crime Branch.

I reached Mumbai and took charge as Chief of the Mumbai Crime Branch on 29 June 1998. Little did I know that my professional and personal life would now be defined as pre-June 1998 and post-June 1998.

On the very first day that I took charge as Chief of the Mumbai Crime Branch, there were two shootouts in Mumbai carried out by the Chhota Rajan gang. The incident was reported in the media as 'Underworld welcomes the new Crime Branch Chief with a shootout'. I immediately sprung to action and resolved that I would take definitive steps to weed out the underworld menace from the city. While the task would be arduous, I was determined to put up a brave and sincere fight against it.

Within no time I got consumed by work with a mission to safeguard the city of Mumbai and free it from the vice-like grip of the underworld. The underworld had run amok in the city for the past three decades; gangsters were targeting and killing people with impunity.

It fell on my shoulders to end this tyranny. I asked myself whether I wanted to succumb to the pressure or treat this as an opportunity of a lifetime to change the crime landscape of the commercial capital of our country.

I decided to take it as an opportunity and got down to work. As I began my journey, I faced a lot of frustration and failures, but I continued relentlessly. The situation on the street was dismal and concerning. Hundreds of businessmen, film stars and other wealthy and prominent citizens were being targeted daily and living in fear. We (the police) were getting unending complaints from helpless people who had been targeted by gangsters. Some were kidnapped, some had received extortion calls, and others, death threats.

The most difficult part was to open the newspapers every morning and read news reports of shootouts and other heinous crimes committed by the underworld. I remember one newspaper headline shouting 'This is the 77th shootout of the year'. Every such headline and article would hit me hard. However, these also served to fuel my resolve further. They gave rise to all the strategies mentioned in the previous chapters and became turning points in our fight against the underworld.

I remember going for solitary walks on Marine Drive which helped me clear my mind, reflect and think afresh about how to overcome my daily challenges. I got some of my most pivotal breakthroughs on those walks.

I deep dived into my work to such an extent that even before I realised it, it took a toll on my health. By age 47-48 I had developed high blood pressure and high sugar (diabetes); it was a gift of the high-pressure work I was involved in. I was working on a 24/7 schedule with no time to spend with family, friends or myself. There was no free time during weekends, no holidays, just continuous work.

Such was the nature of work and amount of pressure that without realising I would carry the work (all the anger, frustration, etc) home, and it would all come out on my family. My wife and two daughters bore most of the brunt of this.

Looking at the sheer number of victims and complainants coming to the police daily, I took steps (which were never taken before) to instil confidence in them. I assured each and every one that nothing would happen to them, and they should not fear any criminal or gangster. It was a huge risk that I took but it went a long way in making the victims feel comfortable and protected. To back my claims, I instructed police officers in police stations and crime branch units to arrange police protection (for the victims) sometimes in civil clothes and in some cases asked them to use the latest technology to help the victims.

Another step I took was to never carry a gun or a bodyguard or any kind of security with me. I thought it would be ridiculous and embarassing if I, as Chief of the Mumbai Crime Branch, was seen with Z scale security while asking people to face the gangsters boldly and to not be afraid of them.

After three years of relentless work (from 1998 to 2001) on a round-the-clock schedule, the Mumbai Police finally conquered and annihilated the underworld. Nothing succeeds like success.

During this strenuous three-year long journey I had unconditional support of the then Mumbai Police Commissioner Ronnie Mendonca, and political leaders who extended unquestioned support to me and my team. During my entire tenure, I never got even one phone call or order from the political bosses that amounted to any kind of interference in my functioning.

The media also started reporting our successes and would report fairly, acknowledging the efforts of the police. This sent out a positive message to society and people regained confidence in the police force.

As a team lead, I had to be sensitive to the needs of my officers as well. While they toiled, pouring their sweat and blood on the field, I had to ensure that they did not need to worry about the health and well-being of their families and the education of their children.

I arranged to build three world-class schools in Gadchiroli, Chandrapur and Thane city. When I took charge as Thane Police Commissioner in February 2005, I saw that the government/police school (which was established in 1920) was in shambles and because of the abysmal state of the school, only 82 children studied there, taught by a lone teacher.

I collected funds from the public and built a 40,000 square foot school in a span of mere six months. Later, another 30,000 square feet were added to the school. Within three years the number of children swelled to 3,000. Half of them were children of policemen paying only 25% of the school fees and in the last 20 years the school has produced students who have all passed with first class and distinction.

The people trusted me and my team and ... shootouts in Mumbai reduced from 101 in 1998 to 48 in 1999 and 26 in 2000 to 18 in 2001 and after 2002 till date the number has been ZERO! This is my biggest reward; it is a huge high for me.

The entire credit for this unprecedented success goes to the brave police officers of Mumbai Police. They not only believed in me but worked like one team and with a mission to eliminate the Mumbai underworld. I am grateful to them and salute them!

◆◆◆◆◆◆

Chapter 15

COLLEAGUES SPEAK

- **Jaywant Hargude, Retired ACP, Mumbai:**

I had an opportunity to work under Shri D. Sivanandhan, then Joint Commissioner of Police (Jt.CP), Crime, Mumbai, as a Police Inspector. It was a memorable period of my life to see his exceptional leadership skill and ability to motivate the police force to control crime in Mumbai and I can proudly say that he has played a pivotal role in curbing gang wars and organised crime in the city.

He was a people's leader in uniform – he could build trust and foster a sense of security among Mumbaikars. He was a caring, compassionate head of our family and would personally help us whenever we were in need. This helped us to work with dedication and sincerity despite it being at the cost of our lives; as he instilled and placed trust not only in us, but also in our family members as well. He is the most popular police officer in the force and is our idol.

A great leader never gives up his services even after his task or tenure is over. After retirement, he founded an NGO called Roti Bank

Mumbai, which is successfully providing meals to needy communities. So far, his foundation has provided more than 20 million meals to people in need.

My best wishes to the Roti Foundation and its founder.

- **Ajit Deshmukh, Retired ACP, Mumbai Police:**

While serving with the Maharashtra State Police Department for 35 years, I was fortunate to be a subordinate officer to respected Shri D. Sivanandhan, an all-time towering personality, who won the hearts of the rank and file under him, setting an example of an ideal leader.

One of the cleanest and most honest officers with unbending principles; he has been an exemplary senior police officer.

It is indisputable that the safety with tranquillity ranking of the metropolis of Mumbai today is attributed unequivocally to him and his dedicated policing efforts that worked to destroy the then prevailing influence of organised underworld gangs.

After his retirement, he has engaged himself in the distribution of food to disadvantaged communities under an NGO called 'Roti Bank' that he created – the only organisation of its kind.

For all his juniors, either regarding their service matters or personal difficulties, Sivanandhan Sir was always someone to look up to, to find the fair way out.

By setting his own example, he inculcated efficiency in the police force under him and taught them to follow the result-oriented method of working.

With his wide spectrum of knowledge and expertise in many subjects, he is known as a popular orator who captivates the audience with his mesmerising eloquence.

Truly, words fall short to describe the multifaceted personality of Sivanandhan Sir.

- **Prafulla Joshi, Retired ACP, Mumbai Police:**

Working with Sivanandhan Sir has been a great experience. In 1983 when I met him for the first time, he was SP, Sindhudurg. He designated me as a PSI in Sawantwadi police station.

He taught me how to effectively discharge my responsibility as a serving police officer who had multiple duties. Thanks to his tutelage and monitoring I learned a lot and achieved my goal to work with him in Crime Branch Mumbai, and at the Thane Commissionerate.

When I was posted in the Crime Branch and would sometimes not perform as per expectations, he would sternly advise and guide me, which pushed me to achieve my goals. When I was in trouble, he helped me, beyond the call of duty.

Not only did he teach me about police work, but he made me a responsible person. He is a caring person with strict principles. He has his personal style of working.

For me he is a mentor, big brother and godfather.

- **Javed Shaikh, Retired ACP, Thane Police:**

Mr. D. Sivanandhan, Retd. Director General of Police (DGP), has dedicated much of his post-retirement life to philanthropy, establishing several welfare institutions.

Throughout his distinguished career, he served with integrity and vision, contributing significantly to the development of police welfare. During his tenure he was majorly responsible for eradicating a considerable number of criminals in Thane and Mumbai.

Serving his country honestly and sincerely, he has definitely left a legacy that is unparallelled.

He channelled his expertise into building educational (Thane Police School) and health care (Police Hospital) institutions, aiming to uplift underprivileged police communities (Police Canteen). He has also contributed immensely to the sports sector.

These institutions have stood the test of time and have become pillars of support, offering resources for those in need. Years after they were built and more than a decade after Sivanandhan sir's retirement, these structures have become monuments and are a shining testimony to his dedicated work for the betterment of the police department and its officers and their families.

- **Rajendra Ghule, Retired ACP, Mumbai Police:**

A Tribute to Leadership: How Shri D. Sivanandhan (IPS) Helped Tame Mumbai's Crime Wave:

From 1997 to 2003, I served in the Mumbai Crime Branch. It was a tumultuous era when gang wars and extortion rackets gripped the city of Mumbai.

In 1998 I had the privilege of working under Shri D. Sivanandhan, then Joint Commissioner of Police (Crime). His tenure marked a turning point in our fight against organised crime.

The late 1990s and early 2000s were a peak period for Mumbai's underworld, with gang violence and extortion plaguing the city.

Under Shri Sivanandhan's leadership, the Crime Branch adopted relentless and innovative strategies to dismantle these criminal networks. With his unwavering support, we brought the crime rate and the infamous gang wars to an all-time low. His guidance was instrumental in our success, often empowering us to take bold steps to restore law and order in the city of Mumbai.

In my career of 34 years as a police officer, I have come across many leaders, but few that matched Shri D. Sivanandhan's calibre.

His mentorship and vision not only shaped my career, but also left an indelible mark on Mumbai's safety. He remains one of the finest IPS officers I've known – a beacon of integrity and resolve in the face of adversity and chaos.

• Bhanu Pratap Barge, Retired ACP, ATS and Crime Branch, Pune:

D. Sivanandhan Sir – a true human being with compassion and a senior police officer who stood firmly behind his junior officers and staff.

Between 1980 and 1983, while I was studying at Fergusson College in Pune, I had the fortune of seeing Sivanandhan Sir, who was then the DCP in Pune. He remained etched in my memory because my relative, ACP Dattatraya Mane, had tied the traditional *pheta* (turban) on him during his wedding. This created not only a fond memory, but also an emotional connection.

I consider myself lucky to have had the opportunity to work with Sivanandhan Sir in Mumbai later in my career. While working with him, I learned everything, from how to collect intelligence properly to how official documentation should be prepared. But more than just police work, the most important lesson I learned from him was how to live life meaningfully and how to remain content. His reassuring words still echo in my ears:

"Whatever is written in your destiny, no matter what happens, you will receive it. Do your work properly — I'm standing with you."

During the 1990s, when gang wars and terrorist activities had gripped Mumbai, D. Sivanandhan was appointed in the city to take control. During that challenging time, through thorough planning, use of modern technology, proper intelligence and the introduction of laws like MCOCA, he not only dismantled organised crime, but also prevented crimes against celebrities before they could even occur, dealing with criminals effectively and decisively.

He rebuilt the lost morale of the Mumbai Police, from constables to senior IPS officers, instilling new confidence.

Be it organised crime, terrorist attacks, cyber-crime or high-level financial crimes during his time at CBI, or intelligence gathering at the Intelligence Bureau (IB), Sivanandhan Sir always had in-depth knowledge and perfect timing for action.

His guidance during the investigation of countless complex and high-risk cases was unmatched — something you rarely see in senior police officers today. Honestly, even ten books wouldn't be enough to document all of it.

Brought up with the right values, he first worked as a professor and then went on to perform brilliantly in the police force, eventually retiring as the Director General of Police, Maharashtra.

Even after retirement, the human within him didn't rest - he continued his service to society by managing three schools with over 4,500 students and feeding lakhs of poor people through his Roti Bank initiative. Words are insufficient to describe such work.

To such a rare and exceptional police officer – I do not pray for his long life for himself, but for society. May God bless him with a long, meaningful life. A heartfelt and repeated salute to him!

- **Prashant Deshpande, Retired ACP, Thane:**

When I was posted as an officer in the Detection Crime Branch of Mumbai Police, the city was going through its worst crime wave. Gang wars were at a peak. The police was entangled in judicial enquiries in encounters. Extortion demands and broad daylight murders was daily news.

The Mumbai Police Force faced harsh criticism and was frustrated. At the time Shri Sivanandhan was posted as Joint Commissioner of Police, Mumbai. With his ability to discover the talents of various officers under him, he reshuffled staff and created great confidence amongst officers by conducting meetings.

He created an atmosphere of group leadership in the Crime Branch. Despite judicial enquiries, his total support encouraged us in taking strict action against the gangsters. Having thorough knowledge of crime, criminals and the legal system and its provisions, he guided us in taking rightful action against those who broke the law.

Mere mention of his name was sufficient to create terror in the minds of gangsters. The introduction of MCOCA was Sir's brainchild. The provisions of the law played a vital role in cracking down on the gangs' financial network.

Working under Sir's command proved to be a turning point in my police career – he trained me to lead a unit successfully, giving me an opportunity to lead the prestigious Bandra Unit of the Crime Branch. Thereafter I worked directly under his command when Sir was leading the Thane Commissionerate and the State Intelligence Department, Maharashtra.

I feel proud that peace in Mumbai city was brought back due to Sir's leadership, continuous efforts and the sleepless nights he spent during his tenure.

◆◆◆◆◆◆

Chapter 16

BRIDGING HUNGER TO DEPOSIT SMILES – THE ROTI BANK STORY

In December 2017, I founded the Roti Bank Mumbai, a Non-Governmental Organisation (NGO) that is committed to ensure that no kid ever goes hungry. Looking back, I never imagined that a simple yet pressing issue – hunger – would define my post-retirement mission. But when you spend decades fighting crime, you learn that hunger is often the seed of desperation that has the potential to lead to lawbreaking. It was clear to me: if we could eliminate hunger, we could reduce crime. And so, Roti Bank was born – not just to feed people, but to create a better, safer society.

The Beginning of Roti Bank

We started Roti Bank as a non-profit hunger relief organisation under Roti Foundation Mumbai. The idea was simple: every day, Mumbai wasted thousands of kilos of food, while thousands of people went to bed hungry. It was unacceptable. We decided to bridge this gap, collecting excess food from restaurants, hotels, and individuals, and delivering it to those in need.

We started with just a few dedicated volunteers and a single van, ensuring food safety and quick distribution. Soon, we expanded, adding more vehicles and people who shared our passion. From weddings to corporate lunches, surplus food now found its way to hungry mouths instead of garbage bins.

A Kitchen for the Hungry

By early 2020, we realised that relying solely on surplus food wasn't enough. Many of our beneficiaries – especially children – needed consistent, nutritious meals. That's when we set up our own kitchen to prepare hot, fresh food daily.

Our focus on school-going children became a turning point. A hungry child struggles to learn, and poor nutrition stunts growth. We decided that our mission wasn't just about filling stomachs – it was about ensuring a healthier, brighter future. With this, our philosophy evolved: it wasn't just about fighting hunger anymore; it was about tackling malnutrition.

A Challenge Like No Other: COVID-19

Then, in March 2020, the world changed. The COVID-19 pandemic and the nationwide lockdown brought unprecedented hunger. Daily wage workers lost their livelihoods overnight. Migrant labourers were stranded. People who had never begged for food before found themselves with nothing to eat.

This was a challenge we could not ignore. Roti Bank, in partnership with Mumbai Police, stepped up. While the city shut down, our vans were on the road. We increased our operations tenfold, delivering over 35,000 meals daily at the peak of the pandemic. With the help of restaurant partners, generous donors, and our own kitchen, we ensured that no one in our reach had to sleep hungry.

Expanding Beyond Mumbai

The hunger crisis wasn't limited to Mumbai, and neither were we. We expanded our operations to Nagpur, Hyderabad, Coimbatore, Chennai, Ahmedabad, and Cuttack. The numbers spoke for themselves:

- In 2018, we served 5 lakh meals.
- In 2020, that number soared to 32 lakh meals in Mumbai alone.
- By March 2025, across India, we have served over 2.5 crore meals and counting.

Each meal wasn't just food – it was dignity, it was survival, it was hope.

A Future Without Hunger

Today, Roti Bank's mission continues. Post-COVID, our focus has been on school-going children, ensuring they receive nutritious snacks daily. We now serve 10,000 schoolchildren in Mumbai, 8,000 in Nagpur, and 175 in the small district of Rayagada in Odisha. Our goal is to build a healthier Bharat by addressing malnutrition at its root.

Beyond schools, we provide 2000 meals daily outside Tata and KEM Hospitals, twice a day, ensuring patients and their families don't go hungry. To enhance nutritional value, we have also introduced fortification in our meals.

From the schoolchildren in Mumbai to schoolchildren in tribal areas of Orissa and Nagpur, Roti Bank is more than just an organisation. It is a movement – a movement to withdraw hunger and deposit smiles.

Because a meal can change a life. And a life, well-fed and full of hope, can change the world.

We are just getting started!

www.rotibankindia.org

ABOUT THE AUTHOR

D. Sivanandhan, is a 1976-batch Indian Police Service (IPS) officer belonging to the Maharashtra cadre. He retired as Director General of Police (DGP), Maharashtra in 2011.

He has had a highly decorated and successful career as a Police Officer, serving as Mumbai Police Commissioner, Chief of the elite Mumbai Crime Branch, Police Commissioner of Thane and Nagpur, and Special Inspector General of Police (IGP) Anti-Naxal operations. Apart from this, he also held several senior positions in the Intelligence Bureau (IB) and the Central Bureau of Investigations (CBI).

In his 35-years of service he has been instrumental in completing several crucial missions, the foremost being the total demolition of the Mumbai underworld during his tenure as Chief of the Mumbai Crime Branch. Under his leadership the Mumbai Police had successfully investigated the IC814 hijacking link in Mumbai.

D. Sivanandhan is a postgraduate in Economics and holds a Master of Arts degree from the University of Madras. He has been decorated with several awards including the Meritorious Service Medal (1993), the President's Distinguished Service Medal (2000) and the Internal Security Medal (1998).

In 2017, D. Sivanandhan was a member of the special task force in the National Security Council Secretariat (Prime Minister's Office) for revamping India's internal and external national security measures. He was a security advisor to the Reserve Bank of India for three years and is on the board of several prestigious companies. He is Chairman of Securus First India Private Limited, a security consultancy company started by him.

He is the co-author of the best-selling book *Chanakya's Seven Secrets of Leadership.*

In 2017, D. Sivanandhan founded Roti Bank Mumbai, an NGO feeding the poor that has served over 20 million meals till date.

◆◆◆◆◆◆

ABOUT INDUS SOURCE BOOKS

Indus Source Books is a niche, independent book publisher in Mumbai passionately committed to publishing good and relevant literature. We believe that books are one of the most important mediums of communication and we seek to bring out publications that help to serve the community and the world we live in.

At Indus Source Books, we celebrate the diverse spiritual traditions, culture, and history of the world and present it to our readers in a contemporary format that retains its essential flavour: "Indian Spirit, Universal Wisdom."

Use the QR code below to visit our website www.indussource.com.

Indus Source Books
42/43C, Balaji Bhavan, Sakal Bhavan Road, Sector 11,
CBD Belapur, Navi Mumbai 400614, INDIA
www.indussource.com | info@indussource.com